SAP NetWeaver™ For Dummies

D1489192

SAP NetWeaver™ Component Checklist

SAP NetWeaver™ consists of various elements and components. This cheat sheet provides some handy lists of the pieces and concepts to help you understand SAP NetWeaver.

The application stack

Each of the tools in SAP NetWeaver inhabit one or more layers of the application stack:

- User interface
- Process logic
- Business logic
- Integration logic
- Application server
- Database
- Operating system

Integration components

- **SAP® Enterprise Portal (SAP EP)** is a set of technologies for creating role-based user interfaces that show you exactly what you need to do your job and make it easier for you to work with business applications.

- **SAP® Mobile Infrastructure (SAP MI)** is like a universal translator for mobile devices. With SAP MI, you can write one interface that can talk to any device, now or in the future.

- **SAP® Business Intelligence (SAP BI)** brings together information, helps analyze and make sense of it, and then distributes both the information and its findings to whoever needs them.

- **SAP® Master Data Management (SAP MDM)** is a system for harmonizing information that is distributed across a wide variety of applications.

- **SAP® Exchange Infrastructure (SAP XI)** is like a railroad system for data and messages traveling between applications. When two applications need to communicate, SAP XI provides a framework to build adapters to each application.

- **SAP® Web Application Server (SAP Web AS)** is the foundation on which SAP NetWeaver is built. It's like the engine behind the scenes of SAP NetWeaver that drives all of SAP's applications and tools.

SAP NetWeaver™ For Dummies®

Cheat Sheet

Development tools

- **SAP® NetWeaver Developer Studio™** is based on Eclipse, and it is extended as a modeling environment through frameworks such as SAP Web Dynpro and development tools such as Java Development Infrastructure. It creates applications that run on SAP Web Application Server.

- **SAP® Composite Application Framework (CAF)** is a modeling and development environment for creating *composite applications* (applications built out of services provided by other applications).

- **SAP® Solution Manager** is SAP's tool for managing the lifecycle of an application and providing a real-time connection with SAP support services.

SAP resources

The following is a quick rundown of some of the resources you have to help you succeed with SAP NetWeaver:

- **Your SAP account representative:** If you're new to the SAP family or don't currently have an account representative, visit www.sap.com/contactsap/directory and contact the SAP office closest to you.

- **The SAP Web site:** For up-to-the-minute information on just about anything you need to know about SAP, check out www.sap.com. The SAP NetWeaver area can be found in the Solutions drop-down list or by visiting www.sap.com/solutions/netweaver.

- **SAP NetWeaver tour:** Check out www.sap.com/company/events for all the updated information about worldwide tour stops.

- **SAP SAPPHIRE conference:** Go to www.sapsapphire.com for all the latest information on how to attend this preeminent SAP conference, and what you'll find at the conference.

- **SAP Business Forums:** Go to www.sap.com/company/events for the latest dates and cities.

- **SAP TechEd conference:** Go to www.sapteched.com to register and see what's on the agenda.

- **The SAP Developer Network:** Go to http://sdn.sap.com to get registered and start discovering more about SAP NetWeaver.

- **SAP partners:** Go to www.sap.com/partners to find out more about SAP's ecosystem of partners that can help with your SAP NetWeaver project.

- **SAP user groups:** Go to www.sapgenie.com/usergroups (not an SAP-owned site) for a pretty good list of user groups, or ask your local SAP representative for contact information.

For Dummies: Bestselling Book Series for Beginners

SAP® NetWeaver™ FOR DUMMIES®

by Dan Woods
and Jeff Word

WILEY

Wiley Publishing, Inc.

SAP® NetWeaver™ For Dummies®

Published by
Wiley Publishing, Inc.
111 River Street
Hoboken, NJ 07030-5774

WILEY

About the Authors

Dan Woods has a background in technology and journalism and now runs the Evolved Media Network, a firm focused on technology communications. He was CTO of TheStreet.com, and CapitalThinking, led development at Time Inc. Pathfinder, and created applications for NandO.net, one of the first newspaper Web sites. Dan has an M.S. from Columbia University's Graduate School of Journalism and a B.A. in Computer Science from the University of Michigan. He covered banking for three years at *The Record* of Hackensack, was database editor for three years at the *Raleigh News & Observer,* and has written six books on technology topics, in addition to numerous white papers and magazine articles. He thanks his wife, Daniele Gerard, and his children, Fiona and Eamon, for their indulgence and support during this project.

Jeffrey Word is the Director of Technology Strategy for SAP, based in Palo Alto, California. Jeffrey has worked at SAP since 2000 in a variety of roles in business development, strategic consulting, and market strategy. Jeffrey previously worked for several IT hardware and software companies in the U.S., Europe, and Latin America. He earned an MBA in International Business from Thunderbird, the American Graduate School of International Management. He also earned a B.A. in European Studies and Spanish from the University of Oklahoma.

Dedications

Dan Woods would like to dedicate this book to his children, Fiona and Eamon, whose mighty minds and love of learning are a constant inspiration.

Jeff Word would like to dedicate this book to Chelsi and Benton for putting up with his crazy schedule and odd behavior during the writing of this book.

Authors' Acknowledgments

For reading versions of these chapters late into the night and on airplanes when they could have been sleeping, for working as hard as the authors trying to take some of the most complex and powerful technology in the world and squeeze an explanation into the *For Dummies* format, and for believing that such a book could really help tell the SAP NetWeaver story, the authors would like to offer special thanks to: Shai Agassi, Peter Graf, Ori Inbar, Matthias Haendly, Pascal Brosset, Amit Chatterjee, Greg Crider, Howard Beader, Roman Bukary, Thomas Mattern, Sunil Gupta, Anders Ranum, Safi Oranski, Tom Ryan, Ivo Totev, Pam Chance, Himanshu Pande, Sami Muneer, Tim Bussiek, Scott Feldman, Sanjeev Agrawal, Peter Tillert, Karin Schattka, Karl Kessler, Henrik Stotz, Werner Aigner, Kaj Van De Loo, Ruediger Buck-Emden, Cay Rademann, Lorra Moyer, Sophie Small, Allison Reed, Kevin Cox, Laura Johnson, David Grasso, Davis Lee, Catherine Courreges, Beca Iniguez, Rohit Gupta, Chris Hanna, Pravin Kumar, and Puneet Suppal.

Extra-special thanks to the talented and tireless Judi Hance for her phenomenal work on the graphics.

Publisher's Acknowledgments

We're proud of this book; please send us your comments through our online registration form located at www.dummies.com/register/.

Some of the people who helped bring this book to market include the following:

Acquisitions, Editorial, and Media Development

Project Editor: Nancy Stevenson

Acquisitions Editor: Katie Feltman

Copy Editors: Jean Rogers, Virginia Sanders, Tonya Cupp

Editorial Manager: Carol Sheehan

Media Development Manager: Laura VanWinkle

Media Development Supervisor: Richard Graves

Editorial Assistant: Amanda Foxworth

Cartoons: Rich Tennant, www.the5thwave.com

Production

Project Coordinator: Courtney MacIntyre

Layout and Graphics: Amanda Carter, Andrea Dahl, Denny Hager, Stephanie D. Jumper, Shelley Norris, Heather Ryan, Mary Gillot Virgin, Melanee Wolven

Proofreaders: Brian H. Walls, TECHBOOKS Production Services

Indexer: TECHBOOKS Production Services

Publishing and Editorial for Technology Dummies

    Richard Swadley, Vice President and Executive Group Publisher

    Andy Cummings, Vice President and Publisher

    Mary C. Corder, Editorial Director

Publishing for Consumer Dummies

    Diane Graves Steele, Vice President and Publisher

    Joyce Pepple, Acquisitions Director

Composition Services

    Gerry Fahey, Vice President of Production Services

    Debbie Stailey, Director of Composition Services

Table of Contents

Introduction

. . . .

*W*e, the authors, would like to think that you're reading this book right now because you've got an insatiable thirst for knowledge about the new SAP integration and application platform, SAP® NetWeaver™. However, we're being realistic. It's more likely that you're sitting there scratching your head about what the heck SAP NetWeaver is and what it can do for you. You probably picked this book up because you want a little help just getting your hands around this puppy.

We explain SAP NetWeaver from the big-picture perspective in this book and break down all the different pieces of SAP NetWeaver into bite-sized chunks. Then we give you a few real-life examples of how SAP NetWeaver works so you can make the all-important leap from theory to reality.

About This Book

SAP NetWeaver is kind of a tough nut to crack. It's both an application platform and an integration platform. Basically, this means that SAP NetWeaver fits on top of and around your existing business applications. You can use SAP NetWeaver technologies to integrate people, information, and processes — inside and outside of your company.

As you go through this book, we take you on a journey through the business software environment in which SAP NetWeaver exists, show you the building blocks of SAP NetWeaver, and give you a glimpse of SAP NetWeaver in action.

Foolish Assumptions

We've made a few assumptions about you, the reader. We figure that you probably work in a company, either big or small. We also assume that you're either in the IT department of the company or one of the IT workers gave you this book so that you'd quit asking so many questions about this stuff.

We also assume that the company you work for either already has some SAP software or is making a decision to buy some right now. Whether you've got a huge SAP installation already or you're evaluating whether to buy a bunch of business applications, you'll need to have an understanding of SAP NetWeaver and exactly what impact it can have on your business.

We don't assume that you have any previous experience with SAP NetWeaver or its components. We also don't assume that you're a techie. On the contrary, we explain things so that a general business person can easily grasp the concepts without all the technical mumbo jumbo that usually accompanies enterprise software explanations.

How This Book Is Organized

This book is designed to help you understand the big picture of SAP NetWeaver, the IT environment in which it operates, general details about the SAP NetWeaver components, and what it looks like in action.

The book is organized to walk you through logical parts and make it easy for you to skip around to topics that interest you without getting irretrievably lost.

Part I: Enterprise Software Basics

Part I explains the environment that SAP NetWeaver operates in. Because SAP NetWeaver sits on top of enterprise applications, we include an overview of the general IT and enterprise software landscape and explain some of the more common arenas that SAP NetWeaver plays in.

Chapter 3 gives you a great high-level overview of the entire SAP NetWeaver platform and is probably the most important chapter of the book. So don't skip it!

Part I also goes into a bit of history about some of the building blocks of SAP NetWeaver and some of the future architecture implications of SAP NetWeaver.

Part II: The Cast of Components

Part II is like a game of blocks, with each chapter covering one SAP NetWeaver building block. We describe each component as a whole and then break them into their individual features. Then we put each component in context with its role in the bigger SAP NetWeaver platform.

We wrote these chapters to be read independently, so feel free to jump around to the ones that interest you most. You can always go back to the other chapters later.

Part III: A Nifty Development Toolkit

Geek alert! Unless you're a super techie or just really feel like you need a migraine headache, don't spend too much time with this part. It's *really* techie and focuses on all the development tools that are part of SAP NetWeaver. We talk about JAVA, ABAP, .NET, and a whole slew of other techie topics that only the propeller heads — programmers, developers, and IT managers — are really interested in.

Part IV: SAP NetWeaver in Action

Telling you what SAP NetWeaver can do and how it does it is the focus of Parts I through III. Part IV is where we begin to make the connection between features and benefits. Here you find a collection of real-life scenarios where SAP NetWeaver adds lots of value to a company. We take you through the explanation of a business scenario and the challenges involved, and then explain how SAP NetWeaver provides solutions. The titles of the chapters are pretty self-explanatory, so jump around to the ones that sound useful to see how SAP NetWeaver works out there in the real world.

Part V: Rolling Out SAP NetWeaver

Part V is where the rubber meets the road. Assuming that you're ready to jump into SAP NetWeaver with both feet, you really need to read this section before you start. It explains the people, information, and tools that you need to get started and gives you a few choice pieces of advice about how to approach your SAP NetWeaver project.

Part VI: The Part of Tens

We think that David Letterman is really cool, so we offer a top-ten list about SAP NetWeaver that you can refer to. (Actually, this is a feature of the *For Dummies* books that we know you've come to love, so we didn't want to disappoint you.) We provide tips for success. For you checklist lovers, this should be enough to start you out on the right path.

Appendix: About the CD

This book is accompanied by a handy CD-ROM filled with additional detailed information about SAP NetWeaver and some demos and customer success stories. It's really easy to use. Pop it in to get a very pretty picture of SAP NetWeaver and all that it does. This appendix walks you through all of this.

What You're Not to Read

First, don't even try to read this whole book in one sitting. We wrote it to be a ready reference that you can browse through and navigate easily to find topics of interest.

That said, we structured the book to cover some basic concepts that you need to understand about the business software and IT world where SAP NetWeaver lives. Then we move through product specifics, all the way down to real examples of SAP NetWeaver in action.

So what *should* you read?

If you're a newbie to the IT world or SAP, read Part I completely to get the big picture. Then browse through Part II, skip Part III entirely (it's a *geek alert* chapter), and dive into Part IV. Use Part V as a reference tool.

If you're an IT professional and have been around SAP for a while, you can skip Chapter 2 and browse through the rest of Part I. Feel free to jump ahead to Part II, challenge your geek credentials in Part III (intended for hardcore techies), and thumb through Parts IV and V.

Icons Used in This Book

To help alert you to some cool or tricky stuff, we include special icons.

This icon signals that we're using a term that's common knowledge in the IT industry, but may need a bit more explanation to help you get the full picture.

Remember icons point out important ideas or concepts that you may want to take extra note of.

TCO Tips are our way of pointing out the various ways that SAP NetWeaver can reduce your total cost of ownership.

We use this icon to alert you to any garden variety useful hints or tricks that can make your life (or at least your work) go a little more smoothly.

Feedback

Because we're so excited about the first edition of *SAP NetWeaver For Dummies* and because SAP NetWeaver is a fairly new topic for the series, we'd like to hear your feedback on your experience with the book. Send us an e-mail with your comments at SAPNetWeaver@EvolvedMediaNetwork.com.

Part I
Enterprise
Software
Basics

The 5th Wave   By Rich Tennant

"This isn't exactly what I meant when I asked for an Integration Platform."

In this part . . .

Yes, this is the strangest *For Dummies* book ever written, unique in that it meets a tremendous challenge: Explain some of the most advanced business software in the world as simply as possible.

To have a shot at getting this right we've got to explain all the basics of enterprise software — you now, all that stuff that everyone just assumes everyone else knows, but then it turns out everyone thinks of it a bit differently? Well, that stuff (you know: integration, abstraction, and so on) is explained in this part, along with the basic ideas behind the way SAP® software is constructed and how SAP NetWeaver™ fits into the world of IT. This part explains some tricky techie things to the digitally unwashed.

Chapter 1

SAP NetWeaver: The New Foundation of IT

In This Chapter

▶ Why we wrote this book

▶ What is SAP® NetWeaver™?

▶ Laying out the IT land

*E*verybody's gotta have a vision. For Columbus it was finding a better route to Asia by sailing west. (Of course, there was a new world in his way.) For Galileo it was inventing a telescope to view the planets and discovering satellites around Jupiter. For you, it might be making sense of all the technoid gobbledygook your company has to deal with day in and day out so you and your IT people don't end up old before their time.

If so, then you'll be glad to hear that at its core, SAP NetWeaver is an ambitious vision for improving Information Technology, including the software and hardware that runs the world of business. But SAP NetWeaver is not just a vision: It's a set of tools and methodologies that can take your company where it needs to go.

Admittedly, SAP NetWeaver is not your normal topic for a *For Dummies* book. It's not a hobby such as yoga, sailing, or personal finance. It's not a word processor or even a programming language. SAP NetWeaver is a super-sized serving of technology and tools made up of products and concepts that are useful to the corporate decision maker and the technologists who work together to solve huge information challenges.

With SAP NetWeaver, you can

✔ Make one portal that gives each user exactly what he needs from all your applications.

✔ Provide a unified view of information from every part of your company and deliver it to employees just when and how they need it.

✔ Knit together into one streamlined interface processes that are distributed in bits across many applications.

And because it is based on the latest technology and approaches to business processes, SAP NetWeaver also increases flexibility and enables change throughout your enterprise. Not bad, huh?

Why Write a Book about SAP NetWeaver?

Even if SAP NetWeaver isn't a typical topic for a *For Dummies* book, SAP and its customers and partners know that it's a topic that sorely needs the *For Dummies* approach, which puts complex ideas and processes into terms everybody can understand. The world of Information Technology has become so vast and complex that it's hard to keep track of all the techie terms and acronyms and how they relate to each other. Enterprise application integration, data warehouses, enterprise portals, business process management, model-driven development, and service-oriented architecture all fall under the umbrella of SAP NetWeaver. Where does the average guy or gal go to even start to make sense of it all?

This book gives you an option to plowing through the conceptual algebra that you read in the *Harvard Business Review* and the *McKinsey Quarterly.* This book helps you avoid the deep complexity of the technology that makes enterprise applications work. Instead, it provides a clear and simple explanation of the entire landscape of Information Technology by explaining how SAP NetWeaver can help you master this complexity and get more value from your investment.

A Technology Symphony

Sometimes it seems like brain surgery is child's play next to grasping the world of enterprise resource planning (ERP). SAP NetWeaver is such an ambitious undertaking with so many dimensions that it is hard even for experienced IT professionals to quickly understand its structure and potential. But here's a starting point: Think of SAP NetWeaver as essentially an orchestra of technologies with many programs and toolkits, each adding its own voice to the composition to allow you to do things that could never be done before.

We dissect SAP NetWeaver in detail in Chapter 3. In Chapter 1 we explain SAP NetWeaver's goals, how to make sense of all the pieces, and what it can do — that is, just what kind of music you can make with it!

SAP NetWeaver 101

When in doubt about the meaning of things, most folks usually revert to the dictionary. So, we start your SAP NetWeaver education with a little definition.

SAP NetWeaver is a set of capabilities that are provided by many different SAP products constructed to work with each other to make applications work together, build new applications on top of existing applications, and lower the total cost of owning applications.

Okay, granted it's a mouthful. So, for you visual learners out there, we drew you a picture. Figure 1-1 shows the most common way that people explain what SAP NetWeaver does.

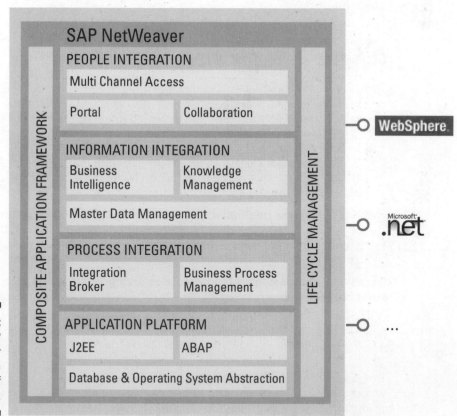

Figure 1-1: SAP NetWeaver offers a wealth of capabilities.

What you're looking at are the core capabilities of SAP NetWeaver: the integration of people, information, and process. When we say SAP NetWeaver has a capability such as *people integration,* it simply means that it enables you to bring people together and help them work more efficiently. Following the same logic, *information integration* means you can bring together information from a variety of locations and have it make sense in the context of what your folks do everyday. Okay, now you can do this last one yourself: *Process integration* means . . . that's right, coordinating the flow of work across departments, divisions, and between companies.

A closer look at Figure 1-1 reveals that each type of integration breaks down into different capabilities. This book has several chapters dedicated to explaining the products that SAP has created to deliver these capabilities.

See Chapter 3 for a detailed overview of which capabilities are provided by which product.

What's in it for me?

So, if a capability enables you to do something, how exactly do you use that capability to get your work done? The answer is that SAP paid attention to how people really do their jobs and designed its products to make technology easier for people to use.

- ✔ **SAP® Enterprise Portal:** Helps create software that brings together all the data and software tools that a person needs to do her job in one consistent user interface.

- ✔ **SAP® Business Intelligence:** Provides tools for information integration, so what your people see is consistent and accurate. (That is, the info somebody in the Sales department sees about a customer matches what somebody in Customer Service or Shipping calls up on the screen.)

- ✔ **SAP® Exchange Infrastructure:** Integrates processes and helps applications talk to one another.

Other products help in different ways. Parts II and III give a detailed explanation of what each product can do, along with examples of how each is used in the real world.

Take another look at Figure 1-1 and you see that the people, information, and process-integration capabilities of SAP NetWeaver all sit on an application platform called the SAP® Web Application Server (SAP Web AS). This is a tool for building and running applications. The SAP Web AS is the technical guts of the platform and the foundation of all the other stuff that goes on top.

Another important part of the SAP NetWeaver equation is the SAP Composite Application Framework (CAF). The SAP CAF is a tool for creating new applications by combining pieces of existing applications to do entirely new things. Finally, Lifecycle Management is a set of utilities that help make the process of installing software, running it, upgrading it, and fixing bugs as smooth as possible. These two boxes were placed on the right and left sides of the box in Figure 1-1 to show that they play an important supporting role in SAP NetWeaver.

Making music with Information Technology

Another way to think of SAP NetWeaver is to understand its goals. SAP NetWeaver is designed to

- ✔ **Enable change** through increased business flexibility and adaptability.
- ✔ **Increase usability** by making it easier for end users to work with all their systems. This increases user adoption, cost savings, and productivity.
- ✔ **Enhance integration** by making it possible for a collection of enterprise applications to work together.
- ✔ **Enable innovation** by allowing new applications to be constructed on top of existing applications.
- ✔ **Save money** by reducing the expense of owning and maintaining your existing systems.

As you find out more and more about SAP NetWeaver, it's useful to consider how every feature helps meet these goals.

Bringing all the instruments together

So, now you understand something about the pieces of SAP NetWeaver and what goals the folks at SAP had in mind when building it. But what, exactly, does this thing do?

To understand that, you have to grasp the importance of a little thing called prepackaged integration. As you'll read more about in Chapter 2, making applications work together is vitally important to most companies. That's where prepackaged integration comes in.

Prepackaged integration simply means that all of the products in SAP NetWeaver were built to work together out of the box. The integration was done at the factory, when the products were created, not after the fact. This represents a huge savings in both money and time when it comes to making applications work together. In the past, companies spent gobs of money just to make programs work together that weren't intended to. SAP NetWeaver eliminates this financial hemorrhage from your IT budget.

Another benefit of prepackaged integration is that SAP NetWeaver comes ready to work with the mySAP™ Business Suite, a collection of enterprise applications. These applications arrive at your office ready to plug into many of the products in SAP NetWeaver, which saves you yet more time and money.

It's important to remember that none of this prepackaged integration prevents integration with products and tools from other vendors. This flexibility simply makes it cheaper and easier to connect SAP systems with each other as well as connecting with non-SAP systems.

So, with the concept of prepackaged integration in mind, you can begin to grasp exactly what can be done with SAP NetWeaver: It is an excellent tool for integrating existing applications and building new ones.

Most people who have used SAP NetWeaver will tell you it can do absolutely anything, but in more practical terms, here's how it's actually being used out there in corporate land:

- ✔ Companies use SAP NetWeaver to create portals that bring together functionality from many different programs and present them in one consistent, easy-to-use interface.

- ✔ Companies use SAP NetWeaver to create one consistent version of the vital data for a company by collecting it from many different applications.

- ✔ Companies use SAP NetWeaver to start a process in one application and then provide one user interface as the process continues through other applications, or even through other companies' systems.

Because companies create these applications based on prepackaged integration, they cost much less to extend and maintain. The bottom line is that these advanced development tools enhance productivity and increase savings.

Want to hear more specifics about what SAP NetWeaver does out there in real-world businesses? The chapters in Part IV describe different scenarios that show how SAP NetWeaver creates real value.

IT: The Lay of the Land

Before we get too far into our explanation of SAP NetWeaver, it's important that you get a feel for the world in which SAP NetWeaver exists, the world of Information Technology (IT to you). So, we devote the rest of this chapter to helping you understand what IT encompasses.

Very simply, *Information Technology* is the application of technology (including telephony and computer technology) to create, store, exchange, and use information in all its forms to help your organization run better.

How big is IT? Well, IT spending accounts for about 3 to 5 percent of the revenues of most companies, which means that total global IT spending runs into the hundreds of billions of dollars, euros, yen, or what have you, every year.

Everybody's a specialist

Now being a big, complex thing (about the size of the known universe at last count), IT naturally has many specialties and subspecialties that essentially fall into the following groups:

- **Data Center and Network Operations:** Involve running the computers, telecommunications networks, and software that run the world. Huge refrigerated rooms containing racks of servers, disk arrays, routers, switches, and network hubs are supported by operators, system administrators, and network engineers, who act as the babysitters and mechanics for the systems behind credit cards, bank accounts, shipping companies, and Web sites, to name a few.

- **End-User Computing:** Involves making the computers and software on our desktops, such as word processors, spreadsheets, and e-mail programs, work for us, rather than driving us crazy.

- **Software Development:** Involves creating new programs using computer languages and many others tools (such as integrated development environments, databases, and networks) to perform calculations or automate processes.

- **Enterprise resource planning** involves great big programs, usually created by software vendors, that automate and organize complex tasks such as accounting, financial planning, customer-service management, supplier interaction, product development, and many other activities.

Understanding the different specialties is a start to understanding IT. The next step is understanding the different types of people and organizations that take care of all this technology.

Who are the players in the world of IT?

The reason that the field of IT exists is that companies need help in solving the problems that all this wonderful technology carries with it — problems of compatibility, communication, and conflicting protocols. The IT industry provides this help in many different forms.

So just who are these wonderful people who solve (or try to solve) all your technology problems? Here's a rundown. *Platform vendors,* or what SAP calls simply *technology vendors,* sell general purpose tools for creating software. This includes

- ✔ **Operating systems** such as MVS, Unix, Linux, or Microsoft Windows

- ✔ **Databases** such as Oracle, DB2, SQL Server, MySQL, or MaxDB

- ✔ **Application servers** such as IBM WebSphere or SAP Web AS

- ✔ **Development tools** to help write programs like Eclipse

- ✔ **Data warehouses** to massage, analyze, and make sense of huge amounts of data

- ✔ **Enterprise application integration** products that send XML messages back and forth between programs

- ✔ **Business process management systems** that allow processes to be described and automated

- ✔ **Portal software** to bring together the functions of many programs into one consistent interface

Application vendors sell programs built on the various platforms, many of which automate specific business tasks such as crunching numbers and writing memos nobody reads. *Suite vendors* sell many different applications that are designed to work together, such as the Office 2003 suite from Microsoft. Large-scale applications meant to help run businesses and bring many suites, applications, and systems into synch are called *enterprise applications.* (That's the business SAP started in.)

Here's a quick rundown of the categories that IT vendors fall into:

- ✔ **Hardware manufacturers** sell computers, printers, networking equipment, storage, and other devices. Examples are Dell, Hewlett-Packard, Sun Microsystems, and IBM.

- ✔ **Platform vendors** sell software toolkits that are the foundation for building and running programs. Examples include SAP, Microsoft, and IBM.

- ✔ **Application vendors** sell programs that people use to get their work done, such as Office-like suites and databases. Examples of vendors are Microsoft, SAP, PeopleSoft, Oracle.

- ✔ **Systems integrators** provide programming and business consulting services to help make all the technology that you spend your hard-earned dollars on work. Examples of these include Accenture, Bearing Point, and Cap Gemini/Ernst & Young.

- ✔ **Analyst firms** study businesses and technology and recommend ways to use technology. Examples are Gartner Research, Forrester Research, META Group, and IDC.

> ✔ **Trade presses** publish magazines and newspapers about technology so that you can try to make sense of it all. Examples are *Computerworld* and *Computer Reseller News.*

In order to understand the subsequent discussion of the IT marketplace and how SAP NetWeaver fits in, look over the rundown of these players in a bit more detail.

Platform vendors: Stack attack

Platform vendors sell general-purpose applications called *operating systems* for creating and running software.

Typically, the concept of a stack explains how the different layers of software that are used in a business work together. The applications at the top of the stack depend on the ones below them. A *platform,* or operating system, usually sits at the base of the stack supporting a series of applications.

Figure 1-2 shows how the applications stack is most frequently described.

Figure 1-2:
A very
simple
application
stack.

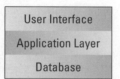

Of course, in the world of IT, nothing is simple. So, we give you another reasonable way to look at an application stack with even more little pieces to contemplate in Figure 1-3.

Figure 1-3:
The
complete
enchilada
application
stack.

In the stack in Figure 1-3, the user interface uses the process logic, which coordinates the business logic, which is protected from messy details by the integration logic, which does its job with the application server utilities, one of which allows the program to talk to the database, and the entire shooting match sits on top of the operating system (the platform).

Finding a vendor in a tech stack

We brought up the idea of the stack because it helps explain the differences between different types of platform vendors. (See, we do have a method to our madness!)

Platform vendors usually play at one or two layers of the stack shown in Figure 1-3:

✔ **The user interface layer** is provided by portal vendors or by tools from application servers that are designed to help construct Web pages.

✔ **The process logic layer** is provided by business process management systems or tools for managing processes in portals or applications servers.

✔ **The business logic layer** is generally provided by application vendors, which we discuss in the next section.

✔ **The integration layer** is provided by enterprise application integration vendors, application servers, or a variety of special-purpose tools such as integration brokers

or systems, for extraction, transformation, and loading of data.

✔ **The application server layer** is provided by application servers.

✔ **The database layer** is provided by (you guessed it) databases.

✔ **The operating system layer** is provided by (yes, now you've got it) operating systems.

Notice how the layers at the bottom are provided by products with the same name. This illustrates an important point about IT. As time goes by, each layer becomes more and more understood, and generally, more and more of a standard, with each vendor providing products with similar, if not the same, functionality. When this happens, the products from one vendor can be exchanged for those of another vendor, without disruption. The products have in effect become an interchangeable part, like a spark plug.

If you take away only one point from our fascinating discussion of stacks, layers, and products let it be this: The first thing to understand when a vendor is explaining its product is in which level of the stack the product operates and how it integrates with all the other pieces of the stack.

Application vendors: Programs to solve business problems

Application vendors sell programs that automate a business process or perform a useful task. For example, Quicken is a program that helps keep track of personal finance information. Microsoft Word is a desktop application that processes your words. Both of these are end-user productivity applications.

This book is concerned with *enterprise applications,* programs that are written to help run businesses. One important thing to remember is that the word "enterprise" doesn't really mean anything more than "for companies."

Application vendors fall into two broad categories: *Independent Software Vendors (ISVs),* companies that typically sell one enterprise application; and *suite vendors,* companies such as Microsoft or SAP that sell many different types of applications.

Now you should know that software is a kind of piggy-back affair: Enterprise applications are usually built on software from a platform vendor, for example. Almost all enterprise applications are based on an operating system and a database. Some application vendors build their own application servers or even their own programming language. SAP did this, which allows it to run its applications on top of almost any operating system.

By building all of its products so that they can work on any database, operating system, and server hardware, SAP gives you the most choices about what sort of database or operating system to use. SAP attempts to be agnostic about such choices, so that customers can do what makes sense for them.

The SAP Basis technology, for example, is similar to an application server. SAP used ABAP, a powerful fourth-generation programming language it invented, to write most of its applications. More recently, SAP is also using the ubiquitous Java programming language to write some parts of its applications. SAP's Web AS performs all of the functions of SAP Basis, as well as supporting both ABAP and Java.

(Don't worry: We explain what all of this stuff is in Chapter 4, which discusses application platforms in use at SAP.)

As you can see, software vendors are liable to stray into each other's territory: SAP and other application vendors frequently build software that falls into the platform layer when it makes sense for them to, and platform vendors have been known to invest in creating applications.

Systems integrators: Rent a brain

Systems integrators are consultants who help companies implement and customize enterprise applications; they also do custom development.

Systems integrators make big bucks by being experts in getting the applications and technologies that companies want to use to work. Systems integrators are also valuable to companies because of their skills in software development and in managing large projects.

At most companies, systems integrators are involved with massive projects where the risk of failure is large. For that reason, systems integrators often bring armies of consultants to bear on a project to move things along as fast as they can run.

SAP also has its own consultants who provide traditional project planning, industry-specific, and product implementation services. These guys can also act like S.W.A.T. teams to help fix urgent problems during implementations and to provide super-expert advice to the frontline experts who work at the system integrator companies.

Analyst firms: Observers from on high

Analyst firms make a living by studying Information Technology and making recommendations to companies about how to use it.

Companies rely on analyst firms for a variety of reasons to help make sense of the complex world of IT and make the decisions that help them keep afloat. Analyst research can help companies rapidly understand new trends. Analysts give advice, for a price, about when to pay attention to certain types of products and when to ignore them. Finally, analysts compare all of the products in a technology space and recommend different products for different circumstances.

Because analyst firms are so influential with companies, IT vendors try to ensure that the analysts completely understand the benefits of their products.

Trade publications: The information newsstand

Trade publications follow the tail of the IT dragon: They publish articles about every aspect of the world of IT, including new product announcements, how technology is being implemented at companies, and how recent news events effect the world of IT.

So, What's Next?

If you've been paying the least bit of attention, you now have a basic understanding of the SAP NetWeaver goals, what it does, and the IT world it lives in. In the next chapter, we take you further into the world of enterprise applications to help you begin to understand SAP's expertise and why you just might need an SAP NetWeaver solution in your own company.

Chapter 2

The Origins of Enterprise Apps

*I*f this book were a symphony, it would now be at the end of the first movement. All the melodies and instruments would have been introduced, and it would be time for the orchestra to really let loose.

In our little symphony, we have introduced SAP NetWeaver — the instruments of the orchestra — and we've offered you the role of both composer and conductor. The world of IT is the auditorium in which our symphony is played and various characters (such as companies that use IT along with vendors and their products) are involved one way or another.

The creative inspiration is the struggle that companies go through to make IT work. In most companies, this involves the battle to reconcile the needs and demands of business users with the capabilities of IT systems. SAP NetWeaver can have a powerful impact on the outcome of that struggle.

So the next step is to really understand how SAP NetWeaver can help. To do that we need to delve a bit deeper into the nature of automation, the cycle of innovation, the economics of enterprise applications, and how the modern suite of enterprise applications helps you understand how enterprise applications provide value.

If we get this right, by the end of this chapter you will know exactly why we're so excited about SAP NetWeaver and what it can do for your business.

Automation and Process: Perfect Partners

Most businesses of any size provide products and services to customers through a complex set of steps in which hundreds or perhaps thousands of people work together. At some point in the business processes, information is entered into a computer program by a person. This could happen when someone takes an order over the phone or enters data from an order form. It's not uncommon, even in these days of technology mania, for that data to be entered by hand into several systems. A financial system may keep track of the money. A manufacturing system may make the product to fill the order. An inventory and shipping system may ship the product to the customer. Entering data by hand into all these systems can create delays and increase the chance for errors.

That's where *automation* comes in. Automation involves taking the delays and error out of the process by replacing error-prone people with a precise description of how a task should be done using computer software. Most of the time, automation simply means shifting most of the burden from the people to the software.

Automation doesn't have to be rocket science to be effective. Much of the value provided by enterprise applications comes through the automation of simple steps added to the automation of other simple steps that can provide huge savings when you look at the net effect on a large enterprise.

The way that all the steps are coordinated is called *process*. Process is the game plan for performing the work of a company. When certain processes become popular in an industry, they become known as *best practices*.

Automating processes is a major focus of *enterprise applications,* which are kind of like pre-packaged, just-add-water best practices. In fact, it's not uncommon for companies to buy enterprise applications just to adopt the embedded processes as their own.

By delivering pre-packaged best practices along with all their applications, SAP provides companies with much quicker implementations, which ends up costing less money.

From SAP's point of view, defining processes properly and automating them effectively is the whole shooting match. SAP NetWeaver builds on the company's 30-year history of automating processes to extend the scope of automation from end to end, across company boundaries and heterogeneous systems.

To help you fully understand the nature of enterprise applications, we'll cover a couple of bases: innovation and economies of scale, both of which play an important role in the way that customers and vendors interact.

The (endless) cycle of innovation

Lots of things move in cycles. The cycle of politics, for example, moves from optimistic promises to broken promises. In the context of business, you encounter the cycle of innovation. The *cycle of innovation* describes the trip that an idea for a business process might take from its initial creation to becoming a best practice.

The cycle of innovation starts when a company creates a new product idea, technique, or process that results in some sort of competitive advantage. Creating a competitive advantage is an important part of success, and maintaining it for as long as possible is another. When a company has an advantage that other companies can't imitate, it is called a *sustainable competitive advantage*.

During the dot com boom, for example, some companies that were quick to provide information about their products on Web sites and allow customers to order online found that they'd tapped into a gold mine not yet overrun with claim jumpers.

As other companies figure out how to apply a technique to their businesses, an innovation such as a Web site becomes what some people call a *next practice*. At this point, the innovation frequently gets its very own name because corporations are name crazy. In the case of product information on Web sites, for example, this became known as *brochure ware*.

At some point, many companies figure out how to do the next practice themselves and it becomes a standard way of doing business, or a *best practice*.

Of course, the Catch 22 is that when everyone is doing the same thing, it ceases to be an advantage. When a best practice becomes a standard way of doing business across thousands of companies, it may become a commodity and be provided by third parties as a turnkey product or service.

For the most part, enterprise applications implement innovations somewhere toward the end of the next-practice phase when a large number of customers express interest in doing business that way. After all, because of the economics of enterprise applications (which we discuss in the following section), it doesn't make sense for enterprise applications to adopt new ways of doing business until a large number of customers are likely to want to buy into it.

SAP is moving further into the business of automating next practices through its xApps™ (cross application) line of products. xApps are more configurable than traditional enterprise applications to automate processes that are less rigid in their definition than best practices by using existing applications as a foundation. We examine xApps throughout the book as they apply to different areas of enterprise computing.

Economies of scale: Technology gets fit

Economies of scale are one of the important reasons that enterprise applications tend to focus on best practices. If you think about it, enterprise applications exist for the same reasons that health clubs do. If you pay the membership fee to use a health club, you have access to a much better set of equipment and facilities than you would if you tried to set up a gym in your house.

The same is true of enterprise applications. If you buy an accounting package, you tend to get much more functionality than if you tried to build it from scratch. You also don't have to worry about the support costs of maintaining the product, fixing bugs, keeping it up to date, and connecting it with other systems and new technologies.

Like huge drug companies, vendors of enterprise applications invest tens or even hundreds of millions of dollars to create their products with visions of a huge, eager market out there somewhere. SAP, for example, typically invests 13 percent of its revenues in research and development of new applications and technologies. It makes sense to do so only if there's a broad enough market for the application so they can recover their investment.

After an enterprise application has become successful, it's possible for vendors to extend it in different directions to encompass next practices or to meet the needs of a particular industry. But the more widely popular the best practices at the core of a product, the larger the market for an enterprise application.

Of course, businesses buy enterprise applications to meet their specific needs. So, during the implementation of an enterprise application, a sum that could amount to many times the license fees is shelled out to system integrators who customize the application to meet the needs of that particular business.

Balancing the ability to customize and integrate a product at the same time and implementing the best practices with the widest appeal is one of the hardest jobs for vendors of enterprise applications like SAP. The arrival of Web services and new ways of organizing software called *service-oriented architecture* are giving vendors new ways of addressing this tradeoff.

We describe SAP's theory of how to make its software generally applicable while being as customizable as possible in Chapter 5 on Enterprise Services Architecture.

Enter the Enterprise Application Suite

Remember how way back in the stone age of computing, everyone had one program for word processing, like Word Star, and another for spreadsheets, like VisiCalc? Maybe that's too far back . . . Remember Word Perfect and Lotus 123? After much consternation and technological warfare, now we have Microsoft Office, an application suite that not only has word processing and a spreadsheet, but also a presentation program, a graphics program, an e-mail client, and a database.

The same transformation that occurred on the desktop also happened in enterprise applications. The equivalents of Word Star and VisiCalc were the earliest enterprise applications (SAP's version written in the 1970s was called SAP R/2®) that focused on automation of the financial, accounting, and controller functions that are so central to running a big company.

The equivalents of WordPerfect and Lotus 1-2-3 were programs such as SAP R/3®, which expanded on the core financial functions and added extensions to help manage business processes related to sales and distribution, materials management, manufacturing, and others. SAP R/3 and programs like it became known as Enterprise Resource Planning (ERP) software.

We can't make this point often enough: If you want to eat lunch with the cool kids, don't pronounce ERP so that it rhymes with *burp* or you'll seem massively uncouth. Say each letter — *e-r-p* — and you'll impress people all over the place.

ERP keeps track of all the financial and accounting information for a complex business and helps with planning, forecasting, and reporting. SAP's most famous product, SAP R/3, existed before the term ERP was invented and had more functions than are in the traditional definition of ERP. For most IT professionals, SAP R/3 equaled ERP because it defined the entire wave of ERP in the 1990s and was wildly popular among the world's largest companies.

The benefit of this generation of software was that the data for all these programs was integrated in one massive database. Although implementing and customizing large ERP installations was sometimes traumatic and expensive, businesses could vault themselves to a higher level of efficiency when everything worked well.

The alphabet soup of TLAs (three letter acronyms, to you)

The first wave of ERP implementation took place in the early 1990s. (Remember the '90s?) This was a time of widespread adoption of Unix as a platform for IT and the growth of the client-server architecture for applications. Then in the mid 1990s, the Internet took off like the hula hoop (remember the . . . never mind), and so did a whole host of new enterprise applications, all of which were conveniently dubbed with a three-letter acronyms (TLAs).

Over at SAP, one way of looking at this evolution is that the modules of R/3 simply experienced a growth spurt, becoming much larger products. Sales and distribution became Customer Relationship Management (CRM). Materials management became Supply Chain Management (SCM).

Another way of looking at the growth of enterprise applications is that the automation of the core processes of business expanded out from ERP in all directions. The result was an end-to-end automation of all the most common processes. Wherever many business were likely to have the same need, a new product suddenly sprang up.

Figure 2-1 shows the way that both business requirements and technology evolved to create the world of many different enterprise applications in which we are now so blessed to live.

The mySAP® ERP products and corresponding abbreviations with birthdays in the mid-to-late 1990s include

- **Customer Relationship Management (CRM):** Focuses on managing interaction with the customer and automating sales, customer service, and order processing.

- **Supply Chain Management (SCM):** Coordinates a complex supply chain of materials and processing across a wide variety of companies.

- **Human Capital Management (HCM):** Describes applications that focus on managing a staff of employees. (Sometimes also called HR, an instance of the rarely-seen two-letter abbreviation.)

- **Product Lifecycle Management (PLM):** Concerns product development and manufacturing from the beginning to the end of the process.

- **Supplier Relationship Management (SRM):** Focuses on efficient procurement of materials from suppliers.

What happened was that, in effect, each VP in a typical organization got his or her very own enterprise application. ERP was for the CEO and CFO. The VP of Sales got CRM. The VP of Manufacturing got SCM. The VP of Human Resources got HR. The VP of Product Development got PLM. And there was much rejoicing.

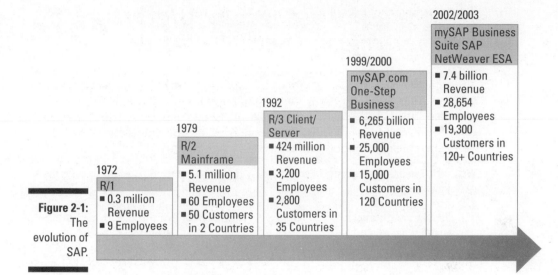

Figure 2-1: The evolution of SAP.

TLA proliferation: The good news and the bad news

The good news about the creation of all these applications is that it meant that the proverbial health club consisting of IT products developed to solve common enterprise problems held a lot more machines. Even a pool.

For almost every common business process, companies now didn't have to develop their own solution. They could buy a product.

The bad news is that the wonderful database integration that ERP had achieved was blasted to smithereens by the growth of TLAs. Each enterprise application now had its own database. This meant that certain tasks were problematic. For example, how could one find all of the information related to one customer? If a company had implemented CRM, ERP, and SCM, it might mean looking in all three applications. This sort of work quickly got old, and then the challenge of integrating these applications reared its ugly head.

The Integration Challenge: Making It All Work Together

So, here we are in the new millennium, with all sorts of technology in place in the bowels of most companies, and still we are not happy.

What would make us happy? What if we could wave a magic wand and have the automation of all the enterprise applications, but go back to the era when every program worked on one integrated database, like the way that ERP started out? This would be very cool.

If this came about, each enterprise application would have access to any piece of corporate data at any time. The process of turning a customer order into cash might start when you place an order in the CRM application and then proceed to the ERP system to keep track of the money associated with the order. Then the SCM system might make sure that the thing being purchased was actually available and route the order to the warehouse for shipping. When the order was shipped, the ERP system would generate an invoice and process the payment.

This is the vision and promise of integration: A process moves from system to system with all the relevant data available at each stage so that the maximum amount of functionality from each enterprise application helps to get the work done. The automation of the process incorporates the fact that a handoff will take place, and the state of the process is kept in a form that is ready to pass from one application to another.

Silos and stovepipes

So, what's the problem? Let's just do this integration thing and be done with it. Therein lies the difficulty, my friend. The fact that each enterprise application is a world unto itself prevents this vision from being easily achieved.

Referring to enterprise applications as a *silo* is a common analogy that reflects the fact that they may be full up with valuable information, but that data is divided by walls. When two enterprise applications are connected, people often use the image of a *stovepipe,* a small channel that allows a limited amount of information to flow back and forth between the silos. (Some really techie people call this point-to-point integration, but for the sake of our discussion we'll just stick with stovepipe, okay?) If you think about it, you realize that a silo is much bigger than a stovepipe, and not much information can flow back and forth between two massive silos through a tiny little stovepipe.

As it turns out, even creating tiny stovepipes is not that easy for a variety of reasons.

Differences in data

The first problem that you may encounter when connecting two enterprise applications is that the data in one is completely different from the data in the other. Here are some examples:

- ✔ One application is concerned with only a mailing address and so the name field may be one long string of text; another application has the last name, middle initial, and first name all in different fields.

- ✔ One of the information sources uses the five-digit ZIP code, and the other uses the nine-digit ZIP code format.

- ✔ One database uses the Social Security Number as a way to uniquely identify a person, but another uses an internally-generated unique number.

These are all simple examples. But how about when one system aggregates data by quarters while another compiles it by months, and both use different currencies? As you can see, when it comes to data integration, the fun never ends.

Brokering data: Not a panacea

If CRM and ERP both have their own records that keep track of customer data, each with different information, moving data from one application to the next isn't easy. Frequently it requires complex programs known as *integration brokers* to translate from one format to another.

To create an integration broker, someone really has to deeply understand the data in both applications so that a translation can be made back and forth without unintended consequences that totally screw things up. For that reason, not only must the differences in the data be understood, but also how each application uses that data.

When the application on either side of a stovepipe integration changes, all this must be figured out again, unless it has been painstakingly documented.

Guess what; it never is.

APIs: A view under the hood

So how do integration brokers do their work anyway? Well, just as you let your friends in your front door when they come over to have a chat, *application programming interfaces* (API) are the way one enterprise application lets other programs talk to it. Using APIs is like lifting the hood of a car and fiddling with the engine. You'd better know what you're doing; otherwise you'll be walking to work the next day.

But complexity is just one problem. Skill level is another. In an integration, the programmer must be very familiar with both applications, which makes the job harder.

Integration: Harmonized technology

Integration is a word that's used throughout the world of IT in many different ways, and with many different meanings. Almost all uses can be boiled down to two meanings.

Most often the word integration means the work done to connect two or more separate things so that they easily work together. Personal finance programs, for example, offer credit card bill integration that allows monthly credit card bills to be automatically loaded into the personal finance program from the Web site of the credit card company. This is a simple integration that allows the information from one source to be made useful in another context. For IT, integration frequently is used to automate manual processes. In personal finance, the integration avoids the need to retype the credit card bill into the personal finance program. Implementing a

few simple integrations like this at a company can save millions every year.

The second and closely related sense of the word *integration* or *integrated* is the idea of working together in an optimized way. People integration means that the people are working together in a better way through some system than if they weren't integrated at all. Process integration means that processes now work together. For static items like information, integration means that information was brought into a common structure that allows the data to paint a larger picture or tell a larger story.

The goal of information integration is to create one version of the truth, a consistent perspective on all activities and deliverables visible to all.

After all, what you can see, you can correct.

All this is made more problematic by the fact that APIs provide a window into a program that seemed reasonable at the time the program was designed, so APIs expose only a fraction of the functionality of an enterprise application. Many of the subroutines and functions used to do work in an enterprise application are not exposed through APIs. So even if you have the programming pluck to get under the hood, you can't always do what you want.

Missing the joke

One final difficulty with stovepipe integrations is that they frequently take place only at the data level. They translate information from one application to another but are oblivious of process. Its like translating a joke from English to French: You might get each individual word translated but still lose the entire context of the joke.

Most of the time, using APIs to enterprise applications provides access to data and to some useful subroutines and functions. What is really at the heart of many integrations is the smooth transition of a process from one application to another. What processes are in an application can sometimes be difficult to understand, and then controlling them through APIs is pretty much impossible.

Stovepipes can work

The good news is that, despite all the gloom and doom we cast on stovepipe integration between enterprise applications, they actually can get the job done. If an integration provides significant business value, the expense of creating and maintaining a complex stovepipe integration can be a wise investment.

Of course, if this expense can be reduced, perhaps you could make even more investments.

Integration toolkits

Because integration has proven so challenging and remains so potentially valuable, an entire industry of products has been created to help with integration applications. The idea is that instead of writing the stovepipe from scratch, it's better to get help from a toolkit designed for the purpose.

We spend much of the later part of this book discussing toolkits in detail. They include systems for passing messages back and forth, for consolidating huge troves of data, and for managing complex processes.

The Total Cost of Ownership Challenge: Putting Spending on a Diet

Total cost of ownership (TCO) is a big buzzword in the software business. You can hear it bandied about in board rooms, at the water cooler, and in grindingly painful budget meetings just before the screaming starts. So what does this TCO thing have to do with enterprise computing? TCO is about all the different expenses involved in owning and running an enterprise application.

Just as operating a car involves more than just the purchase price (think insurance, gas, fender benders), the cost of software goes way beyond what you paid for the license. You pay for customizing the software that you bought and then pay for maintenance. You pay the fees that vendors charge to provide upgrades as well as the cost of the hardware and networks required to run it. The biggest cost is usually the people who are maintaining all this technology.

So why should you be upset at having to spend all this money? Here it is in bold type: **More than 70 percent of most IT budgets are eaten up by costs related to running existing systems.** This means that your company is probably paying a huge bill every year just to stand still. Less than a third of your spending probably goes toward innovating with IT to get ahead of the competition.

What lurks behind TCO?

When you look at the hefty sums spent on TCO, you realize that a huge amount of the TCO cost is spent on maintaining stovepipe integrations.

It's easy to see why. Stovepipe integrations are expensive to create and expensive to maintain. They require highly skilled people to figure them out in the first place, and someone has to scurry to make things work when any little thing changes. When the integrations are between products created by two different software vendors, you don't even want to know what it will cost you. If integration toolkits are part of the picture . . . you get the idea.

So to really get at the drivers of TCO we have to look at not just the cost of the application or the integration platforms, but the cost of integrating both of these together. You can begin to understand this big picture by looking at Figure 2-2.

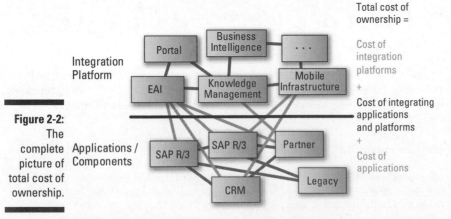

Figure 2-2: The complete picture of total cost of ownership.

TCO is, then, the cost of your applications, plus the cost of your integration platforms, plus the cost of integrating your various integration technologies and then using them to integrate your applications. This is the case unless, of course, you buy this all as a complete, integrated technology platform — such as SAP NetWeaver.

Cutting TCO down to size

Vendors have taken a powerful interest in reducing TCO because that's what their customers want . . . and want to pay for. The question is, how can they reduce TCO?

One way to do this is to avoid as much customization and integration as possible. This, of course, undermines some of the benefits of integration and the need for certain company-specific functionality.

Another way to reduce TCO would be to outsource the entire IT operation, throw it out of house, make it somebody else's problem. Although this makes the situation simpler from an accounting standpoint because lots of smaller costs and relationship tabs are replaced with one big check, it really just shifts the burden of reducing TCO to the outsourcing firm. Perhaps they will be better at playing the game of keeping expenses down (perhaps not), but it is still the same game.

So, the eternal question remains: How can companies spend less on TCO and more on innovation?

Why Do You Need SAP NetWeaver, Anyway?

You knew this was coming: The point of this book is to show you how SAP NetWeaver changes the rules of the game for IT. It reduces TCO and increases the potential for innovation by leaps and bounds. It sounds wonderful — the greatest thing since sliced bread. But how does it do it?

Figure 2-3 shows how using SAP NetWeaver to achieve specific goals — creating interoperability between applications and platforms, using products that are integrated out of the box, using products adapted to specific industry needs, and other features such as integration hubs and Web services — can add up to significant reductions in TCO.

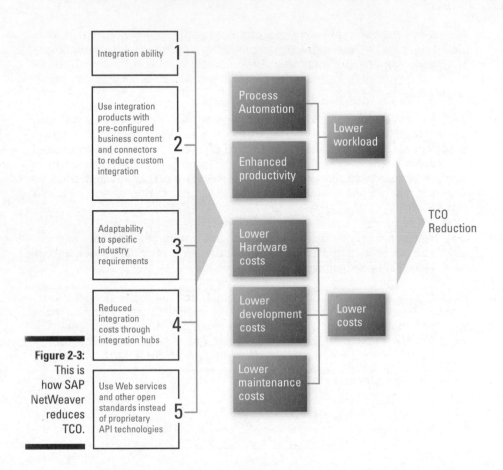

Figure 2-3:
This is
how SAP
NetWeaver
reduces
TCO.

The theory of SAP NetWeaver starts with the concept of pre-packaged integration. What if all of the stovepipe integrations that we've mentioned so far could be delivered by a standardized product? Then the economies of scale would kick in. Everyone could work out on the health club's new wonder machine that is dedicated to integration and pay a much smaller cost than if they had to buy the whole machine themselves.

Pre-packaged integration: Buying stovepipes off the shelf

The key question is, can integration be productized? The answer is yes, much more so than is done with current integration platforms. And here's how it will work.

Productized integration starts with a suite of integration tools all designed to work together. Hey, isn't that SAP NetWeaver you're talking about? Why yes it is, at least part of SAP NetWeaver . . . .

A platform for integration: It's all in there

SAP NetWeaver has all the individual integration technologies that you need, packed together in one neat package. Do you want a portal? Got it. A data warehouse? Check. How about a messaging system? No problem. Interested in complex business process management? Taken care of. What about an application server to run all this? SAP NetWeaver has that covered, too.

Now when you think of how all these systems are built by the same vendor to use the same mechanisms for identifying users, so-called single sign-on, the same methods for administration, plus the same cycles for upgrade and maintenance, you can actually hear the sound of TCO shrinking and profits expanding.

Fertile ground: Development environments

But that's not all, not by a long shot. See, you really can't buy a stovepipe off the shelf and expect it to work the second you get it home and unwrap it. In essence, what you're buying is a kit for building a stovepipe with 80 to 90 percent of the work done for you. But how do you complete the work? You need a development environment, and SAP NetWeaver just happens to have many different tools for the job.

SAP NetWeaver has a traditional development environment that allows developers to write code in languages such as Java, which are used to build stovepipes from scratch.

But the development tools in SAP NetWeaver leave traditional tools in the dust. For example:

- At the easy end of the spectrum is SAP NetWeaver Visual Composer, an environment that allows you to create user interfaces by using a simple drag-and-drop interface.

- Web Dynpro is an environment for modeling user interfaces to increase developer productivity and reduce the cost of maintenance.

- The Composite Application Framework is another model-driven tool that allows you to knit together applications from the kind of services that we discuss shortly in the section "Composing a Service Symphony."

A model of business efficiency

You may have built models of monsters, cars, and airplanes as a kid, but model-driven tools are kind of different. (No glue or tiny paint brushes are involved, for example.) You can use models as a way to manage the complexity of stovepipes and the applications themselves.

Modeling describes what a program should do by defining relationships between simplified components, rather than piling up mounds of code. For a user-interface modeling system, for example, the components used for modeling might be buttons, text boxes, and so on. After the relationship between the components is described or modeled, the description or model is then used to generate the program.

In most model-driven development environments, a little traditional code has to be written here and there, but most of the application is generated by the model. This means that when it comes time to fix or improve the program, you have much less complexity and code to understand and maintain. This is a leap forward in TCO reduction — trust us. Plus, code generated by these tools tends to have fewer bugs and requires less upkeep than code written the old-fashioned way.

mySAP Business Suite integration

The final piece of progress in pre-packaged integration is the way that SAP NetWeaver and the mySAP™ Business Suite (SAP's version of ERP, CRM, SCM, and all the other enterprise applications) are built to work together. Figure 2-4 shows you how the mySAP ERP is at the core of the applications, interacting with the other mySAP Business Suite solutions that surround it.

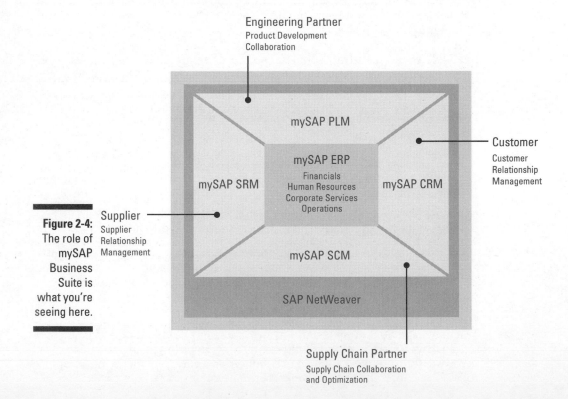

Figure 2-4: The role of mySAP Business Suite is what you're seeing here.

As it turns out, 70 or 80 percent of all stovepipes run through core enterprise applications such as ERP and CRM. SAP has used SAP NetWeaver to build those stovepipes in advance so that its version of enterprise applications come with stovepipes already between them. These are not stovepipe kits but working integrations that are supported as products that can also be opened up and customized. This is the final blow to high TCO because it has the effect of sharing, through packaging the solution as a product (referred to as *productization*), as many integration costs as possible.

Of course, SAP is a realistic company: The folks know that not everyone buys only SAP applications and that many customers purchase enterprise applications from other vendors. That's why SAP NetWeaver is an *open platform,* meaning that the product embraces standards such as Web Services Description Language (WSDL) and Business Process Execution Language for Web Services (BPEL2WS), which make it a great platform for building stovepipes back and forth between any application, regardless of vendor.

Innovation, at your service

So, having hunted down and contained TCO to as small a box as possible, the next requirement for SAP was to make the other part of the budget, the bucks spent on innovation, as productive as possible.

To understand how SAP's approach to enterprise applications works, go back in time and look at what Microsoft did with its ubiquitous Office Suite. Excel, Word, PowerPoint, and the other members of the Microsoft Office Suite all started life as separate products. But gradually they started to share components for common functions such as formatting text, spell checking, and so on. These days, about 70 percent of the code in Microsoft Office is shared.

SAP is using SAP NetWeaver to make the same transition with its mySAP Business Suite of products. In each successive version of mySAP Business Suite that comes along down the road, SAP NetWeaver will contain more and more of the shared code.

Actually, this trend has been underway for a couple years. The SAP® Enterprise Portal will be used as the user-interface layer. The SAP® Web Application Server is the application server on which the mySAP Business Suite solutions operate. As each year passes, more and more of the mySAP Business Suite will draw on parts of SAP NetWeaver.

Web services, the universal three-pronged plug
The careful design of a product family is only part of the story. The method by which this shift will finally happen is vitally important, and services are the key.

In our Microsoft Office example, all the code is running on a personal computer and mechanisms — like shared libraries and dynamic linking — are used to share certain functions. But with enterprise applications, it's a lot more complicated. Programs may be running on different computers, or the same program may be running on several computers for load balancing purposes. *Web services* provide a different approach to sharing. Web services are a standard way for applications to talk to one another by using the Internet. Essentially, with Web services, an application that has some data or functionality to share exposes itself as a service to the outside world. With Web services, the program you are calling on can be on the same computer or halfway around the world, and the programs never know it.

What is happening with the mySAP Business Suite is that instead of each application being one huge collection of functionality (usually called a *monolith*), enterprise applications are delivered as a set of Web services with some user interfaces built with SAP NetWeaver on top of them. The idea is that the important part of the application is no longer the user interface, but the reusable Web services. A user interface is provided, of course, but this is just a starting point. This Web services-based structure makes much more of the application useful for integration or for building a new kind of application called a *composite application,* which is an application built out of Web services provided by other applications.

But hold on there pardner, you may be saying to yourself. Aren't APIs the same as these Web services you are talking about? Not at all. APIs are complex entities accessible through a programming language such as Java. Web services are self-describing platform- and language-independent gateways to functionality designed to work over the Internet. There's a lot more to it than this, and the theme of reusable Web services will be explained throughout the book, but the bottom line is that Web services were built for sharing.

What we're talking about is service enablement, a fancy way of saying that functionality inside each application is available to other applications as a "service." The other important aspect of the *service-enablement* of the mySAP Business Suite is that we now have the experience of doing it the hard way with stovepipes. Now we know more about what kind of functions should be exposed and how to allow the processes of an application to be visible.

Composing a service symphony

But, as you may have guessed, this service-enablement is a lot more complex than just sharing code. The services that are exposed across the applications and SAP NetWeaver also open the door to a new kind of innovation that has never been possible before.

It is now possible to build a so-called composite application by using the services of the mySAP Business Suite and SAP NetWeaver as building blocks. What happens is the conveniently named SAP Composite Application

Framework (CAF) provides a development environment in which all these services can be combined, through modeling, into new applications. Of course, new services can be created by using Java and other languages if they are needed, but most composite applications come from existing services.

Say, for example, you want to create an application that changes a sales order in the CRM system, and then make sure the same changes are reflected in the ERP and SCM systems. A composite application can use Web services to get at the information in all three applications, but provide one user interface for the end user to get this done.

Composite applications open a whole new universe of possibilities for innovation. The SAP CAF in effect provides a way to create applications that use services to carry a process forward by using data and functionality from the entire mySAP Business Suite and from SAP NetWeaver.

Composite applications can be developed faster than traditional applications because they have a running start; that's because they're built on top of other applications, so they already have 80 percent of the functionality they need. They are easier to maintain and configure because they are based on models, not low-level code. Because composite applications can use all the functions of SAP NetWeaver, like the collaborative features of the portal and the ability to manage documents from SAP® Knowledge Management, composite applications can automate processes and integrate information in ways never before possible.

The possibilities are so vast that SAP has already discovered areas in which composite applications can be made into products that people will pay good money for. These packaged composite applications are being sold as what SAP calls SAP xApps, or cross applications. The name emphasizes that they can be cross-functional for an entire organization and also cross application boundaries.

Enterprise Services Architecture

In this exciting world of modeling, Web services, and composite applications, many new things are possible. Processes that are not currently automated, such as devising strategy or analyzing and executing mergers, will be supported more fully by software. Extremely complex and dynamic relationships between companies will be defined and automated in days or weeks instead of months or years using a suite of Web services. A vast landscape of IT opportunity is opening up.

SAP has developed *Enterprise Services Architecture,* a concept and vision that acts as a roadmap and a set of principles to make sense of the possibilities that services and SAP NetWeaver provide. Enterprise Services Architecture is nothing short of a comprehensive blueprint for how to organize your IT landscape.

Figure 2-5 shows how the previous generation of 3-tier client/server is reorganized by Enterprise Services Architecture, which separates enterprise applications into layers to provide role-based user interfaces, more flexibility, and a faster response to changing events. In Chapter 5 we'll explain this in greater detail.

Now that you have the big picture firmly in your head, the next chapter will explain each of the SAP NetWeaver components, which will no doubt become lethal IT weapons to the enlightened readers of this book.

3-tier Client/Server Architecture

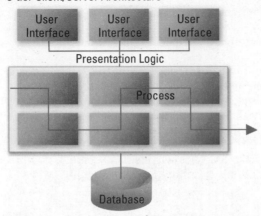

Enterprise Services Architecture

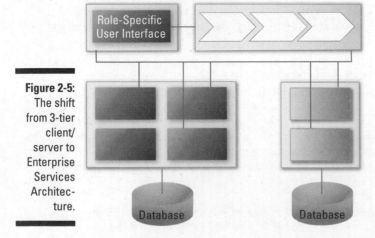

Figure 2-5:
The shift from 3-tier client/ server to Enterprise Services Architecture.

Chapter 3

Meet SAP NetWeaver

*I*n an orchestra, each instrument has a different job. The composer or arranger assigns parts to flutes, tympanis, and trumpets, and each instrument has a special role. The rhythm generally stays with the percussion crowd. The violins and French horns may carry the melody along. But during the concert, all instruments add to the harmony of the piece.

The various components of SAP NetWeaver work the same way. Each is a powerful instrument that can make many different kinds of IT music, but each also has one thing that it does particularly well. Each uniquely talented component has the most value when playing well with others to solve a problem.

In this chapter you look at each component from the perspective of how it meets the goals of SAP NetWeaver, what sort of integration its provides (people, information, or process), where it fits on the application stack, and how it relates to other components.

We also look at where SAP NetWeaver is going as a product. SAP NetWeaver first arrived on the scene as a set of components which we describe here. In the future all these component tunes will come together in one unified work. In other words, in 2004 SAP NetWeaver will become less like a collection of components and more like a platform.

This goal of this chapter is to show you enough about all of these IT instruments that you can become a regular Mozart of business data.

Giving SAP NetWeaver the Once-Over

In this chapter we fill your brain with visions of millions of lines of code and hundreds of person-years of work. How do we achieve this amazing feat? Well, this is a book about an SAP product, and SAP is all about processes, so here is the way it works — we show you each component of SAP NetWeaver related to four characteristics of the product:

- ✔ **Goals:** How the component helps achieve SAP NetWeaver goals of increasing usability, supporting integration, enabling innovation, and saving money.

- ✔ **Integration:** How the component helps integrate people, information, and processes.

- ✔ **The application stack:** What areas of the application stack the component primarily inhabits, as shown in Figure 3-1.

- ✔ **The big picture:** How this component is designed to work with other SAP NetWeaver components.

| User Interface |
| Process Logic |
| Business Logic |
| Integration Logic |
| Application Server |
| Database |
| Operating System |

Figure 3-1: The application stack.

We'll also take a look at *identity* — that is, how the new version, SAP NetWeaver '04, will change the way the product is defined and packaged for the IT community.

Along the way, we also briefly explain the larger domain of the world of IT and its relationship to each component.

The References section of the CD-ROM included with this book contains detailed, real-life customer examples. You'll find examples for all the products discussed in this chapter: SAP® Enterprise Portal, SAP® Mobile Infrastructure, SAP® Business Intelligence, SAP® Master Data Management, SAP® Exchange Infrastructure, and SAP® Web Application Server.

In this chapter you take a tour of almost all the different kinds of functionality that the IT world has to offer. Get ready, get set . . . go!

The Fast-Moving Parts of SAP NetWeaver

This chapter gives you a bit of a different take on SAP NetWeaver, focusing on the products that it consists of, rather than its capabilities.

Why? Well, because the most common way to think about SAP NetWeaver is to think of its capabilities for people, information, and process integration, as shown in Figure 3-2.

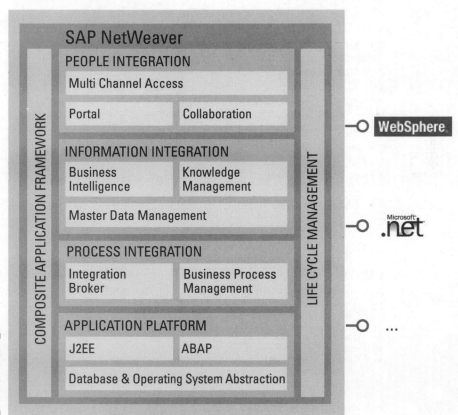

Figure 3-2:
SAP
NetWeaver
capabilities.

Imminent integration

Looking at SAP NetWeaver this way is a component-oriented sort of mindset. So is categorizing the capabilities in terms of people, information, and process integration. This is a view of the parts, not of the whole. As we explain shortly, the SAP NetWeaver '04 view of SAP NetWeaver is much more about the benefits of the integrated platform. This will be covered in the final section of this chapter, "What Can SAP NetWeaver Do for You?"

But frankly, you can't feed a population on ideals, and you can't build a system with a collection of capabilities, which are a description of the kind of work that is done. You need software products and toolkits that you can grab onto and use to do the work and build a new world (or at least a new solution for your business).

In this chapter, you get a tour of all the SAP NetWeaver components. Even though all these components will eventually grow together, we start with a component perspective because an understanding of the parts provides the basis for an understanding of the integrated platform. To pander to the left side of your brain, we organize the components into two different categories: integration tools and development tools.

Integration components are software products that help perform the work of enterprise applications by providing a powerful engine or platform for a specialized type of functionality. In SAP NetWeaver you'll find the following integration components:

- SAP Enterprise Portal
- SAP Mobile Infrastructure
- SAP Business Intelligence
- SAP Master Data Management
- SAP Exchange Infrastructure
- SAP Web Application Server

Development and management tools help create and operate software. In SAP NetWeaver these are the development and management tools:

- SAP NetWeaver Developer Studio
- SAP Visual Composer
- SAP Composite Application Framework
- SAP Solution Manager

Each of these tools is a world unto itself, so we'll review these components one by one.

It's about a central access point: SAP Enterprise Portal

Applications are frequently organized around a function, such as accounting or purchasing. Some tasks that involve several functions force users to jump from application to application to get their jobs done.

Now, it's human nature to quickly get weary of Madonna music videos and of moving from screen to screen in applications that look and work differently. This wastes a lot of time and requires really boring training for each of the different systems. SAP Enterprise Portal (SAP EP) is a set of technologies for creating role-based user interfaces that solve this problem. SAP EP shows you exactly what you need to do your job and makes it easier for you to work with business applications by bringing functions from many applications together into one place.

Like the arrival/departure screen at an airport, portals are also a central access point, the one place people go for important information. By harmonizing the look and feel of different types of applications from different vendors, you make your users much more productive, and, along the way, you save tons of money.

SAP EP starts by providing one place where you can access all those different programs, but SAP EP can do fancier integrations. When that happens, all of the information and applications underneath them are hidden, and the user interface looks like one unified program that was built just for you, like My Yahoo! or My MSN, only better. SAP EP even allows you to tweak that interface so that you can decide exactly what you want to display, and you can hide things that are totally unimportant.

SAP EP also adds some features that are not available in other applications. For example, SAP EP provides workflow features that help you keep track of which step you are at in a process. SAP EP supports collaboration among large groups of people by providing shared folders, discussion forums, and e-mail lists.

The most important parts of SAP EP are the knowledge- and content-management features. These allow you to store, categorize, and search through *unstructured documents,* meaning word-processing files, presentations, spreadsheets, and all the other documents you shuffle around on a daily basis.

SAP EP is really about integrating applications from the users' point of view, at all levels, and in the process bringing many useful things into one organized place.

How SAP EP helps meet SAP NetWeaver goals

SAP EP helps make applications more usable by creating role-based interfaces that are all about what the user needs to see to do her job. Therefore, SAP EP helps save money by making workers more efficient, because there's no more wasted time (and forgotten passwords) jumping from application to application looking for information.

But SAP EP doesn't stop there. SAP EP's collaboration functionality helps with people integration. The knowledge-management capabilities and ability to bring information from many different applications into one place are an example of information integration. SAP EP also provides a little bit of help for process integration with its workflow capability.

Some SAP EP examples

Employee self service is one of the most popular ways to use SAP EP. In this sort of deployment, all of the services that a company offers its employees, from making human resources information about health care and pension plans available, to simple modifications like changing an address, all happen in one place. This can save lots of money by reducing the burden on the HR staff, who otherwise have to answer all of these questions one at a time.

Another popular self-service use is an external portal in which a company enables all of its suppliers to keep track of shipments, invoices, and payments through a Web site, which saves the Receiving and Accounts Payable departments a lot of time, paperwork, and headaches.

How SAP EP works

SAP EP works by providing a page layout template that cuts a page into a bunch of different areas. Each area can be filled with HTML or with special programs called *iViews*. (In case you schmooze with different vendor types, other companies call these sorts of programs *portlets*.) iViews talk back and forth with other applications or information sources and then present the information to the user. iViews can also send messages to each other, so that a change in one iView can cause other iViews to change.

It's sometimes easier to think of SAP EP as a facelift for older applications. It really just displays existing functionality or information in a Web-friendly way, and then allows you to perform a whole new set of activities with the same old systems.

As you can tell from this explanation, SAP EP is mostly about the user-interface layer of the stack, though SAP EP also provides some services in the integration and process logic layer.

Does SAP EP play nicely with other SAP NetWeaver components?

Here's the good news: SAP EP is designed to work with all SAP NetWeaver components. iViews can call out to each and every one of the SAP NetWeaver components to invoke their services. The bad news? Well . . . hmmm . . . there isn't any.

In fact, SAP EP has been designated as the user-interface layer of the future for all SAP products. As time passes, every one of SAP's applications will use SAP EP to build its user interfaces.

The SAP EP, like all other SAP NetWeaver components, runs on the SAP Web Application Server (SAP Web AS).

SAP Mobile Infrastructure helps mobile devices talk

Every type of different mobile device out there, such as a cell phone, pager, or PDA, has a different user interface. If you want your employee self-service portal or some other application to talk to these mobile devices, you have to write a special interface for each one. SAP thinks that's crazy, and so they invented SAP Mobile Infrastructure (SAP MI), which is like a universal translator for mobile devices. With SAP MI, you can write one interface that can talk to any device, now or in the future.

Here's how it works. First you use the tools that SAP MI provides to describe a user interface. Then, when a remote device connects to your SAP MI interface, SAP MI runtime recognizes the type of device and sends the right commands to allow that device to work with your application. Simple, huh?

Taking integration a few steps further

SAP MI makes things easier on developers because they only have to write one interface to support many different devices. (We all want to make life easier for developers, right?) Such mobile interfaces bring applications out to people wherever they are, especially if they can't be chained to a desk and do their jobs (like folks who work on the shop floor or sell stuff on the road).

SAP MI helps with SAP's goals of people and information integration by making business applications and crucial information more accessible. It can also help with process integration by reducing delays in distributing information.

How do you use SAP MI?

So, you want some examples? How about this: Use SAP MI to extend project management information to people, wherever they are, to reduce delays and bottlenecks. Or provide your sales force with access to the Customer Relationship Management (CRM) system through mobile devices, another classic application of SAP MI.

Just how does SAP MI work?

SAP MI applications are built in the SAP NetWeaver Developer Studio and they run on the SAP Web AS and on a mobile device. SAP MI resides in the user-interface layer of the application stack. A user interface is designed using a set of predefined elements, such as text boxes, buttons, and so forth. The relationships between these elements are specified or *modeled,* meaning that the relationships between the elements are defined by the developer using a graphical tool, and kept track of using what is called *metadata.* The metadata description is then used to generate code for the various mobile devices that are supported. This modeling approach is used all over the place in SAP NetWeaver because it is so much more efficient for developers and makes changing the code so much easier.

SAP MI and all the other SAP NetWeaver components

Certain components of SAP NetWeaver tend to have relationships with others — isn't that sweet? SAP MI primarily has a special bond with the SAP NetWeaver EP. Usually an SAP MI interface is a special version of an already existing interface in SAP EP.

But that does not have to be the case. SAP MI is a flexible enough environment that any application, not just portals, can use it to connect to all sorts of devices.

SAP Business Intelligence: There is intelligent life out there

Perhaps after a lengthy meeting where exactly zilch gets accomplished, you doubt that business and intelligence go hand in hand, but SAP is out to prove you wrong. SAP Business Intelligence (SAP BI) brings together information, helps analyze and make sense of it, and then distributes both the information and its findings to whoever needs them.

SAP BI falls into a category of products called *data warehouses.* The basic functions of SAP BI are like most data warehouses. For example, imagine that a company has 20 different divisions, managed by five different CRM systems. All of the forecasting data might be consolidated in a data warehouse. This happens first through a process known as *extraction, transformation,* and *loading,* in which the information is basically copied into the data warehouse and put in a normalized form. (A *normalized form* involves pouring all the records from all the different CRM systems into one standard format.) The data is then rolled up into summary information, and precalculated structures called InfoCubes are created that allow complex questions to be answered rapidly.

The process of looking for interesting nuggets of information in data warehouses is called *data mining*. Fancy models are created and used for analysis or to alert the company to different sorts of events that the data may reveal, such as falling sales in a particular region.

But SAP's vision goes far beyond what is typically included in a data warehouse because it is so well integrated with other mySAP™ Business Suite solutions and other SAP NetWeaver components.

For example, SAP BI goes light years beyond the standard reporting that you might be accustomed to (you know, the stack of incomprehensible green and white dot-matrix reports stacked under your desk gathering dust). The trick is to do all the rocket science in the guts of SAP BI and display the relevant results in simple, easy-to-read graphics that anyone can understand and use. After all, analytical tools are pretty much worthless if you have to have a Ph.D. in advanced mathematics to use them.

One of the major uses of SAP BI is for performance and operational measurement. Because of the power and flexibility of the data warehouse and modeling tools, you can finally compare many different parts of your business as apples to apples.

SAP BI has many other capabilities. Information can be distributed out to smaller collections of data called *data marts*. Advanced tools for creating reports and queries from SAP BI allow you to easily import that data into other SAP applications and SAP NetWeaver components. Special packages of what SAP calls *business content* allow SAP BI to reach into applications such as CRM and perform complex analysis, all without having to build everything from scratch.

Meeting SAP NetWeaver goals

At this point, you should know you're in the presence of royalty, because SAP BI is the king of information integration. It's a flexible repository that can create a unified and normalized view of information from any number of sources. You can store vast quantities of data in SAP BI, which can then be analyzed and the results delivered wherever you need them.

SAP BI has helps improve usability by providing one consistent view of information, rather than requiring users to jump around in many different systems and dig around for the data they need.

How you use SAP BI

A classic example of SAP BI application is where you use SAP BI to consolidate sales data from many different divisions into one consistent format so it can be analyzed with advanced tools. You might examine buying trends across geographic or demographic groups. For example, a huge soft drink vendor might want to know everything that a fast-food chain buys from them around the globe on a weekly basis in order to minimize shipping costs. Or an athletic shoe manufacturer might want to analyze daily sales of a certain sneaker, broken down by retail outlet and by ZIP code, and then combine that information with advertising data to see what ads are most effective.

The ability of SAP BI to collect information and provide an audit trail of its origin and how it was transformed make it the perfect tool for compliance with new laws such as Sarbanes-Oxley, which mandate stringent and auditable reporting on corporate performance.

How SAP BI works

So what does SAP BI do to work its magic on your data? It's actually no mystery. SAP BI first creates a copy of all of the data in the repository. Then, using rules for transformation and various modeling techniques, the information is brought together and cleaned up into nice, neat information objects. These are then combined into InfoCubes to support what is known as *Online Analytic Processing (OLAP)*. OLAP is kind of a super query-handling machine (that can deal with more complex queries than everyday database systems) based on precalculation of partial results in InfoCubes. OLAP also lets you take a look at data based on several criteria at once. Trust us, it's cool.

Okay, back to SAP BI. SAP BI has a distribution mechanism called *Open Hub Services,* which distributes portions of data out to those smaller collections of data, the data marts. SAP BI offers lots of query- and report-generation tools that you use to produce very nice looking, useful reports.

In case you wonder where SAP BI lives, it operates at the database layer of the application stack, with a large number of functions for reporting and analysis in the user-interface and application layers.

How does SAP BI work with other SAP NetWeaver components?

SAP BI, unlike all the other SAP NetWeaver components, is powered by solar energy. Well actually no, it runs on the SAP Web AS, just like every other component.

Here's a rundown of its relationships with other SAP NetWeaver family members:

- ✓ SAP BI is tightly integrated with SAP EP.
- ✓ SAP BI can generate various types of queries and reports and save them directly as iViews, which can be included in the portal.
- ✓ The results of SAP BI Web applications can be stored in the content-management repository.

> ✔ SAP BI applications can be included in collaborative elements like chat rooms and discussion forums and also distributed to mobile devices through SAP MI.

Building harmonies from information with SAP Master Data Management

SAP Master Data Management (SAP MDM) is a system for harmonizing information that is distributed across a wide variety of applications. In a way, it is a toolkit for building real-time, read/write data warehouses for what SAP calls master data. *Master data* is data that is not connected to any one particular transaction, such as customer information, product descriptions, and charts of accounts.

In a data warehouse, all of the information is copied into a central repository and SAP MDM enables this mode of operation, which it calls *content consolidation*. But it also allows other modes such as *data harmonization,* in which the data in all the distributed repositories are made consistent. Under data harmonization, for example, the old and new addresses of a particular customer might be made consistent in all systems.

Essentially, *centralized master data management* is a scenario in which the master data no longer resides in the distributed applications, but instead, you access it from one central repository.

Furthering SAP NetWeaver goals

Integrity in people is a really important thing, and it's no less important in your data. SAP MDM is all about information integration in real time to ensure data integrity. While data warehouses are primarily about reporting, getting master data into a consistent format can help greatly with application and process integration. Reducing data errors and inconsistent data can mean huge savings because you prevent errors. Consistent data means that integration and maintenance costs also drop.

Some SAP MDM examples

Companies that have many different purchasing systems often end up with identical parts from the same supplier. The tricky part is that these things may be called something different in every system. Because the different divisions don't know that they're buying the same thing, they don't get a volume discount from the supplier. SAP MDM can harmonize all the different part numbers so that the company can get the real picture of what it's buying, how much it's paying, and who it's buying from. Knowledge is power (or, in this case, savings).

How SAP MDM works

SAP MDM lives in the database and integration logic layers of the application stack. It uses the *metadata* (that is, data that describes the structure and location of data in each distributed repository) management and storage capabilities of SAP BI and the messaging, data mapping, and business-process management capabilities of SAP Exchange Infrastructure to transport and transform the data. A variety of special-purpose tools allow you to configure SAP MDM to automatically find duplicates or transfer information about relationships discovered between records to other programs.

SAP MDM gets along with other SAP NetWeaver components

Stop us if you are tired of hearing this, but SAP MDM, like all SAP NetWeaver components, runs on the SAP Web AS.

SAP MDM relies on SAP BI and SAP Exchange Infrastructure to do its job. It can provide master data to any SAP NetWeaver component.

All aboard SAP Exchange Infrastructure

SAP NetWeaver Exchange Infrastructure (SAP XI) is like a railroad system for data and messages traveling between applications. When two applications need to communicate, SAP XI provides a framework to build adapters to each application, sort of like railroad tracks that switch from one data format to another and route the flow of messages. Using all of these features, messages can flow back and forth with high levels of security and guaranteed delivery. Plus, by using a messaging hub like SAP XI, you don't have to rewrite every interface each time you make a change to one system or the other. You just change one interface to SAP XI and save loads of time and money.

You can send messages back and forth on this high tech railway line to synchronize databases, integrate processes, remotely call functionality, and perform business-to-business integrations, all asynchronously or in real time.

As if that weren't enough, SAP XI also has advanced business-process management capabilities. This allows your systems to monitor complex series of events and react to them automatically, which is the key to success in many different integration scenarios. How would it work? Well, for instance, the SAP XI business-process management capabilities could help a supply chain management system schedule a product for manufacturing only when all of the parts have been received from suppliers. SAP XI can wait and monitor messages over days, weeks, or months, and then initiate the right automated response.

First stop: Meeting SAP NetWeaver goals

SAP XI is a powerful engine for application-to-application (A2A) integration and process integration. It is a flexible modeling toolkit for replacing custom coding with configuration and code generation, which, believe us, can save you big time on development and maintenance costs.

Also, by managing the integration of applications and business processes at one time, with the same tool, you can actually connect technology with a business need and tell the systems when to talk to each other, what to say, and how to say it, according to which step of the business process you're in.

How you use SAP XI

Say you have to exchange sales orders between a purchasing and a sales-management system. You have to pass around order acknowledgements and change orders and many other documents between these systems in a common format so that the system can read them electronically. SAP XI does all that, and in the process it eliminates the need for redundant manual entry of data.

SAP XI works this way

SAP XI sets up housekeeping in the integration and process logic layer of the application stack. This whiz kid has an integration repository that is used to store descriptions of messages, an integration directory that helps the system find message types and mappings, and an integration server that sends and transforms XML messages. The integration server has engines that make adapters, business process management, and data mappings work. Oh, and one added bonus: SAP XI also allows you to use Web services to send and receive messages.

Traveling along with other SAP NetWeaver components

SAP XI functionality is like the universal slicer and dicer of SAP NetWeaver, because it can be used by almost every SAP NetWeaver component. Portals can use information from SAP XI messages, SAP Web AS can use Web services fuelled by SAP XI or process the messages directly. SAP BI and SAP MDM use SAP XI to move information back and forth from distributed repositories.

SAP XI runs on the original version of Microsoft Basic. Okay, there's no fooling you: Like all SAP NetWeaver components, SAP XI runs on SAP Web AS.

SAP Web Application Server

SAP Web AS is the foundation on which SAP NetWeaver is built. It's like the engine behind the scenes of SAP NetWeaver that drives all of SAP's applications and tools. The mySAP Business Suite solutions are written in ABAP and run on top of SAP Web AS. SAP EP is Java code that runs on top of SAP Web AS. SAP Web AS is as essential to the well being of SAP NetWeaver as coffee is to jump-starting corporate America every day.

SAP Web AS is as tightly connected to the SAP NetWeaver development environment as the IRS is to your income. That's because it is such a core part of building applications and tools. It's also the way that customers create custom code for their own applications.

It can be tricky to understand SAP Web AS because many of the development components operate at both development time and runtime. Keeping the distinction in mind between the development time and runtime capabilities of SAP Web AS can help.

At development time, all of the work to create applications is done through SAP NetWeaver Developer Studio, which we explain in the next section on tools. The code is then executed at runtime on SAP Web AS.

The following are important points to understand about SAP Web AS and its capabilities:

- **SAP Web AS supports two languages at the same time.** Kind of like a UN translator, SAP Web AS supports Java code that meets the J2EE 1.3 specification and ABAP code, which is SAP's language for business applications.

- **SAP Web AS is a fully developed application server, comparable to IBM's WebSphere or BEA's WebLogic.** SAP Web AS has capabilities for load balancing, communicating with the Internet, connecting with databases, building Web pages, and creating Web services.

- **SAP Web AS supports the SAP Web Dynpro environment for creating user interfaces through modeling and code generation.**

How SAP Web AS meets SAP NetWeaver goals

SAP Web AS gives you two big perks for the price of one. First, you get more value out of the ABAP applications (SAP R/3®, mySAP Business Suite) you have in place; second, you can now easily extend the functionality of those and other systems by using a much more common language: Java. By combining ABAP and Java, SAP Web AS gives you this great single environment in which to work with applications, regardless of what language they were written in. This saves a whole lot of time, money, and effort for developers — just ask one.

SAP Web AS is directly involved in all three types of integration: people, information, and process. Web services created on SAP Web AS can bring a legacy application into the portal, provide information to a data warehouse, or help SAP XI communicate between applications.

How SAP Web AS is used

SAP Web AS does everything from running mySAP CRM to executing custom Java and ABAP code. But keep in mind that the typical use of SAP Web AS is invisible to the user.

Getting under the hood

In this section, you noodle around in SAP Web AS to see what makes it tick. SAP Web AS is involved with all levels of the application stack, and it has the following groups of components:

- The Internet Communication Manager, which talks back and forth with the Internet.

- Runtime engines for Web Dynpro, Java, and ABAP to execute code written for those platforms.

- Web Services Infrastructure, which has all the plumbing to support deployment of Web services.

- The Open SQL database abstraction, which ensures that any relational database can sit underneath SAP Web AS.

SAP is a member of the Java Community Process and is a leading definer and implementer of all Java standards. What does that mean for you? Well, as a result, SAP Web AS is one of the most open and standards-friendly platforms.

Development for SAP Web AS is aided by the Java Development Infrastructure, a suite of tools for development that is explained in detail in the later section, "SAP NetWeaver Developer Studio's toolkit."

How SAP Web AS works with other SAP NetWeaver components

SAP Web AS is the foundation of SAP NetWeaver components and mySAP Business Suite solutions and is involved in helping all of them do their jobs.

Development Tools: The SAP NetWeaver Construction Set

So, you're probably thinking, this stuff all sounds great; how can I get some? With these tools you can build applications that leverage all the components. In fact, SAP has a full suite of development tools you use for different purposes:

- **An integrated development environment for Java coding:** When you really want to get under the hood and tinker, SAP NetWeaver Developer Studio provides an integrated development environment for Java coding, with many different extensions for those times when you want to do weird and wonderful stuff.

✔ **SAP Composite Application Framework:** A model-driven development environment for creating composite applications, which use services provided by existing applications as the foundation for building new applications.

✔ **SAP NetWeaver Visual Composer:** This tool provides the user-interface modeling environment for the SAP Composite Application Framework (quite a mouthful, but trust us, this is the easy one).

✔ **The solution manager:** This central service platform uses a combination of software and services to help move a program through its life cycle and keep it updated and running smoothly through all phases: from installation, through testing, deployment, monitoring, management, and finally into a comfortable retirement.

Of course, people often say it can't be that simple, and indeed, it isn't. But after you discover what these tools can do, we think you'll be amazed at their potential.

SAP NetWeaver Developer Studio's toolkit

As far as development tools go, all roads lead to the SAP Developer Studio.

SAP NetWeaver Developer Studio is based on Eclipse (www.eclipse.org), which is a super toolkit for building development tools. (Programmers love building toolkits.) IBM came up with the Eclipse framework and decided in a generous moment to share it with the rest of the world. So now others, SAP included, use it to create development environments of their own.

The SAP NetWeaver Developer Studio has an environment for building programs in the ubiquitous Java language, with all its support for editing, managing source code, and building and debugging programs that developers have come to know and love. Special features for development of Web services are also provided.

There's more good news: As time goes by, the SAP NetWeaver Developer Studio will become even more of a modeling environment and other languages besides Java will be supported.

Breaking new ground

The SAP NetWeaver Developer Studio is used by all sorts of SAP developers. In fact, Developer Studio is essential to those creating SAP products, as well as systems integrators and developers creating their own applications.

The SAP NetWeaver Developer Studio has been pushed to the outer limits as a development environment through a set of capabilities called the Java Development Infrastructure (JDI). The JDI supports features such as a Java Dictionary of data types and definitions, tracking of dependencies between modules, and automatic rebuilding of libraries, which are features that SAP has found critical to making users productive over its 30-year history of developing software.

Where SAP really breaks new ground is in how you can use SAP NetWeaver Developer Studio as an application modeler. The SAP NetWeaver Developer Studio supports a user-interface framework called SAP Web Dynpro, which allows programmers to specify in a simple way, without using Java code, what a user interface should look like and how it should act. The Java code to create this user interface is then generated automatically. You can then improve and customize the generated code with additional Java code to fill in any gaps.

SAP didn't want to leave the hot wireless technology out of the loop, so SAP NetWeaver Developer Studio has a similar environment for creating user interfaces for wireless and handheld devices: the SAP MI.

SAP NetWeaver Developer Studio also includes special environments for developing portal interfaces, which are key to almost every project you tackle.

Helping SAP NetWeaver users in many ways

The code you write in the SAP NetWeaver Developer Studio makes the triple-play of people, information, and process integration by helping programmers be more productive. Essentially, programmers spend as much time as possible adding value and as little time as possible dealing with trivial details. In this way, the SAP NetWeaver Developer Studio supports innovation and saves your company money.

How it works with other SAP NetWeaver components

The SAP NetWeaver Developer Studio creates applications that run on SAP Web AS. Code from the SAP NetWeaver Developer Studio can exist at any layer of the application stack.

SAP Composite Application Framework

The SAP Composite Application Framework (SAP CAF) is a modeling and development environment for creating composite applications. (You probably guessed that, right?) *Composite applications* are essentially applications built out of services provided by other applications.

Composite applications are very hot in the current IT environment because they help you accelerate development by leveraging and reusing existing applications.

SAP CAF allows you to define applications using role-based or process-based modeling. Here's how it works:

- ✔ SAP NetWeaver Visual Composer, the new UI modeling tool, helps build front ends.

- ✔ Flexible objects called *guided procedures* help move a user through a process one step at a time.

- ✔ The existing functionality of SAP NetWeaver, mySAP Business Suite solutions, and that from other vendors is accessed through an object access layer.

- ✔ Features for managing collaboration and communication are built in. A control center allows a user to see all of the roles she is playing within several composite applications and navigate the applications based on those roles.

SAP CAF has the effect of allowing almost an entire application to be modeled rather than coded by hand. This is good news, because when it comes time to change the processes or user interfaces of an application, the change happens through adjusting the model, not through the tedious task of manipulating code. This also means that you easily can modify and optimize applications to better support your business processes.

How you use SAP CAF

You create SAP xApps™ using SAP CAF, building these applications on top of SAP NetWeaver, mySAP Business Suite, and other non-SAP applications. SAP CAF uses their roles, guided procedures, and collaborative functions to automate cross-functional processes such as product definition and resource and program management.

What goes on inside SAP CAF

SAP CAF has a metadata repository that contains information that describes the objects, roles, and user interfaces, as well as the relationships between all of those things. This metadata is then used to generate the code that runs on the SAP Web AS. In this way, a small amount of metadata can be used to generate hundreds and thousands of lines of code. And hundreds and thousands of lines of code would warm the cockles of any developer's heart, right?

How SAP CAF works with other SAP NetWeaver components

SAP CAF is like the ringmaster of modeling. It uses all SAP NetWeaver components as services. Through the object access layer, for example, you can make the search features of the SAP Knowledge Management component part of any object in the SAP CAF. The same holds true for collaboration features and the ability to send and receive messages using SAP XI.

SAP CAF has special features for controlling applications that allow for on the fly adjustments. Guided procedures create flexible processes that walk a user through an interface composed of services or screens from existing mySAP Business Suite solutions.

Solve your problems with SAP Solution Manager

SAP has graciously handed its customers the same tools for managing the life cycle of an application that it uses to manage its own products. For 30 years, SAP has developed, installed, configured, and upgraded software in heterogeneous, multiplatform environments. And it's no slacker in development, is it?

With SAP Solution Manager, you can keep track of the versions of installed code, separate local customizations from the core product, get an installation and packaging framework for components of an application, and take advantage of a systematic approach to patches and upgrades.

SAP Solution Manager also provides a framework for configuration and management of an application in a high-availability environment. This means that it provides monitoring of the mySAP Business Suite solutions, SAP NetWeaver components, and applications from other vendors. It also reaches inside applications to monitor the processes going on inside. By all of these means, Solution Manager helps improve the productivity of your operations staff and reduce maintenance costs.

How might you use SAP Solution Manager? A good example would be to manage the upgrade of any of the mySAP Business Suite solutions using the best practice process templates and automatic detection of required upgrades based on your existing software. You could also use Solution Manager to package and distribute a custom application that you're rolling out to all the data centers of your enterprise.

How SAP Solution Manager works

So, how does SAP Solution Manager manage the three-ring circus of development? It uses services from SAP support such as EarlyWatch, which gives notice of important upgrades, combined with business content about best practices for implementation and a monitoring system, along with an issue tracking and project-management framework specifically designed to support complex IT operations.

Supporting SAP NetWeaver components

SAP Solution Manager is the installation and upgrade program for mySAP Business Suite solutions, SAP NetWeaver components, and all the applications you build using them.

What Can SAP NetWeaver Do for You?

The point of integration technologies is to help companies win in today's brutally competitive marketplace. No matter how cool all of these technologies are, if they don't help you make more money, save more money, and beat the competition, then they probably aren't worth your precious time and IT budget.

A key question you should be asking, then, is how doesSAP NetWeaver help your business win? While a detailed answer to this question would differ from company to company, a basic set of principles can explain how SAP NetWeaver enables companies to build competitive advantage.

Introducing . . . SAP NetWeaver '04

Remember we told you how the component mindset of SAP NetWeaver, which presents SAP NetWeaver as a powerful set of individual instruments, is going to shift with the SAP NetWeaver '04 vision? That's when it becomes a unified platform for integration and development.

This distinction is not just marketingese: It provides many significant benefits for customers. So you can understand the brave new world of SAP NetWeaver '04, here's a breakdown of what it contains.

Synchronized release

SAP NetWeaver solutions and components are delivered here in a *synchronized* release cycle, whereby all SAP NetWeaver components are delivered in a single package. The first such release is SAP NetWeaver '04, which delivers

- SAP Web AS 6.40
- SAP EP 6.0
- SAP XI 3.0
- SAP Business Information Warehouse (BW) 3.5
- SAP MI 2.5

Remember that in addition to these components, SAP MDM, SAP NetWeaver Developer Studio, SAP Solution Manager, and SAP CAF are always integral to SAP NetWeaver.

Unified testing

The whole set of SAP NetWeaver '04 components has been tested and validated together by SAP — something that is simply not possible for *all* the potential combinations that could occur when you're dealing with random releases of different components.

One platform powering all SAP solutions

In 2004, the following SAP applications are built upon and ship with the synchronized SAP NetWeaver '04 technology base: mySAP ERP, mySAP Supply Chain Management (mySAP SCM), and mySAP Supplier Relationship Management (mySAP SRM), among others. In 2005, all SAP applications will ship on the SAP NetWeaver '05 platform.

The result? Reduced complexity. The synchronizing of, for example, SAP BW with your mySAP SCM solutions, or your mySAP CRM and portal solutions, or your mySAP SRM solutions and the SAP XI. The need for different sets of adapters and plugs-ins simply goes away and everything is handily streamlined.

It's just better for customers

Bean counters take note! There are numerous administrative, TCO, and QA benefits to this synchronized approach, including

- All of these SAP NetWeaver components are now based on the same version of SAP Web AS (Release 6.40) and so share a common technical foundation. This simplifies a wide range of infrastructure activities, including administration, monitoring, and user and security management. Everything can use the same operating system release, as well as the same DBMS release. Reduce complexity in an IT landscape and you reduce TCO.

- Many parts of SAP NetWeaver can be run within a single physical server if a small configuration is sufficient, thus reducing the number of systems and databases for you to administer.

- Many parts of SAP NetWeaver can be run within one management entity, the SAP Web AS system, with its shared database, shared central services, common external IP address, administration, and so on. An SAP Web AS system can be a single small box running just one instance of the SAP Web AS, but it can also scale up to multiple big computers with many instances of the SAP Web AS that run together as one logical (albeit huge) unit.

Whether you're working with SAP NetWeaver today, or one of the next few versions, each shares certain key advantages for businesses that you'll read about right now.

Business Process Evolution: The better mousetrap of competitive advantage

Let's talk mousetraps for a second. Say you work at a company that is a leader in the marketplace. How did that happen? In today's hypercompetitive markets, most of the time the answer is that your company found a better way to build and sell the same old mousetrap, rather than inventing an entirely revolutionary mousetrap. Just look at Dell: It didn't invent the computer or any of its parts, it just innovated better business processes to sell computers. Dell found cheaper and better ways to build computers and get them in the hands of its customers.

In other words, your company has to develop better processes that can be executed faster and more efficiently than your competitors, leaving them in the dust. Processes such as customer service, manufacturing, procurement, and human capital management have turned out to be much more sustainable advantages over time than shorter-term advantages, such as patents for ideas that are easily copied.

Technology and data: The great equalizers

In today's world, the availability of technology and information is a great equalizer. Everyone has access to oceans of data, and technology keeps getting cheaper and better. If the secret sauce for beating the competition is better processes, the ugly truth is that the recipe for the sauce doesn't stay secret for long. Your company's competitors quickly figure out, using technology and information, how to imitate your best practices and catch up.

On top of that, business conditions change awfully fast. In this new century, boom and bust cycles have compressed. Information moves faster and markets are more and more efficient, putting the squeeze on everybody. (Just do a quick count of ulcers among high-level managers and you'll see what we mean.)

So in this environment, what is the sustainable advantage? Okay, listen closely: What you need to win is the ability to adapt processes as rapidly as business conditions change. Adaptable businesses innovate faster and beat competitors to market. Companies that spend their time and resources innovating are more profitable, and they provide their shareholders with a greater return on equity.

You heard it here, first.

SAP NetWeaver enables business process evolution

You know, it's amazing how often companies understand what they have to do to change their processes, but the rigid and costly nature of IT prevents them from making those changes. SAP NetWeaver changes this equation by breaking the IT bottleneck.

One strong theme that runs through our descriptions of all of the SAP NetWeaver components is the way that each component can be adapted to account for change. Whether it is modeling, or configuration, or just a beautifully designed product that helps manage complexity, each SAP NetWeaver component is ready to evolve as your business does. As you see in Chapter 5, SAP has a general theory of how applications should be constructed to be flexible called Enterprise Services Architecture. Enterprise Services Architecture is how SAP NetWeaver can amplify the power of the mySAP Business Suite solutions.

So what does this mean for you? Well, it kind of depends on who you are:

- **CEO:** SAP NetWeaver allows flexible implementation of business strategies so companies can adapt rapidly to changing business conditions.

- **IT professional:** SAP NetWeaver empowers IT types to drive innovation into business processes across the entire enterprise by taking an existing IT infrastructure that enables work and turning it into an enabler of change. (CEOs like things like that.) SAP NetWeaver is also built to evolve with ease, which makes change cheaper and less risky.

- **CIO:** CIOs and their fellow travelers use SAP NetWeaver as the platform of choice to better align IT with their business and support business process evolution. As we point out in the Chapter 2, TCO is made up of the cost of applications, tools, and integrating it all together. The prepackaged integration of SAP NetWeaver drives TCO as low as it can possibly go, helps reduce complexity, and still allows you to integrate with non-SAP systems.

✔ **Developer:** For developers and architects who love gadgets, SAP NetWeaver represents the ultimate whiz bang toolkit. SAP NetWeaver is by far the most advanced platform for business computing in terms of model-driven development, business-process management, and abstraction at all levels. By becoming an expert in SAP NetWeaver, developers learn cutting-edge technology and lead change at their companies.

No matter who you are, by reading through this chapter you take quite a tour through technologies that are likely to change the future.

In the next chapter, you find out about the roots of these technologies in the past 30 years of development at SAP.

Chapter 4

The Birth of a Solution

In This Chapter

▶ Examining the enduring problems of enterprise applications

▶ Understanding the SAP use of abstraction

▶ Reviewing the ancestors of SAP® NetWeaver™

▶ Explaining how SAP NetWeaver evolved

▶ Looking ahead to the next generation of challenges

After giving SAP NetWeaver the once-over, it's reasonable to ask the question: How did SAP come up with this thing? Indeed, SAP NetWeaver wasn't just thought up one day out of the blue. SAP has been struggling with most of the problems that SAP NetWeaver addresses for the past 30 years. SAP NetWeaver is the most comprehensive solution put forth to date.

In this chapter, we take you back in a technology time machine so you can see how the universe of enterprise applications was formed. What are the nagging problems that have always faced those who build the technology? How have the problems been solved over the decades?

The goal of this chapter is to help customers who have earlier versions of SAP technology to understand why what they have works the way it does and how it will work with SAP NetWeaver. If you're from the younger generation and don't have any earlier technology in place, you'll get a better understanding of the roots and history of the current tools by reading this chapter.

This is important not because you need a history lesson, but because the modern IT environment has become so complex that every company is now, by necessity, a software company. The problems that used to face software vendors now face you, so understanding the structure, design, and rationale for solutions such as SAP NetWeaver is important.

The Age-Old Problems of Application Development

If you look at the systems at almost any large company, you can see different layers of technology stretching back almost all the way to the early days of mainframes. Even when antique devices such as punch cards are no longer visible, the architectures that they used, such as batch processing, are still in place. It's as if the modern IT department is being haunted by the ghosts of technology past. (Play Twilight Zone theme music here.) Punch card readers, spinning magnetic tapes, and disk drives the size of washing machines still cast an aura on the way IT works.

Things are no different when you look at the history of enterprise software. One of the fundamental drivers of SAP's success is that the company faced complex problems head on from day one. When those thrill seekers Hans-Werner Hector, Deitmar Hopp, Hasso Plattner, Klaus Tschira, and Claus Wellenreuther left IBM to start Systems Applications Products in Data Processing (the English translation of the official name of SAP), they brought with them an approach to problem solving that was forged in the salt mines of mathematics and engineering. Several of the founders were Ph.D.s, and perhaps because of this, throughout its history, SAP has been methodical to the extreme.

So get in the Wayback Machine: At the time of SAP's founding in 1972, the world of computing was dominated by IBM mainframes. The whole idea of writing software products for general consumption was new and innovative. IBM rejected the offer of SAP's founders to start a company focused on application development as a project within IBM, so SAP's founders went off on their own.

If SAP had been founded in the United States, the problems it faced would have been simpler. But as a European company, SAP had to provide solutions for companies that span international boundaries and routinely handle multi-currency transactions, customs regulations, and different tax regimes. So, by a fluke, SAP's products were born in this environment and learned to support all of these dimensions and in many different natural languages, as well.

American competitors didn't face such problems until they were years into their product cycles, which made adapting to a more complex world more difficult for them. So SAP never solved just one problem at a time. Its products always had to solve many different versions of the same problem, which is at the heart of why enterprise applications are so hard to build.

Why are enterprise applications so darn hard to make?

Creating enterprise applications and software products in general is a difficult proposition, even for the simplest of products. That's because in order to be successful, enterprise applications have to anticipate the ways in which client needs will differ and allow for configuration to solve their unique problems. The ideal situation is that a new product arrives at a client, and the client can change settings in the blink of an eye to make the product do exactly what is needed without having to write a single line of new code.

In the best case, the way that new software will fit into your company's environment has been anticipated before you install the software. If you need to connect to the accounting system, the programs to move data back and forth are already there. If you need an interface for connecting different departments, such as allowing the Customer Service department to check on the status of an order, it is already built in. If you want to offer an interface in one language for one location and a different language for another, you just have to change settings, not write new code.

Now wait a minute . . .

All this is much easier said than done. Take a look at the problem of collecting address information for a customer in an enterprise software product, for example.

The first screen your customer service staffer might see is a simple form with fields for address information. But in what language will the questions be asked? Okay, so there must be some way to allow the question to be asked and answers to be entered in different languages. But wait; what about the different format for addresses and ZIP codes? Okay, so the screen must allow for different fields in different forms. But wait again: What if the country has a language that reads from right to left instead of from left to right? Okay, so each screen might have a different layout. What if they use a non-Romance language, such as Chinese, which doesn't use an alphabet at all, but ideographs that require two-byte characters?

One approach to solving this problem would be to write a different screen for each country. But if you do that, you have created a maintenance nightmare. If you want to upgrade the process of collecting an address, you may have to update 50 different programs.

Happily, most enterprise applications have settings in configuration files that control all of these challenges. If you want your screen to collect addresses in German, you change the setting and all of the German language text is retrieved and put on the screen.

So far, so good. The challenge then becomes, how can an enterprise application be created that follows instructions to change its behavior in the ways we've talked about? And once an enterprise application has been made configurable, how can it be extended to meet new requirements when they rear their ugly heads? Customers always have needs that are not anticipated, so the software has to allow for some special processing to occur. But if extensions are allowed for, how can they be maintained when you move from one version of the address collection screen to the next?

What's an enterprise software vendor to do?

Playing the business content game

The reason that enterprise applications are so complex is that they are general-purpose systems for solving specific problems. Buying an enterprise application is not like buying a car or a refrigerator; enterprise applications aren't a final solution when they arrive at your company. They must be adjusted to meet your specific needs. In fact, enterprise applications are more like a configurable toolkit for building exactly the car or refrigerator you want.

Making choices

You can meet the specific situation at one company by setting the right values for all of the possible different choices. For a contact information screen, for example, you might tell the enterprise application to collect addresses in English, using United States ZIP codes, with two lines for the address so there's space to add an apartment number or office/department number, and lines for the numbers for home, office, and cell phones. Another company might specify addresses in French using the Canadian postal code.

SAP calls settings and methods of configuration such as these *business content,* and most SAP products come with a huge collection of preconfigured settings for customers to choose from so they don't have to reinvent the wheel each time and set each one manually.

One of the cheapest ways to close the gap between the enterprise application that comes out of the box and exactly what your company needs is using packages of business content that make the enterprise application meet a specific situation or need. It's like having a component for a car accessory ready to install. If you want satellite radio, you use a kit to install it in your car.

The equivalent for an enterprise application might be an interface for a portal that allows employees to update their own addresses. The business content would be a set of screens, a workflow between them, and other settings that offer a ready-made capability to allow employees a self-service system. The self-service information may differ, but the infrastructure of employee information is there to give you a headstart.

The more business content that is available, the easier it is to make an enterprise application do exactly what your company wants it to do. SAP has hundreds of different packages of business content for all of its products.

The second way to make an enterprise application meet your needs is for the application to have the flexibility to allow you to create your own business content. And if that approach isn't good enough, writing code can always get the job done.

One of the main goals of SAP NetWeaver is to ensure that making an enterprise application that works for your company involves business content, rather than custom programming.

Managing the whole enchilada

One screen used to enter an address may have many different dimensions. But imagine how complex something like building a general-purpose application for keeping track of the finances of a multinational company becomes. Managing the complexity of gathering requirements, designing the solution, and then communicating that solution to developers is daunting, to say the least.

Smart technology companies ensure that systems integrators and developers are as productive as they possibly can be by providing them with the best tools for writing business content and custom code — tools that reduce the possibility of errors. These tools must allow developers to write programs that can run on multiple operating systems (IBM, Microsoft, Sun, Linux) and against multiple databases (Oracle, Sybase, IBM DB2, Microsoft SQL Server, mySQL, MaxDB). Technology companies have to keep track of all of the different versions of the programs it writes, and the ones its products interact with. Upgrades to one version of a product have to be checked so they don't break other versions. Software products also must be able to deal with the fact that multiple versions of the same application might be communicating with each other. Testing all of this software in all of the different configurations is a huge task.

The point is that enterprise software products are impossible to create and manage without calling into play clever techniques that reduce a huge and incredibly complicated situation into smaller, simpler, and easier-to-handle pieces. Designing this software in a way that reduces costs and allows for more flexibility and change is really what SAP NetWeaver is all about.

The SAP Way: Abstract and Conquer

If there is a silver bullet, a secret to creating great enterprise applications, it is the proper use of abstraction. If you understand abstraction, then for the most part you've got a handle on SAP technology and can impress people at the drop of a hat.

So what is *abstraction*? Fundamentally, it consists of presenting a problem on a need-to-know basis to cut down on inherent complexity.

Almost all abstractions have two sides: a simple model of what someone needs to know and the complex mess underneath that is managed by the technology delivering it. When you push the power button on your computer, the power surges through the microchips and disk drives, and all sorts of programs start loading, but the screen only shows you the simple result of all this stuff (usually a blue sky, a green field, and some weird music). That is what most abstractions are like: Push a simple thing like a power button and it sets off a chain of complex events that produce something a user can actually use.

The idea is that the user of the abstraction gets to think of the problem in very simple terms because the implementer of the abstraction (in this case, SAP) manages the complexity behind the scenes and reduces the problem to the simplest terms possible.

The Ancestors of SAP NetWeaver

To solve all of the gnarly problems in enterprise application development, SAP went crazy and created abstractions at every level of the application stack. Trust us, this is very good news for you.

Which database is under there, anyway?

One of the first abstractions SAP created allows seamless access to data. The current version, Open SQL, allows SAP to write its programs in one way, using routines for data access provided by Open SQL. At development time, the programmer (the user of the abstraction) never has to know if there is an Oracle database or a IBM database or a Microsoft database underneath Open SQL. At runtime, the Open SQL layer magically knows which database is present and translates the request into the right form. But the programmer can remain blissfully ignorant of what's going on behind the scenes.

It's important to note that all abstractions have to exist both at development time, when the behavior of the system is defined, and at runtime, when the programs execute and the task of the abstraction is being carried out. That's why most of the abstractions used in enterprise applications have components to support both development and runtime use of the abstraction.

Way back when...in the early days of SAP, data wasn't stored only in databases, but could also be contained in files. But because of abstraction, the application code never really had to know whether a file or a database was being used. In this way, the Open SQL layer for data access has proven to be a whiz kid, vital to the success of all SAP products.

It's so abstract . . .

But SAP didn't stop there. Besides Open SQL, SAP has abstractions for every part of an enterprise application. Here's a list of the abstractions that preceded SAP NetWeaver. (You'll see shortly what these consist of and what they've become in SAP NetWeaver's generation.)

- SAP Basis
- ABAP
- Remote Function Call (RFC)
- Dynpro
- SAP GUI
- ABAP Business Workflow
- Report Writer
- ABAP Query
- Application Linking and Embedding (ALE)
- IDocs
- ABAP Workbench

If you looked at these abstractions, you'd see a progression. The first abstractions of SAP dealt with providing the programmer with a way to write code so that it could run on as many different platforms as possible. Open SQL, SAP BASIS, Dynpro, and ABAP Business Workflow fall into this category.

The next step was abstractions that supported access and integration. RFCs allow other programs to access the guts of SAP R/3®, for example, while Report Writer and ABAP Query provide simple gateways to access the information inside SAP R/3.

The last step was to extend the abstractions to handle new architectural forms, specifically the transformation from the mainframe to the three-tier client/server architecture. Enter SAP GUI, which existed to allow platform-independent development under the client/server model. Application Linking and Embedding, which helps move information between instances of SAP R/3, and IDoc, which allows programs to exchange information through structure document formats, supported a configuration in which multiple versions of SAP R/3 were in place and needed to be synchronized.

ALE solved the problem of running many copies of SAP R/3 for different purposes. This was required because the original vision for SAP, one application that integrates business information and processes on top of one database, changed as time passed and the abstractions had to change to keep up.

The New Kid on the Block: SAP NetWeaver

So, in walks SAP NetWeaver, the latest and greatest response from SAP to changing conditions in technology, architecture, and customer needs. A simple way to understand SAP NetWeaver is as a collection of new and improved versions of the traditional abstractions of SAP, with handy extra features thrown in that address new problems and take advantage of new opportunities.

So why now, you may ask? Well, in part SAP NetWeaver became necessary because the world of IT took off in many different directions. For example:

- The proliferation of enterprise applications made integration of applications as important as the functionality of the applications themselves.

- Heterogeneity across platforms and applications became an inevitable and accepted fact. Companies routinely used platforms from vendors such as Microsoft, Sun, Linux, and IBM and different vendors of applications such as SAP, Peoplesoft, Oracle, and others. That meant that any viable application or tool had to be built to work with other applications and tools from different vendors.

- New technologies such as the Internet, HTML/HTTP, application servers, portals, Web services, and Business Process Management appeared on the scene, creating standard abstractions for existing layers and inventing brand-new abstractions for areas such as mobile devices.

- New toolkits for special-purpose functions such as content management, enterprise application integration, and data warehouses became a standard part of the IT infrastructure.

- XML data standards started popping up in almost every industry.

At the same time, the breadth and complexity of the IT infrastructure was growing, the pace of change in business also outstripped the ability of the previous generation of technology to keep up. Businesses were increasingly held back by the inability of their IT systems to support and optimize new business processes.

Into this breach, SAP NetWeaver has arrived as an evolution of the previous generations of abstractions. SAP NetWeaver components have essentially evolved to meet the demands of the current marketplace. What follows is the lowdown on what abstraction ancestors and their corresponding functions have become in SAP NetWeaver.

Open SQL becomes . . . Open SQL

Open SQL in SAP R/3 and Open SQL in SAP NetWeaver have the same job. Because of Open SQL, you can write a program once and run it on many different databases. Open SQL provides an abstraction of data access, as well as a dictionary for data and data types. Open SQL in SAP NetWeaver, however, is available for both ABAP and Java.

Open SQL should not be confused with *JDBC*, which is another way to abstract databases from Java. Open SQL has a more complete and well-designed abstraction that prevents platform dependencies from sneaking in, which defeat the purpose of the abstraction by linking your code tightly to one specific database program. Platform dependencies are usually hidden until you try to run the code using another database and the program just doesn't work.

ABAP and SAP Basis become SAP® Web Application Server and Java

ABAP is a fourth-generation programming language invented by SAP to improve the productivity of programmers writing business applications. Originally, SAP wrote its applications using assembler language and created abstractions by using macros. ABAP was inspired by Cobol; as ABAP evolved, it adopted object-oriented features, similar to Java. Features of ABAP that are friendly to business applications include standard functions for conversions between currencies, calendar functions, internationalization features, and many other things that you need to create an enterprise application. ABAP also made it very easy to attach a user-interface dialog screen to application logic.

Basis is an abstraction of the operating system. It's very similar to an early version of the Java Virtual Machine, except that it was designed to run ABAP, not Java. All of the things applications need from the operating system, such as the ability to create processes, dispatch tasks, open files, send e-mail messages, open connections to other programs through a network, display the time of day, and so on, happen through the abstractions provided by the

SAP Basis layer. SAP Basis is the container for the runtime versions of all the other abstractions.

The ability of SAP Basis to be an abstraction of various operating system activities is standardized in a layer known as the *application server.* Developers love application servers because they provide lots of help in writing applications and also allow a developer to write a program once and have it run on many different operating systems. SAP's new application server, SAP® Web Application Server (SAP Web AS), is based on the J2EE standard for the Java programming language and related technologies. This thing specifies a virtual machine and a variety of other open standards that provide abstractions for operating system functions, network access, process control and interaction, and user-interface development.

What SAP had to invent in SAP Basis and DYNP (the runtime for Dynpro, an abstraction of the character-based terminal screen of the sort that existed before the windowing environments became popular), now is defined as a standard in J2EE. SAP Web AS) is one of many application servers that implements the standard. SAP Web AS differs from all other application servers in that it supports both Java and ABAP, along with all of its runtime features.

Figure 4-1 shows the way that the features provided by SAP Basis have been preserved and extended by SAP Web AS.

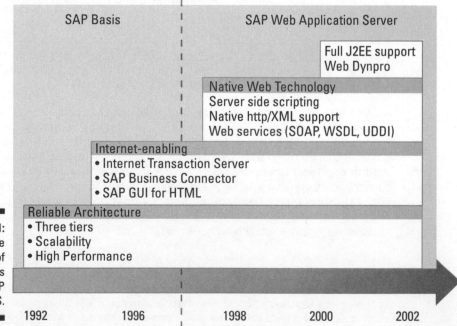

Figure 4-1: The evolution of SAP Basis into SAP Web AS.

RFCs become Web services

Remote Function Call (RFC) is a way that an enterprise application allows other applications to invoke its functionality. (In the case of SAP, RFCs allow external programs to invoke the functionality of mySAP™ Business Suite solutions.) RFCs allow developers to create their own abstractions and to present them to others. Business Application Programming Interface (BAPI) are RFCs that SAP promises to keep as stable as possible.

In SAP NetWeaver, Web services, which are based on a standard controlled by an independent group, become the standard way for applications to present their functionality for use by other applications. While RFCs could be invoked from any platform in the past, a user had to figure out what each RFC did by examining the Business Object Repository of the mySAP Business Suite solutions. Web services are easier to understand because they are self describing. You can find out much of what you need to know about how a Web service works by looking at the Web Services Description Language file, which describes the XML used to communicate back and forth with a Web service.

Dynpro and SAP GUI turn into . . .

. . . SAP Web Dynpro, SAP® Enterprise Portal, and SAP® Mobile Infrastructure.

Dynpro, an abstraction of the character-based terminal, allowed a programmer to create all the elements of a dialog screen, including a layout for a user-interface screen and labels and text fields to be placed on it. The dialog screen would then work on all the different sorts of terminals without modification.

SAP GUI was created to support client-side processing using the Unix x-Windows environment and Microsoft Windows. SAP GUI allowed a user to log on to an SAP application such as SAP R/3, and then download the interface definitions that would then run on the client. When a user asked for some functionality to be performed by the application, a request would be sent from SAP GUI to BASIS, and the appropriate task would be dispatched. The results would be sent back to SAP GUI. One efficiency measure of SAP GUI was that only the changes were sent back and forth, not the entire screen.

This user-interface abstraction layer has also become taken over by standards. HTML and HTTP play the role that Dynpro and DIAG, the transport protocol for Dynpro, used to play. SAP GUI's job is taken over by the browser. The SAP Enterprise Portal (SAP EP) provides the runtime on the server side as well as a framework for gluing the user interface to the application logic. iViews in SAP EP are small Java programs that assemble information from applications and other data sources, present it to the user, and then handle the response. Other features of the portal, such as client-side eventing, allow different parts of the screen to send messages back and forth so the information onscreen can remain synchronized.

SAP Mobile Infrastructure is a modeling and runtime abstraction of mobile devices such as cell phones, PDAs, and other handhelds. It allows one interface to be specified and then rendered on many different devices.

ABAP Business Workflow becomes Workflow in many flavors

ABAP's Business Workflow helps define a series of steps that guide a user through the dialog screens and function modules in an ABAP program. ABAP Business Workflow lets you model business workflows, which are chains (sometimes even graphs) of related transactions that need to be executed in a certain order by several users. The steps taken can be controlled based on the state of the application. The tasks assigned to a particular user can be viewed in a sort of inbox structure. The workflow engine keeps track of the whole processing and proper distribution of work items. Developers who use workflow engines end up writing a lot less code, can change the code faster and with fewer errors, and can create programs using graphical tools.

The importance of an abstract workflow and process control system is recognized at various levels of SAP NetWeaver. The ad hoc workflow in SAP EP provides a very simple way to manage transitions from one user-interface page to another. The business workflow capability of SAP Web AS provides a more robust workflow language that can handle . . . well, more complex workflows. The most advanced such capability in SAP NetWeaver is the Business Process Management (BPM) feature of SAP® Exchange Infrastructure, a full-feature process modeler that can handle responses to asynchronous events.

ALE and IDocs become . . .

. . . SAP Exchange Infrastructure, SAP Master Data Management, and XML.

Application Linking and Embedding (ALE) is a system for communicating between different instances of SAP R/3. In the early days of SAP, most customers had only one instance of SAP R/3. But as SAP R/3 grew in functionality and was sold to larger and larger companies, it became common for a customer to have several installations of SAP R/3. ALE allowed certain types of master data — that is data, say about the chart of accounts or describing products, that is not linked to a particular transaction — to be transferred between instances of SAP R/3. ALE was based on RFCs and at the time solved the problems of pushing data from one application to another.

IDocs are a format for exchanging information. Frequently, ALE works by sending IDocs from one SAP R/3 instance to another. IDocs are also used to send information back and forth between certain RFCs.

In SAP NetWeaver, this functionality has grown up into a powerful architecture for sending and receiving messages. Enterprise Application Integration is the name for this type of product. SAP's version is called SAP Exchange Infrastructure, and it is a robust system for sending and receiving messages with features such as guaranteed delivery of messages, routing and broadcasting of messages from a central hub, and mapping of one message format to another. XML has replaced IDocs as the way to format messages. SAP Master Data Management is a product specifically for keeping distributed copies of data in many different applications in the same state. It is a product that meets the original purpose that ALE was designed for.

Report Writer and ABAP Query become SAP Business Intelligence

Report Writer and ABAP Query are simple tools that help with reporting and querying. Report Writer is a feature of the SAP R/3 controlling module that allows reports to be designed and laid out in a declarative fashion. ABAP Query is an interface for query by example and query-using forms that worked through the Open SQL layer.

The need for information consolidation and analysis has spawned an entire field known as data warehousing and a collection of complex data manipulation and analysis tools called Online Analytical Processing (OLAP). SAP® Business Intelligence (SAP BI) is a comprehensive data warehouse that allows information from a variety of sources to be collected, cleaned, and consolidated. The SAP BI OLAP functionality then allows rapid analysis and drill down of the consolidated data. SAP BI also has an advanced report-writing capability and an Open Hub component that allows distribution of portions of the data warehouse to smaller collections of data called *data marts*.

ABAP Workbench becomes SAP NetWeaver Developer Studio

ABAP Workbench is transformed in SAP NetWeaver into the SAP NetWeaver Developer Studio (Dev Studio), which provides a complete integrated development environment for Java in the same way that ABAP Workbench does for ABAP. Dev Studio also brings over from ABAP Workbench its advanced features for building a large and complex program out of components. In Dev Studio, this is called the Java Development Infrastructure.

ABAP's Life Cycle Management features become SAP Solution Manager

For years, SAP has had a well-organized set of tools for helping you manage the development, installation, configuration, upgrade, and operation of a product at a client site. The ABAP versions of these capabilities have been updated in SAP Solution Manager, which is a central way to manage your installation when it comes to patches, upgrades, and monitoring.

Summing It Up: Transformation Themes

Several themes run through the evolution of SAP NetWeaver:

- ✔ **Standardization:** For the SAP Web AS, for Web Dynpro, and for Web services, open standards play an important role in defining SAP NetWeaver functionality.

- ✔ **Productization:** Toolkits or parts of toolkits such as Report Writer or ALE have become large products with many-faceted functionality.

- ✔ **Modeling:** Finally, at every turn, in products and in toolkits, modeling is taking a more prominent role, showing that the SAP way of conquering complexity through abstraction is alive and well.

SAP NetWeaver: Modeling new frontiers

If you look at what is different about SAP NetWeaver compared with the abstractions used in SAP R/3, the rise of modeling may be the most striking difference — even more important than the rise of standards.

Modeling is important because it provides a way to conquer even more complexity than simple abstractions. In *modeling,* a set of simple abstractions or components is used to define the universe of a program being developed. Then a model is created by defining connections between those components. Web Dynpro, for example, has a whole set of components that define common user-interface elements like buttons and text boxes.

The models, which are stored as metadata, are then read by a special program that then generates all of the Java code needed to create an application that works just like the model says it should.

For Web Dynpro, for example, this means a program that generates code for SAP Enterprise Portal iViews and other components based on the model. This process can be thought of as making the model *executable*.

Web Dynpro works within SAP NetWeaver Developer Studio, as well as other modeling environments such as SAP Mobile Infrastructure.

The most ambitious foray into executable models is the SAP Composite Application Framework (SAP CAF), an environment for modeling entire applications, not just the user interface, from application and platform components exposed as Web services. There is no counterpart to SAP CAF in previous versions of SAP technology.

Speaking a new language

Another new frontier for SAP NetWeaver are languages for BPM. Such languages hold the promise to make the configuration of how programs work much easier and perhaps could allow business analysts instead of programmers to control most of the logic. SAP is participating in standards efforts for specific types of BPM languages like BPEL4WS, which is a joint effort by Microsoft and IBM to merge their two previous efforts at creating such a language. If the standards creation efforts succeed, such a language could be used in every SAP application and every SAP NetWeaver component.

Web services make sense of things

The new world that SAP NetWeaver lives in is a lot more complex than the old world of previous generations of SAP technology. But, on the other hand, more tools, more standards, and more products exist now to help manage the complexity. Web services are the key elements for managing and encapsulating the complexity, and to make sense of how to properly use Web services, SAP has created an entire theory called Enterprise Services Architecture (which is, conveniently, the topic of the next chapter).

Chapter 5

A Blueprint for the Future

*Y*ou may have gotten the idea that SAP is like some extremely methodical child prodigy that plans and designs everything to the nth degree. You'd be right.

In previous chapters we survey the tools and products included in SAP NetWeaver and how SAP has painstakingly designed its technology over the last three decades. Now it's time to look at SAP's master plan for the future.

Although the capabilities of SAP NetWeaver are vital to understand, they are really only part of the story. The rest of the story will, quite simply, change the world of IT. The growth of enterprise applications and new developments in technology such as Web services is going to change the way businesses use technology as profoundly as e-mail changed communication. (How many stamps have you licked lately?)

As you might expect, SAP is on the case with Enterprise Services Architecture, a general theory of how to make Web services work for businesses. In this chapter we look at how Web services and other forces are reshaping the world and how Enterprise Services Architecture controls how they can be put to work in your business.

A Simple View of the Big Picture

Here's a question for you: Where is enterprise technology headed? The answer awaits you in the following sections.

Enterprise evolution

First, the basic building block of IT, the enterprise application, started out life as a big container for automating complex business functions. Programs such as Enterprise Resource Planning (ERP) and Customer Relationship Management (CRM) collected data and processes and allowed large enterprises to become more methodical and more efficient.

But the success of enterprise applications has led to an entirely new set of demands that is forcing the whole structure of enterprise applications to change. That's because companies today want to automate not only the standard processes that exist in every business, but also the processes that are uniquely their own. Nobody can afford to do this all by writing custom code, so companies are increasingly looking to vendors to solve this problem with the magic bullet of better technology. Increasing competition and customer power has led to all sorts of other demands, such as the need to support outsourcing relationships and processes that flow through your own company's walls and across many different companies.

Companies have spent big bucks on enterprise technology, and existing enterprise applications have brought a lot of benefits to companies. So, SAP and all other technology vendors have to find a way to take the existing set of enterprise applications and use them to meet the current and future demands. Enterprise Services Architecture is SAP's plan for answering the challenges its customers face in the most affordable and efficient way possible.

The nature of the Enterprise Services Architecture beast

So we've danced around the nature of Enterprise Services Architecture, and you're probably anxious to hear a clear definition of it. Fair enough. We think a simple analogy to an automobile provides the quickest inroad to understanding the essence of Enterprise Services Architecture.

Think of two elements of a car: the machinery and the controls. The machinery under the hood includes the engine, brakes, transmission, and all the other components that make the car work. This is the realm of mechanics and engineers. The controls on and around the dashboard include the brake, accelerator, steering wheel, speedometer, and so on, which provide the driver with the control and information that she needs to drive safely. The dashboard is the domain of the driver.

At its most fundamental level, Enterprise Services Architecture is an explanation to the mechanics and engineers of how to build the machines under the hood so that the best possible dashboard can be created for the drivers at the lowest possible cost.

Okay, so this analogy may be a tad oversimplified (like a kid playing with blocks compared to brain surgery), but keeping it in mind can help you navigate the complexities and maintain a clear focus during our explanation of Enterprise Services Architecture.

So, still want a techie definition? *Enterprise Services Architecture* is a set of fundamental principles and guidelines for creating a flexible computing environment with the greatest business value at the lowest possible cost.

Who Needs Enterprise Services Architecture?

The simplest answer to the question of why businesses need Enterprise Services Architecture is this: It helps businesses take advantage of the incredible possibilities created by the invention and adoption of Web services.

Web services are revolutionary because they are becoming the standard way for one application to talk to another. Absolutely every technology vendor has jumped on board the Web services bandwagon.

Web services rule!

You can appreciate the vast importance of the rise of Web services by looking at the evolution of online services such as AOL and CompuServe. Since the Web arrived, people have been able to access information from any place by using *browsers* instead of proprietary methods used by the online services. The Web uses standard ways of formatting and transmitting information to and from a browser — HTML and HTTP, respectively — over the Internet. (We're sure you've heard of it.) Broad acceptance of open standards has led to phenomenal growth and has replaced proprietary technology for the most part.

Web services provide a way to allow applications to talk to one another that is platform independent and isn't controlled by any one vendor. A company, for example, could create a Web service that allows it to check credit history. If this Web service were included in various applications, then employees would easily be able to find the credit history of a potential customer. It wouldn't matter if a program were running on Unix, Linux, Microsoft Windows, or a mobile device; anybody could access the same Web service.

The same transformation in online navigation that was led by the creation of the HTTP and HTML standards is now possible on a massive scale for applications. Proprietary methods of connecting and integrating applications of all types will be replaced by standard methods based on Web services. Much more integration will be possible. As applications present themselves to the world as Web services, the cost of connecting applications together drops and companies will be able to work together in many ways that were previously way too expensive. For example, with Web services it may take only days to connect two systems running in separate companies, instead of weeks or months.

Like the Web itself, Web services have revolutionary potential. They represent a huge opportunity for companies that need a competitive edge. Enterprise Services Architecture is quite simply the road map to help IT take advantage of Web services to gain flexibility and reduce their costs.

How do Web services work?

An easy way to understand Web services is as a flexible and configurable plug and socket for applications, just like the plug that you use to connect your computer to a wall outlet.

When one application wants to allow other applications to connect and access some of its functionality or data, it describes the way that its plug works by using a standard form called *Web Services Description Language* (WSDL). Other applications take a quick look at the description and then plug in.

After the connection is made, WSDL also describes commands that control the flow of information back and forth over the connection. The information moves back and forth as messages formatted in XML, a standard language that can describe almost any data format.

Like HTML and HTTP, Web services are based on a standard definition that is not controlled by any one company. That's one of the reasons that Web services became so popular so quickly. Another reason is that Web service connections between applications are much cheaper to create and maintain than earlier approaches to making such connections. Unlike some of those earlier methods, Web services are reusable, which means that one Web service can be used by any number of other applications. And, one application can provide many different Web services.

This revolution is already underway. Web services exist for all sorts of reasons. FedEx and UPS publish Web services for package tracking. Google and Amazon provide Web service interfaces to create front ends to their sites. These are just the first few drops in an imminent downpour of Web services usefulness.

Is it safe?

Of course any new technology always has a flip side to it. The power of Web services to connect one application to another also opens up the door for abuse. How many connections are really needed? Why bother connecting applications at all? Should any rules exist for how one application connects to another? How can all this happen with the appropriate level of security and reliability?

Web service standards will help address issues of security and guaranteed delivery of messages, but on many of these questions, standards will be silent. It's up to the business people who use this powerful technology to do so correctly. This hasn't been lost on SAP: Another way of thinking of Enterprise Services Architecture is as a common-sense set of rules for using Web services.

What Can Your Business Do with Web Services?

Businesses are attracted to Web services like ants to a picnic because, if used properly, Web services open the door to flexibility. But to understand fully why businesses care about Web services, step back a bit and look at the IT infrastructure at most companies.

Once upon a time . . .

Let us tell you a fairy tale about the evolution of IT at most firms. It goes something like this.

Back in the dim, dark days of computing, around the late 1980s, mainframe applications gave way to more modern client/server applications. First, large systems like Enterprise Resource Planning (ERP) came along to automate and control financial and administrative processes. Then, based on the efficiency and productivity that were magically produced in successful ERP implementations, the scope of automation naturally expanded. Every Vice President (VP) got his own wish for an application identified with a three-letter abbreviation (TLA). The VP of Sales got Customer Relationship Management (CRM). The VP of Manufacturing got Supply Chain Management (SCM). The VP of Product Development got Product Lifecycle Management (PLM). The VP of Purchasing got Supplier Relationship Management (SRM). And all was well.

So, for a while, everyone was happy because all the new applications automated previously manual functions. But it didn't take long for the people to get restless. They realized that sometimes an important business process started in CRM, moved to ERP, and ended up in SCM. Few of these enterprise applications could easily share data with each other, and almost none were able to support the idea of managing a cross-application, cross-functional process. There was unrest in the kingdom of IT.

Companies did the best they could to bridge the gap between these applications and used expensive techniques to connect one application to another. A partial solution to this problem appeared in the form of human integration, as shown in Figure 5-1. The brains of the wisest people in the kingdom who had access to all the information from different systems became the hubs for the cross-application integration of processes.

At about this time, *Enterprise Application Integration* (*EAI*) products emerged to help with making application-to-application connections, but even with such products, making connections remained expensive and difficult. EAI, as it turned out, provided only a fraction of the capabilities that the people needed to connect applications. That's because the focus of EAI on sending, receiving, and routing messages and mapping one format to another meant that it lacked the ability to solve the top-to-bottom application integration problem including the user interface, process innovation and optimization, information integration, and collaborative functionality.

The fact that companies frequently used enterprise applications from different vendors, either by choice or because somebody had stormed the battlements (known today as a merger), compounded this problem. At many companies, many different installations of an application similar to ERP were in place.

At this point in the story, companies often had a significant investment in technology that extended automation from one end of the enterprise to the other, but it was quite difficult to make the applications talk to one another.

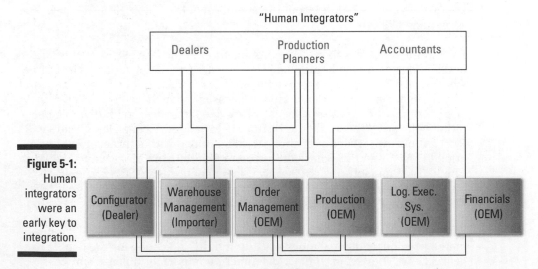

Figure 5-1: Human integrators were an early key to integration.

Process optimization and a thing called "the hub"

So here you are today, with competitive forces in every industry running rampant across the land. Even when a company gets some sort of advantage, it doesn't last as long as it used to. Companies are feeling brutal pressure from both customers and investors to cut costs, but at the same time increase market share. What's a company to do?

It's a process

Companies have increasingly started to analyze and optimize the processes by which they run their businesses as some Holy Grail of success. But seldom does the ideal process fit neatly within one enterprise application. More often, the ideal process crisscrosses application and functional boundaries like a hockey player storming the field. When asked to implement such processes, the IT department frequently has to explain that "it will be expensive and take a long time." (Stop us if you've heard that one before.)

This emphasis on processes has also created a desire to change the way applications appear to users and how they work inside. Go back to the automobile analogy for a second.

Right now, each enterprise application is like its own car. It has an engine (the application) that does the work and a dashboard (the user interface) that lets the business people drive it around town.

But business people don't think in terms of applications. What business people want in their heart of hearts is one user interface to show how their role is helping to carry out a process, not one per application. A single user interface or dashboard might have to show what's happening in the engine of one enterprise application at the beginning of a process, another in the middle, and another at the end. Business people want to see a dashboard that helps them drive a process from beginning to end, regardless of how many different engines have to get involved.

Businesses also increasingly want to extend their processes across company boundaries so that the engines running at other companies can be brought into the process. Such connections can be used to make processes run more smoothly or to outsource activities that used to take place inside a company.

Making this happen requires creating lots of connections between applications and between applications and user interfaces. Before Web services, the cost of creating and maintaining all these connections made reaching the full potential of cross-application integration so expensive that it became practically impossible. But now companies increasingly use Web services as a way to make their existing architecture more process-centric and to extend automation across applications and company boundaries.

Breaking up is hard to do

A huge danger lurks in all these possibilities. Most IT professionals remember the early days of BASIC programming when programs frequently had little structure, lots of GOTOs, and a large amount of complexity. *Spaghetti code* was the name for such programs, and they were almost impossible to maintain. Changing one line could have an unintended effect and break the whole thing.

Breaking a program is one thing. Breaking an entire complex of integrated enterprise applications is a much more costly mistake and can do horrible things to your company.

Okay, so to understand how you can avoid spaghetti complexity in favor of a design that allows efficient and reliable management of many-to-many application connections, dive a bit deeper into our analogy.

To really represent how Enterprise Services Architecture works and where all the work of managing the cross-application processes happens, think about the layer between the dashboard and the engine. It's made up of wires and connectors that reside, for example, in the steering column of a car. It's the *hub* in your enterprise system. The hub is the layer that manages all the connections to the engine portion of the enterprise application. The engine portion can be thought of as the part accessible through the steering column of Web services. The hub portion uses these Web services to connect many engines to user interfaces as needed.

Figure 5-2 illustrates this structure. The row of enterprise system boxes is unified by the two horizontal layers, one above and one below. One of these layers is the portal, which handles the user interface. The other layer is the hub — the integration broker and master data management layer — that connects all the enterprise systems together.

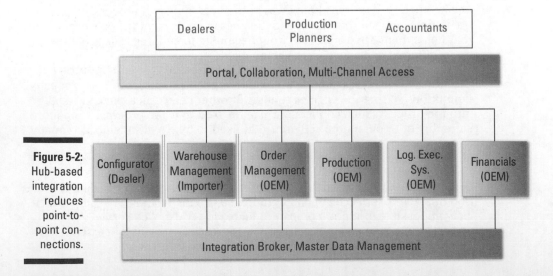

Figure 5-2: Hub-based integration reduces point-to-point connections.

Back to Enterprise Services Architecture

Many companies recognize the potential of Web services but are hesitant to undertake an ambitious program until someone points out a couple things: a comprehensive theory of how Web services will be implemented on top of existing programs and how the new user interfaces will be created without turning the entire infrastructure into a mass of unmanageable complexity. The hub is the first step in understanding how Enterprise Services Architecture solves the problem by describing what each element and each layer in the world of IT must do to make Web services work on your particular race course.

What Will SAP Do with Web Services?

To the big brains at SAP, Web services represent the key to allowing customers to actually use the applications that they've spent lots of money on over the past ten years and gradually make a transition to a better architecture.

The problem facing SAP is that applications such as ERP were once the center of the universe. Business processes were automated within these applications. Now corporate strategy and related business processes are the center of the universe, and as we point out, these frequently cross application boundaries. In Enterprise Services Architecture, processes are managed increasingly in the hub. Now each application's job is to provide the hub with help to manage processes as they pass from application to application. This means that the hub can make connections between lots of applications. (Integration is just another name for making the connections.)

Shifting gears

SAP is doing lots of things to adapt to the possibilities of Web services:

- Making every application ready to provide and consume Web services
- Basing integration on Web services and providing all the supporting tools needed to do that
- Changing the way applications are created to take advantage of Web services
- Prepackaging the connections between applications, between tools, and between applications and tools so that as much integration as possible is available out of the box
- Using a hub and supporting services to manage cross-application processes and many-to-many connections based on Web services
- Reducing the cost of owning applications and changing them to adapt to new processes

While we're doing lists, here's a list of the problems that Web services solve for SAP in adapting its approach to integration. Web services

✔ Allow the existing set of applications, including legacy, SAP, and third-party applications to more easily and cheaply participate in cross-application and cross-enterprise processes by using either adapters or native support.

✔ Make extending any existing enterprise applications with new functionality much easier for SAP.

✔ Simplify the creation of versions of enterprise applications for specific industries.

✔ Simplify the creation of new applications that automate processes beyond the scope of existing applications.

Implementing a new vision

At the beginning of 2003, Hasso Plattner, co-founder and CEO of SAP, addressed a company meeting and explained the workings and the significance of Enterprise Services Architecture. For anyone who missed it, here's a quick rundown.

"We developed the technology to build applications which predominantly sit on services. They do not have their own database. They use services," Plattner said. "Many applications are providing services, and we can now reuse these services and build new applications." Plattner then pointed out that banks and credit card companies were among the first to offer services to other applications.

"We have our strengths, we maintain our strengths, and we add new capabilities. This is why I believe Enterprise Services Architecture is more important or probably at least as important as our invention in the early 1990s of the three-tier client/server architecture," Plattner concluded.

What makes all the qualities possible that Hasso is so proud of is the user interface that has been permanently separated from the engine and the hub that allows one user interface to connect to many different engines. Now the needs of the drivers (the business users) to execute, monitor, and control processes are the major factors in designing a new user interface, not just how one particular engine operates.

Where's This Web Services Stuff Headed?

But Web services are not enough by themselves. The key to making Enterprise Services Architecture work in practice is to have the best set of tools for taking advantage of Web services so that you can create great user interfaces. Enterprise Services Architecture explains the structure of how great user interfaces are created. SAP NetWeaver is the set of tools that you use to create both the hub and the user interface.

The previous sections explain the current state of IT. The following sections look at the likely long-term effects of Web services.

Business objects replace applications

One key benefit of Web services is that they hide and manage complexity. An application uses the WSDL description to figure out how to call a Web service. The details of how the Web service works are not really that important.

Over the long term, useful Web services will become more important than applications. Some Web services will be used over and over in many different user interfaces. For example, at some point a customer Web service that allows customer data to be stored and retrieved is likely to be common. One can easily imagine Web services that represent invoices, expense reports, and purchase orders. Hasso Plattner (you remember Hasso from the earlier section "Implementing a new vision," right?) calls such Web services *natural business objects*. It's likely that the growth of Web services will help to define and possibly create a standard set of such objects.

The implication is that in the future companies probably will not buy applications. Instead, they will purchase Web services and user interfaces, and then meet their own specific needs by assembling shiny new user interfaces, perhaps creating a few custom Web services for special purposes.

A quick word on economics

If businesses are headed for the Web services world and the ability to publish and subscribe to Web services becomes as easy as finding and accessing a new Web site, economics will shift as well. Things are likely to head toward the aggregation and commoditization of certain kinds of services. Web services will be created for common purposes, such as processing credit card transactions or searching the Web. Some of these Web services already exist. As more companies use Web services as the basis of their architecture, a market for other common services, such as filing tax returns or preparing and processing invoices, will be created.

The world in which Web services is used in such a pervasive way is sometimes referred to as the *service grid*. The service grid is like a hub for Web services to manage connections between companies, like the power grid that connects your utility company's service.

Another way to think of Enterprise Services Architecture is as the road map that leads from where businesses are today to the service grid of the future.

So How Does Enterprise Services Architecture Work?

When you understand all about how enterprise applications and Web services evolved, Enterprise Services Architecture is actually a pretty simple concept. We milk our analogy of the car one more time to complete the explanation.

Applications versus Enterprise Services

The engine of the car is the functionality of the enterprise application. Inside the engine is all the programming codethat does the work of automating business processes. What Web services do is allow these engines to present a small bit of their functionality for use in a dashboard (the user interface or by calling on other applications. *Application services* is the name for the Web services that expose services from an engine or an enterprise application.

Although application services perform some useful task, such as deleting an order from the CRM system, the business user doesn't usually need to see them. To display application services on a user interface would be like showing the workings of each sparkplug to the driver of a car. The driver just doesn't need to know that much information.

Instead, *enterprise services* are the kind of services that are proudly displayed on your enterprise user interface. These services are meaningful to the business user and reflect how your company thinks of its business. Figure 5-3 shows how enterprise services exist in the hub layer and use application services.

For example, an enterprise service that's used for canceling an order invokes the application service to delete the order from the CRM system. It also checks the SCM system to see whether any parts have been ordered; the financial system to see if an invoice has been created; and any other system that was involved in the creation of the order. An enterprise service is essentially a higher level service that could use many application services to get its job done. When a business user presses the Cancel Order button on the user interface, the enterprise service manages the complexity of that activity and doesn't leave it to the business user to figure out what else needs to be done.

One other thing: It's possible that in some cases an application service has such general applicability that business people use it in practice as an enterprise service.

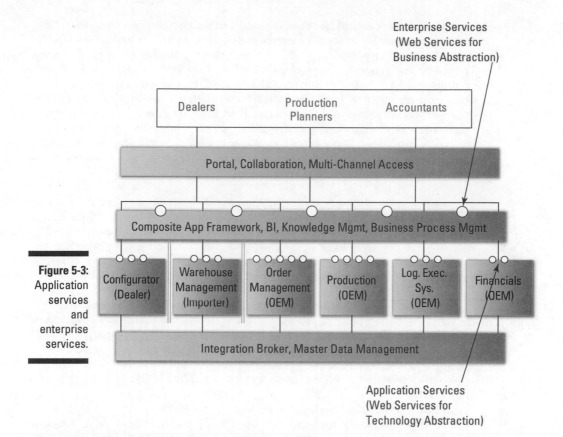

Enterprise Services
(Web Services for
Business Abstraction)

Application Services
(Web Services for
Technology Abstraction)

Figure 5-3:
Application
services
and
enterprise
services.

Enterprise services and application services are the way that Enterprise Services Architecture organizes Web services to make them useful. However, they aren't the only way that Web services are used. The service grid will introduce many more of these, and simple utility functions such as displaying the date and time will become Web services as well.

The role of composite applications

Two more important points can help you get a handle on understanding Enterprise Services Architecture.

First, an enterprise application can provide application services and still work the same way that it always has with the user interface that came with it in the first place. That's why Enterprise Services Architecture isn't disruptive and allows for incremental creation of new services.

The second point is that the user interface so far has been given three jobs: creating the user interface, implementing cross-application processes, and managing the many-to-many Web services connections between applications. These last two functions have been called the hub, but the hub is actually much more than that. The hub also allows for the creation of enterprise services from application services. It orchestrates all the application and enterprise services into new applications that manage a process flowing through many different engines, using many different powerful tools. This user-interface layer provides quite a lot of functionality and power. The user interface actually enables the creation of a new kind of application called composite applications.

Composite applications are constructed using Web services as building blocks. Composite applications make sense because they bring together all the useful functionality of existing enterprise applications. Composite applications save you the hassle of building a new application just to replicate existing functionality. Most companies have too many repositories for basic customer information already. It doesn't make sense to create another one.

Look again at Figure 5-3 and you'll see that it introduces this new layer to the hub that contains a bunch of tools starting with the SAP Composite Application Framework. A composite application may use the services from many existing engines — that is, enterprise applications. The hub may first aggregate different application services into an enterprise service and then the composite application can use those enterprise services to do the work.

If you need new custom Web services, you create them in the user interface layer. A new composite application is born using a combination of application and enterprise services, along with other services and capabilities provided by all of the rest of SAP NetWeaver. This includes functionality for creating portal interfaces, managing business processes, and many other tasks (which we describe shortly).

Keep in mind that the efficiency of this structure is very important. Composite applications leverage as much as possible of existing enterprise applications. Note also that a composite application is free to span as many enterprise applications and be as process-oriented as it needs to be. This means that the user interface is not tightly bound to one engine.

Three families of composite applications

You may have only one family (and sometimes one is more than enough!) but Enterprise Services Architecture has three families of composite applications.

The first type is composite applications that are products. They are part of mySAP™ Business Suite and extend and enhance existing enterprise applications. In this family of applications, the composite application structure is used to create new functionality by using the services from just a single enterprise application. When you need new features in ERP, for example, it's easier to add them by using the composite applications approach than to break open the single application and add more code there. Composite applications are also used to create special versions of enterprise applications to solve problems for specific industries. In a composite application for the utility industry, for example, the existing enterprise applications are enhanced with new Web services that help manage power generation.

The second family of composite applications is xApps™, which are focused on creating new processes that aren't part of existing enterprise applications. These processes are frequently focused on highly collaborative areas that span the entire enterprise, such as resource and program management, mergers and acquisitions, or product definition. xApps may have more new functionality than composite applications that extend existing enterprise applications, but they also use the natural objects and other application services from existing applications.

Finally, the third family of composite applications is *custom composite applications,* which are built by companies using SAP NetWeaver to solve problems specific to their business. The biggest distinction between the other two families and this one is that the other two are actually products supported by SAP, but this family is custom code. The same approach is used, however. Existing application services and enterprise services are supplemented by new Web services that are created to meet special needs.

All three families of composite applications are created using the SAP Composite Application Framework (SAP CAF), a tool in SAP NetWeaver. Figure 5-4 shows how the first two families of composite applications use the hub provided by SAP NetWeaver to support different types of innovation. *Best practices* innovation improves existing processes, and *next practices* innovation introduces new ones.

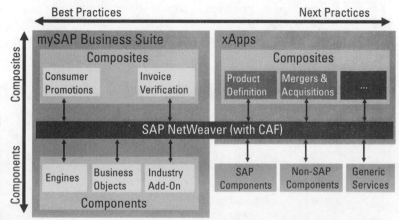

Figure 5-4: Support for innovation from SAP NetWeaver.

Heterogeneous Integration (Easy for You to Say)

SAP wants to make sure that Enterprise Services Architecture lowers your total cost of ownership by delivering SAP NetWeaver and all its enterprise applications with instant, pre-packaged integration.

Does this mean that only SAP tools and applications can participate in the perks of Enterprise Services Architecture? Not at all. Web services are universally accepted, and at all levels SAP's application and tools are ready to integrate with Web services, wherever they come from. This is a key requirement for success in a world in which most companies are awash in technology from many different vendors.

So, keeping this universal approach to integration, how do mechanics and engineers build the applications under the Web services hood to enable the creation of the best possible user interface? Here are some guidelines:

- Expose useful functionality from enterprise applications as application services.
- Use the hub in the user interface to pull together the application services into enterprise services.
- Create an environment for composite application development based on application and enterprise services, using as much additional existing functionality as possible to create new applications.

Building a Better Interface

As you discover in the previous sections, the user interface is a little complex. Now we expose its innards and explain how SAP NetWeaver helps you create interfaces and enables Enterprise Services Architecture.

SAP NetWeaver lurks behind the interface

Okay, here's a surprise: All of SAP NetWeaver is actually inside the user interface.

In terms of Enterprise Services Architecture, the way to think of SAP NetWeaver is as a tool for building your enterprise user interfaces. Essentially, you use SAP NetWeaver to integrate enterprise applications and build composite applications.

SAP NetWeaver is one way to build software that follows the recommended structure of Enterprise Services Architecture. SAP NetWeaver is *not* the same thing as Enterprise Services Architecture.

With all its functionality (which we explain in Chapter 3), SAP NetWeaver gives a significant leg up to companies that want to integrate their IT infrastructure at the lowest possible cost. SAP lowers costs for integration by providing prepackaged integration between all the SAP NetWeaver tools and all the mySAP Business Suite Enterprise Applications. None of this prepackaged integration prevents creating connections with non-SAP applications.

A key benefit of SAP NetWeaver is that it creates an environment that allows businesses to unleash the power of Web services and manage the complexity inherent in using them, all according to the structure of Enterprise Services Architecture. Composite applications lend themselves to rapid improvement because Web services by their nature can be easily reused. By adopting Enterprise Services Architecture and using SAP NetWeaver to implement it, you can gain unprecedented flexibility while keeping costs under control.

A whole new way of programming

Enterprise Services Architecture is a whole new ballgame when it comes to designing applications. SAP NetWeaver is a whole new toolkit for building those applications. To bring these two together, SAP has created a new *programming model*. This is the fundamental approach and basic building blocks that programmers use to create programs. The new model bridges Enterprise Services Architecture and SAP NetWeaver so that programmers have a ready-made paradigm for achieving the former with the latter.

Using Web services based on existing applications (both application services and enterprise services) is a big part of this new model. But the complete model goes way beyond that. The ultimate goal of this new model is to lower the costs of developing and owning software. SAP will use this new model to build its products, and customers will use the new model to extend and customize SAP products and to create custom applications of their own.

Everybody has goals and a programming model is no different. Here are the goals of the SAP programming model:

- ✔ Increase the use of modeling in application development to express relationships between services. This means that more of an application can be generated automatically, instead of being programmed by hand. This speeds development and makes programs easier to change.

- ✔ Increase the number of reusable components in an application. One set of tools would be used to manage master data in all applications. A tax engine might be created to perform tax calculations. Commonly used functions would be carried out with shared components and standard approaches.

- ✔ Make SAP NetWeaver and the tools that it provides the foundation of all SAP products.

- ✔ Use the portal as the user interface for all products.

- ✔ Accelerate user interface development through the use of patterns.

- ✔ Employ business process management tools to control and customize the behavior of programs, ensuring a clear separation between process control and business logic.

- ✔ Use a consistent approach across all applications to such challenges as reporting, integration of desktop applications, and data access.

- ✔ Adopt a single approach to storing all different kinds of data, taking into account the different needs for transactional data, replicated master data, and unstructured data such as documents.

At its heart, this new programming model maximizes the amount of each program that is composed of reusable components, anticipates as many potential problems as possible, and provides a standard method of solving them. The result of such a model is a new kind of software that is far easier to change and far less costly to develop and maintain.

This programming model will show up on the desks of programmers in the form of new libraries and tools for the SAP CAF and SAP NetWeaver Developer Studio.

Incremental adoption: Taking it step by step

One common mistake that people make when considering the adoption of Enterprise Services Architecture is thinking in terms of a big bang approach. Although Enterprise Services Architecture is a comprehensive theory that offers suggestions about how to improve every corner of your company's infrastructure, the nature of Web services and SAP NetWeaver allow you to make the changes gradually.

For example, here's one approach to incremental adoption:

1. Start small by using the SAP® Enterprise Portal to implement a role-specific user interface that assembles all the information from different enterprise applications to help automate a cross-functional process.

2. Provide more power for such portal interfaces by creating custom Web services with the SAP® Web Application Server.

3. Using SAP® Exchange Infrastructure, create a platform of reusable Web services that extend the power of many different applications to new audiences.

4. Combine new Web services with those from existing enterprise applications to create a comprehensive composite application that automates an end-to-end process by using the SAP CAF.

Figure 5-5 illustrates such a staged implementation. The next section gives you a more specific example focused on the (surprise!) automobile industry. (Gentlemen, start your dashboards!)

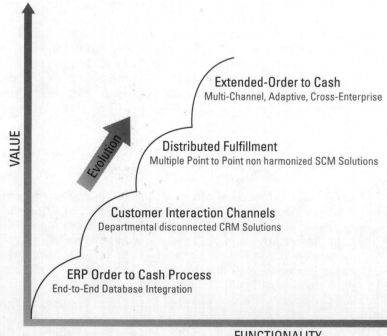

Figure 5-5: Staged implementation of Enterprise Services Architecture.

Motor City Driven by Enterprise Services Architecture

Like many industries, the automotive industry is under extreme competitive stress. IT departments have to justify more than ever the value of the projects that they undertake with a hard case for return on investment (ROI). Increasing levels of process integration inside a company have to be constructed on an existing hodge podge of infrastructure. Processes involving external partners have to be integrated through direct connections or through industry-sponsored exchanges. New technologies such as radio frequency IDs (RFIDs) come into play. The IT infrastructure must manage complex international supply chains and support outsourcing arrangements.

So, what can SAP NetWeaver bring to the mix? A lot.

Accelerating new vehicle development

Accelerating new vehicle development by improving the flow of information in an organization provides a way to beat the competition at its own game. The typical automotive manufacturer needs to recognize market trends and customer whim far enough ahead of the curve to incorporate customer expectations into new vehicle models. It's hard to shrink research and development cycle times when product definition teams don't have good access to market research. Other challenges include poor collaboration among these teams; high processing costs due to data that isn't integrated; difficulty introducing new products into the supply chain; and poor coordination between manufacturing and management that results in inadequate and costly engineering change management and follow-up process steps. What's an industry to do?

SAP NetWeaver can help address these problems in the following specific ways. It can enable a company to do the following:

- ✔ **Create an environment where people can access any information from any source — including unstructured information sources.** SAP® Business Intelligence (SAP BI) and SAP® Knowledge Management (SAP KM) significantly improve decision making by providing structured and unstructured information and analysis capabilities to enable product design teams to take correct action in less time, more efficiently, and with greater clarity and accountability.

- ✔ **Exchange information with external partners (design or purchasing, for example) and allow for seamless access to operational data.** SAP® Enterprise Portal (SAP EP) and collaboration capabilities help reduce processing time by helping efficient collaboration between internal and external product definition team members through one integrated platform.

✔ **Central master data management feeds operational systems and provides for data harmonization.** SAP® Master Data Management (SAP MDM) and SAP NetWeaver collaborate well, reducing processing costs and enhancing collaboration with partners by providing synchronized information (for example, by using product IDs or business partner IDs) when structured data is exchanged in the design collaboration stage (PLM) or in Requests for Information/Quotation (SRM).

✔ **Enable seamless integration into Supply Chain Management (SCM) and manufacturing systems for a successful new product launch from first idea to start of production.** SAP NetWeaver business process management capability and SAP® Exchange Infrastructure (SAP XI) significantly reduce development and new product ramp-up costs by supporting engineering changes with process management tools. They also provide a tighter integration of product development data into production and supply chain execution systems.

✔ **Allow the creation of composite applications that automate innovative processes that are enabled by services from SCM, PLM, ERP, and other collaborative technology.** The SAP CAF can recombine services that are accessed through SAP XI from the core enterprise applications to knit together new processes that cross traditional boundaries. This provides the engineers, designers, and senior management with more information in context so that they can do their jobs and produce a new vehicle.

The Bottom Line of Enterprise Services Architecture

Enterprise Services Architecture is a new model of IT infrastructure. As Figure 5-6 shows, the transition from the mainframe era to the client/server era was largely a matter of replacement. The transition to a services-oriented architecture, by contrast, leaves current systems in place. This architecture extends the current infrastructure and adds a new level of flexibility at the same time.

Of course, Enterprise Services Architecture really means little if it doesn't help your company succeed. When you combine the general principles of Enterprise Services Architecture with the technical power of the SAP NetWeaver components, you get the ability to build flexible solutions that can be rapidly changed or grown to meet your changing needs.

IT is transformed from a bottleneck to an enabler of change, and therein lies the greatest value of Enterprise Services Architecture and SAP NetWeaver.

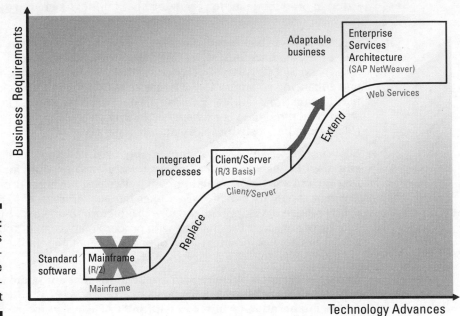

Figure 5-6:
The stages
of IT infra-
structure
develop-
ment

Chapter 6

The Evolution of mySAP Business Suite

*I*f you've worked in an organization with SAP applications in place, you probably have more than a nodding acquaintance with mySAP Business Suite. This is SAP's collection of enterprise applications that has been developed to automate the core processes at every level of your business.

Now SAP NetWeaver and Enterprise Services Architecture have a profoundly positive impact on the way that SAP will create mySAP Business Suite solutions in the future. This relates to both how they are packaged and delivered to customers and your ability to customize and configure them at a low cost.

The burning question that we address in this chapter is, how will the mySAP Business Suite solutions be transformed as they evolve from version to version, and what will the applications look like in the end? (That got your brain cells racing in anticipation, didn't it?) Enterprise Services Architecture describes the shape of this transformation, and SAP NetWeaver is the enabling platform for change.

The Short Answer

The short answer is that as SAP releases each new version of mySAP Business Suite, SAP NetWeaver becomes a bigger part of how each application works. In addition, more and more enterprise Web services will be provided to you right out of the box. As this change takes place, composite applications and SAP xApps™, which we describe in greater detail in the following chapter, will become more essential in making SAP software do what it does.

Perhaps the most important thing to keep in mind is that the transformation of the mySAP Business Suite solutions will be gradual and offered as a choice to existing SAP customers. It's *evolution* rather than *revolution*. After all, too much is at risk on all sides for any hurried transition to be forced down customers' throats. Billions of dollars and euros have been spent on putting thousands of instances of SAP technology in place. Moving this installed base forward will happen as customers choose to improve their situations by adopting new versions of mySAP Business Suite solutions.

This chapter explains (the long answer) how those new choices will be offered and how applications will change in the process.

The Starting Point

Now it's time for the details about how the applications will change and affect your life. First, you need to know that Enterprise Services Architecture describes the ideal world that SAP NetWeaver helps create. But nobody solves their business problems with an architecture, the same way that nobody lives in a blueprint for a house. Enterprise applications such as those contained in mySAP Business Suite are the house. They move the bits of data from room to room in your business and get stuff done.

Each new version of mySAP Business Suite will have more power to implement Enterprise Services Architecture and provide costs savings and increased flexibility. Remember, though, that the new house will get built one brick at a time.

Brick by brick

Here's a summary of the transformation:

✔ Today the current versions of mySAP Business Suite solutions all use SAP NetWeaver as a platform to a varying degree. All the versions run on SAP® Web Application Server (SAP Web AS), and several use other pieces of SAP NetWeaver, such as SAP® Business Intelligence (SAP BI), SAP® Exchange Infrastructure (SAP XI), and SAP® Enterprise Portal (SAP EP).

✔ Successive versions of the mySAP Business Suite solutions will use more and more components of SAP NetWeaver to do their jobs. SAP XI will help more solutions reach out to other applications. SAP® Mobile Infrastructure (SAP MI) will extend solutions to the field, and so on.

✔ With each new version of the mySAP Business Suite solutions, more and more functionality will be provided via application and enterprise services (which you can find out about in Chapter 5). These Web services will be used as building blocks for creating new composite applications.

✔ As each new version of mySAP Business Suite solutions comes out, business content and modeling will control ever larger parts of each SAP NetWeaver enterprise application, paving the way for low cost customization and specialization for specific industries.

✔ Using SAP NetWeaver as a foundation, composite applications will play a larger and larger role in the way that mySAP Business Suite solutions are constructed, delivered, and customized.

✔ As a result of all of these changes, the flexibility of the IT infrastructure will be dramatically increased. The lower cost and decreased difficulty of reconfiguring solutions to meet business needs will create a more nimble enterprise that can evolve and innovate at a rapid pace.

Want a visual? Okay, Figure 6-1 shows how different parts of the application stack will work before and after the transformation caused by SAP NetWeaver, Enterprise Services Architecture, and composite applications.

Without SAP NetWeaver

Applications written in ABAP.

UI, Database, Operating System managed through abstractions in ABAP.

Business content controls configuration of application.

Integration primarily hard coded.

User Interface
Process Logic
Business Logic
Integration Logic
Application Server
Database
Operating System

With SAP NetWeaver

Applications written in ABAP with major portions provided by SAP NetWeaver Components like Enterprise Portal and Exchange Infrastructure, and many others.

UI, Database, Operating System managed through abstractions in ABAP and SAP NetWeaver Components.

Business content controls much more of the application . . .

Hard coded integration replaced with business content or open standards.

Figure 6-1: mySAP Business Suite solutions with and without SAP NetWeaver.

Do you need another way to look at it? You may remember how Microsoft Office was at first just a collection of applications — Word, PowerPoint, and Excel. Each of these had a somewhat independent life up to a point. Now they all share the same clip art database, the same spellchecker, the ability to share data with the other applications, and many other features. Plus, Microsoft has added quite a few new applications to the suite along the way. That's kind of what mySAP Business Suite and SAP NetWeaver will be like in the near future.

For everything there is a time

So this is the big picture, but exactly when will this transition hit for any specific product? Well, software vendors, SAP included, don't generally announce five-year plans for specific functionality of any application, so we can't give you an exact answer. Generally, the only lists of specific features that are absolutely clearly specified are those in the current release and those in the next one.

That said, here's what SAP has announced:

- ✔ In 2004, SAP NetWeaver '04 will be bundled and delivered with the mySAP Business Suite solutions.

- ✔ You'll be able to buy SAP NetWeaver user licenses separately so that you can plug it into the version of mySAP Business Suite (or its predecessor, www.mysap.com) that you've already got running.

- ✔ SAP NetWeaver '04 will be very well integrated with each of the mySAP Business Suite solutions, and future versions of mySAP Business Suite will become even more integrated and dependent on SAP NetWeaver.

Almost all the SAP NetWeaver components are backward-compatible to any SAP® R/3 system later than version 3.1I, including the www.mysap.com and mySAP Business Suite solutions. This kind of backwardness is good: It means you don't have to worry about doing a lot of customization to get everything working.

The rest of this chapter describes the big picture of how mySAP Business Suite solutions will evolve because of the possibilities created by SAP NetWeaver to fulfill the vision of Enterprise Services Architecture.

Why is this such a big deal? Because SAP does a lot of thinking about what should come next for each product and is very careful about releasing such information. Unfortunately, *For Dummies* books aren't yet part of this process, although the authors have put that in the suggestion box.

By the way, this chapter is *not* a product announcement. Really, it's not. Not at all. Nope.

It is however, worth reading, so get going already.

Is SAP NetWeaver only about the future?

All this talk about successive versions and incremental progress and fulfilling visions could easily give you the wrong impression that SAP NetWeaver is still on the drawing board. That's not at all true. SAP NetWeaver is here now. All the SAP NetWeaver components that we have mention are working products and can be purchased and used to make your business run better today (and we show you how to do just that in Part IV).

The point of this chapter is to show how the mySAP Business Suite solutions will make even more use of SAP NetWeaver as time goes on and how increased used of Web services will pave the way for a composite applications approach. Got it? Good. Moving on. . . .

SAP NetWeaver Meets mySAP Business Suite

So, now that it's perfectly clear that we aren't making a product announcement but are in fact explaining the pattern that product announcements are likely to take (fine distinction), we can get this show on the road.

How exactly will SAP NetWeaver and mySAP play together going forward? Here's the SAP sound bite: mySAP Business Suite solutions will increasingly use SAP NetWeaver components to do their work, which has the effect of merging the solution and the integration technology to create a prepackaged application that is easily configured to meet business needs. The innovation is that integration technology is not an afterthought, but part of the application.

SAP NetWeaver is already friends with mySAP Business Suite

All mySAP Business Suite applications use SAP NetWeaver already. The first way that SAP NetWeaver is used by mySAP Business Suite is through the SAP Web AS. All mySAP Business Suite applications run on the SAP Web AS, taking advantage of its support for both Java and ABAP.

The next most popular way that mySAP Business Suite solutions use SAP NetWeaver is through the SAP EP. mySAP Customer Relationship Management (CRM) currently uses the SAP EP for its user-interface layer. Many other mySAP Business Suite solutions have part of their interfaces in SAP CRM, and as time goes on, SAP CRM will be the interface layer for all of them. (When, exactly, is something that this book doesn't address, because that would enter the forbidden realm of the product announcement.)

Right now, most of the mySAP Business Suite solutions can provide some sort of data to the SAP EP, through the BAPIs if in no other way. But many go way beyond that and come with business content that configures the portal to provide a specialized view of the solution for a particular industry or advanced function.

After SAP EP, the next most frequently used part of SAP NetWeaver is SAP BI. In fact, over 6,000 companies around the world already use SAP BI to collect and analyze data from SAP and non-SAP systems alike.

SAP XI is also in widespread use with mySAP Business Suite solutions. For example, mySAP Supplier Relationship Management (SRM) uses SAP XI to move purchasing data, such as purchase orders and confirmations, happily back and forth between business partners.

The importance of business content

Now and then we highlight something that's really important for you to understand. (Not that we don't think you value every single word we say equally.) Well, consider this highlighted: It's critical to understand the importance of enabling mySAP Business Suite solutions to use SAP NetWeaver components. Here's why.

Generally speaking, *business content* (collections of settings, configurations, and programs such as iViews that tailor one or more SAP products for a particular purpose) has traditionally reduced the cost of implementation and customization as well as making it easier to keep customizations up to date from one release to the next. Business content is collected in business packages, for example with campaign management features for the marketing staff, business packages for asset finance, and leasing help to keep track of financing and leasing of movable assets, as well as hundreds of others. Now, however, business content is expanding in scope, which means that traditional custom code is being replaced by standard business content right and left. This means that it will be much easier and cheaper to change mySAP Business Suite solutions to make them do exactly what you want without rewriting code. Custom code won't be available for user modifications, but business content will be.

For example, the SAP EP business content, which consists of iViews and other configuration settings, taxonomies, and other elements that customize an application, is in a standard form. Remember how abstractions are used to manage complexity? Well, using business content means that you're using an abstraction to control the behavior of an application. The bottom line is that more of the application becomes available for you to modify.

But this is the technology side of business content. What your boss wants to hear is that business content reduces the cost of implementation dramatically. The whole process of customization is streamlined and accelerated. The custom configured idea of business packages replaces the laborious nature of hard coding. Instead of starting with a blank slate, a business package gives customers a huge head start. Business packages are also maintained and upgraded as SAP NetWeaver and the mySAP Business Suite improve with each version, which reduces the cost of maintaining customizations through upgrade cycles.

The bottom line: Expect more business content coming at you from all directions.

Existing applications will become better acquainted with SAP NetWeaver

So, if mySAP Business Suite applications are already using SAP Web AS, SAP EP, SAP BI, and SAP XI to some extent, what's next?

Well, at first, the updates will be more of the same. All these products will just be used to a greater extent by mySAP Business Suite. Just as SAP completely converted the mySAP CRM interface to use SAP EP, so will the other mySAP Business Suite solutions, for example.

The next step is that other parts of SAP NetWeaver will adapt to help the applications do what they do well. mySAP Business Suite solutions will use SAP MI to support mobile devices. SAP Business Intelligence will analyze the data in any of the mySAP Business Suite solutions with much more preconfigured business content for each application. SAP® Master Data Management (SAP MDM) will come ready to manage the master data of several instances of a mySAP Business Suite application across the world.

So here's how to think of this evolution: SAP NetWeaver will start enabling the mySAP Business Suite solutions and offering help based on each component's special talents. Then, SAP NetWeaver will start affecting the way that the applications are constructed.

SAP NetWeaver: Adding tools to existing toolkits

Some people say that you should do what you know best. The first way that SAP will help with the core functions of the mySAP Business Suite is by adding on to the functionality that is similar to SAP NetWeaver components.

In certain applications, such as mySAP SRM, the earlier technology for data exchange with suppliers was the Business Connector, a tool for moving data back and forth between applications. This approach works pretty well for simple data exchange. But, SAP XI is now offered as part of mySAP SRM. It can do everything that Business Connector can do, and lots, lots more. When customers who have seen the difference and the easy migration path to SAP XI considered upgrading, you could time their decision to upgrade with an egg timer.

Keep in mind that the existing way of doing things will still work, but new ways of working will become possible. This dual-functionality situation will probably be supported for a long time.

The second way that SAP will affect the mySAP Business Suite solutions is through growing the parts of the applications controlled by business content and modeling, based on the principles of Enterprise Services Architecture.

Figure 6-2, which shows how the different components of SAP NetWeaver relate to different layers of the application stack. This gives you an indication of the type of help each component might give to mySAP Business Suite solutions.

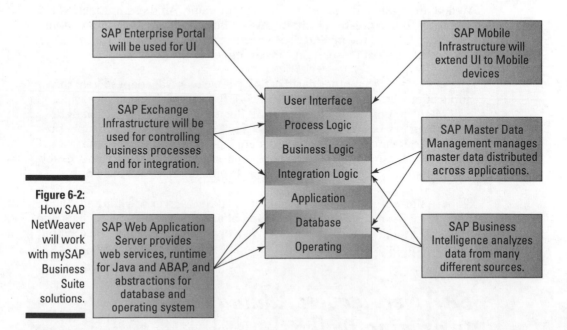

Figure 6-2:
How SAP NetWeaver will work with mySAP Business Suite solutions.

Opportunity pounding on your door

As we note earlier in this chapter, a quick look at the situation facing SAP makes it clear that change has to happen one step at a time. SAP has thousands of customers using all sorts of different versions of the mySAP Business Suite and SAP NetWeaver in all sorts of different industries all over the world. For each product, when a new version is being planned, SAP will go through an analysis and ask the following sorts of questions:

- ✔ Can any parts of this application be improved by tighter integration with SAP NetWeaver?

- ✔ Can any parts of this application be replaced with SAP NetWeaver components?

- ✔ What impact would these changes have on users?

- ✔ What benefits would any changes have for users?

- ✔ How can any changes be made in an orderly manner that provide a smooth migration path for existing customers?

These questions are just some of the factors in play when planning a new version of an application. Other biggie factors include developments in technology, what the competition is doing, government regulation, and specific developments in different industries.

The right plan is based on opportunistic evolution that balances everything. It keeps a product moving forward with new features that provide new possibilities, without leaving any customer in a really tough spot.

SAP does want its customers to evolve and use newer versions of its products, but only if the new products provide more value. (Trust us, we have this from the horse's mouth.) SAP's actual goal is to make SAP NetWeaver components overwhelmingly attractive by making it easier and cheaper to do what you need to do.

mySAP Business Suite Applications Embrace Composite Applications

Now look at how SAP NetWeaver will take a bite right out of the center of the applications. To understand this transition and why it's taking place, take a look at the way SAP developed its applications in the past and the way it will develop them in future.

How things work now

Most mySAP Business Suite solutions work through a complex interaction between components and modules written in Java and ABAP, SAP's language for writing mySAP Business Suite solutions.

Okay, in Chapter 4 we described how abstraction helps manage complexity, by providing a container with a simple interface to the outside world, and handling the complex stuff inside. The components and modules of any application are part of that divide-and-conquer strategy. One component may handle a specialized task such as tax calculations or an important object such as a sales order. Modules may have specialized jobs within a component but interact in simpler ways.

The way that the outside world uses the functions in these components and modules is either through connecting them to the user interface or by creating interfaces to them for other programs to use. These interfaces for other programs are called application programming interfaces (APIs). SAP's name for this sort of programming interface are Remote Function Calls (RFCs) or Business Application Programming Interfaces (BAPIs). The only difference between RFCs and BAPIs is that BAPIs follow certain rules and are guaranteed to be upward-compatible as new versions are released.

So, to really understand the changes that are taking place now, take a look at the way that the process for creating the current versions of mySAP Business Suite solutions worked:

1. SAP gathered business requirements together to determine what the application should do.

2. Architects and programmers designed components and modules on SAP Web AS to manage the complexity of the problem and deliver the functionality needed by using the abstraction layers over the user interface, database, and operating system provided by SAP.

3. SAP connected the components and modules to user interfaces and exposed them to other programs through RFCs and BAPIs.

4. All this functionality was then packaged up in a very neat little box and delivered to the customer, who could control the application through changing parameter files, adjusting the user interface, and writing programs that used the RFCs and BAPIs.

What this approach led to was applications that were controlled by custom ABAP code that might have provided some flexibility through parameter files and other approaches to configuration. But ABAP code was king, the primary mechanism to manage the complexity of the application and carry out the work that you needed to get done.

The future

So what's down the road for SAP applications? The main thing is that SAP NetWeaver and Enterprise Services Architecture create a new programming model for mySAP Business Suite. The steps that SAP will take to create a mySAP Business Suite application from now on will be these:

1. The business requirements are gathered to determine what the application should do. (Of course, this always is the first step.)

2. The architects and developers design services that manage the complexity and deliver the needed functionality. The way that services work will be described in metadata.

3. The architects and developers will make the services work by using some combination of three approaches: by programming them in ABAP or Java; by using a framework for application modeling; or by using other services.

4. The application will use the services, along with modeling frameworks, for user-interface and business-process management by using metadata to describe what the application should do. Based on these descriptions, most of the ABAP and Java code that's used for the application will be generated automatically. (If your head is spinning with technology terms, just hang in there. Read on in this chapter for a bit more detail about terms such as *modeling frameworks* and *metadata*.)

5. The application will be packaged and delivered to users who will now not only be able to change the user interface and the parameter files, but also have access to the metadata that describes how the application works. This metadata is business content that controls more and more of the application as time goes by.

Here is the bottom line: As time goes on, more and more mySAP Business Suite solutions will be delivered as business content. So, in the end, through business content executed on SAP NetWeaver, the parts of a solution that a customer can control become much larger in scope. Figure 6-3 shows how much more business content will be available after mySAP Business Suite starts using more of SAP NetWeaver.

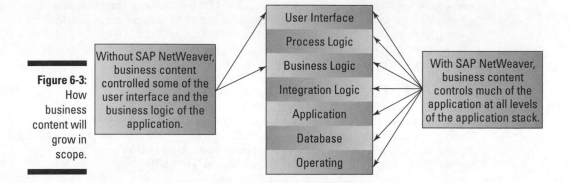

Figure 6-3:
How
business
content will
grow in
scope.

Who cares? SAP cares because these changes allow your company to deliver mySAP ERP along with customized applications for specific industries at a much lower cost. Upgrading software, supporting many versions, and working with partners also become easier and cheaper.

Composite applications snuggle up to mySAP Business Suite

So, how will composite applications change the future of the mySAP Business Suite? Well, here's the secret in a nutshell: mySAP Business Suite solutions are going to be extended with composite applications. That really sums up the whole change, so you can go back to work now. (Just kidding.)

Composite applications are built on services provided by other applications. To build a composite application, you start by looking at other applications for services that will help you do the job you want to do. The composite application fills in whatever extra functionality it needs with services from various applications and, voilà, a new application is born.

As time passes, more and more of mySAP Business Suite will come with all sorts of services out of the box. New functionality will be created using all these services to do the job that needs to be done. So one difference between composite applications and the new form of mySAP Business Suite is that more of the services will belong to mySAP Business Suite instead of coming from other applications. In this sense, mySAP Business Suite solutions may be based on services (as are composite applications).

The secret to making this all practical is that modeling will replace programming. If you're interested in modeling, this book has plenty of places to read about it. Chapter 6 talks more about the new programming model of composite applications, which makes heavy use of modeling and metadata. Chapter 9 covers SAP Mobile Infrastructure and how SAP has modeled mobile devices. Chapter 10 discusses SAP Business Intelligence and how the data in an enterprise is modeled. Chapter 13 discusses SAP Web Application Server and the Web Dynpro environment for modeling user interfaces. Chapter 15 (which covers SAP NetWeaver Visual Composer) and Chapter 16 (which discusses the SAP Composite Application Framework) show some different ways that SAP has created environments for application modeling

mySAP Business Suite of the Future

The mySAP Business Suite of the future is an environment in which more and more of the application comes as business content on top of SAP NetWeaver, made up of user interfaces, application, and enterprise services, and other elements all glued together with a modeling approach.

Millions of lines of code make up the current set of mySAP Business Suite solutions and thousands of installations worldwide. The process of change will be gradual, but its impact will be very positive. It will increase what every customer can do with mySAP Business Suite solutions and reduce the cost of doing it.

Chapter 7

Composite Applications and SAP xApps: Flexible and Reusable Innovation

....

....

The products SAP creates provide such a dizzying number of business applications and supporting technology that you could get a headache just trying to get a handle on it all. Think of this book as a bottle of aspirin, because we explain things in simple, easy-to-understand terms.

Because all the power of SAP NetWeaver™ is brought to fruition in composite applications and SAP xApps, we take it especially easy on you in this chapter. These sorts of applications bring Enterprise Services Architecture, SAP NetWeaver, and mySAP™ Business Suite into an orderly package that can help your business. (Aren't you feeling better already?) Not only can you do things that you are doing now better, faster, and cheaper, but you will be able to perform tasks that were never before possible and embed within software new processes that were formerly only sketched out on whiteboards or dinner napkins.

Quite simply, composite applications and SAP xApps are where SAP NetWeaver and Enterprise Services Architecture come together to create business value. This chapter explains why that matters and how it all works.

How Composite Applications Work

The simplest way to define a *composite application* is as a Frankenstein's monster kind of creation, constructed primarily by building on parts of existing applications. But unlike Frankenstein's monster, the parts of the existing applications are not removed piece by piece. They serve the existing application and the composite application at the same time. This has been theoretically possible for years through the use of an *Application Programming Interface (API),* which allows one program to use the functions and data of another program. As a practical matter, however, APIs are linked to a particular programming language, don't adhere to any standard, aren't self describing, and are used mostly to integrate one application with another. These limitations have made the reality of composite applications harder to achieve than bringing poor, dead Frankenstein to life.

Web services to the rescue

Enter Web services, which change everything. *Web services* provide a standard way for one application to talk to another application that is language independent and based on an industry standard. Furthermore, Web Services Description Language provides a Web service the ability to describe itself, so that both programmers and other programs can easily figure out what a Web service has to offer.

In the world outside of SAP, when people talk about *composite applications,* they mean building new applications out of existing applications using Web services instead of APIs to allow other programs to use their functionality.

But SAP is a world unto itself, so when SAP talks about *composite applications,* a whole lot more comes into play. That's because SAP has solved not just part of the problem, but the entire problem. Yup, you heard it here, first.

Here are the elements SAP adds to this Web services picture:

- **Enterprise Services Architecture:** The theory that provides the blueprint for how all the enabling technologies and applications come together in a coherent design. The way that enterprise services are constructed from application services using this architecture explains the job that Web services must do to create a successful composite application.

- **SAP NetWeaver:** The platform on which you can construct composite applications. Besides the simple creation of Web services, which is not really that hard, SAP NetWeaver provides solutions to difficult problems that come up when creating composite applications. SAP® Enterprise

Portal, for example, solves user-interface problems such as disparate application interfaces, training gaps, and ease of use. SAP® Master Data Management helps manage distributed master data. All the other components solve crucial issues so that, as much as possible, any composite application built the SAP way comes from handy existing toolkits.

✔ **mySAP Business Suite:** A huge collection of functionality that is just sitting there, waiting to be reused by composite applications. Other vendors applications can be used in composite applications as well. Right now, you can access quite a bit of the functionality of mySAP Business Suite and other underlying solutions through Web services. More functionality will be Web-service enabled with new versions of each enterprise application. mySAP Business Suite solutions will also use more and more of SAP NetWeaver in the future, which will make your job of customization and reuse easier still.

✔ **SAP Composite Application Framework (CAF):** Quite logically, SAP CAF has a lot to do with how composite applications come together. SAP CAF is a model-driven development environment that makes creating composite applications much easier. To create an application with SAP CAF, you simply describe what the application should do, rather than write code in a programming language. It's like giving your order into a fast-food drive-through speaker and picking up a neat package of finished food, rather than having to cook it all yourself. After you create the model of a program, the SAP CAF generates almost all of the programming language code automatically.

The SAP CAF approach makes composite applications much easier to build and far less costly to update and maintain because the sort of business content that is created during modeling is much easier to modify and maintain than custom code.

Now, with all this thinking, applications, and technology firepower, composite applications have become more than just an interesting theory; they've become a compelling new direction. The elements that SAP adds to the simple core concept are what make SAP CAF sing.

Making a difference in your business

So, you're probably sitting there in your office or cubicle wondering, so how will SAP NetWeaver change my business?

To understand how SAP NetWeaver can change your business, you need to understand the three types of composite applications that may make a difference:

✓ **Custom-built composite applications:** The applications you build yourself with the SAP CAF and perhaps help from SAP or another systems integrator. (Later in this chapter we give an example of a very advanced composite application built with SAP CAF by an international apparel company.)

✓ **Composite applications in mySAP Business Suite:** These applications are used to enhance or extend the functionality of the mySAP Business Suite. The composite application approach could be used to create a new application that uses functionality from many different mySAP Business Suite solutions, or to use bits of one application to add to its functionality and flexibility to another program. mySAP Business Suite extensions for specific industries or for specialized functions will be built this way.

✓ **SAP xApps:** These applications are packaged composite applications, meaning that they are created, sold, and supported as products. SAP xApps are created both by SAP and by partners who use the functionality in SAP NetWeaver and mySAP Business Suite, but have expanded and customized SAP NetWeaver and mySAP Business Suite to solve unique challenges. SAP xApps are frequently focused on helping companies adopt innovative ways of doing business, sometimes called by those who come with catchy buzzwords, *next practices,* and they can save you time, effort, and money.

Figure 7-1 shows how SAP NetWeaver relates to the different forms of composite applications.

In the rest of this chapter we explain the advantages of composite applications done SAP style and work through some examples.

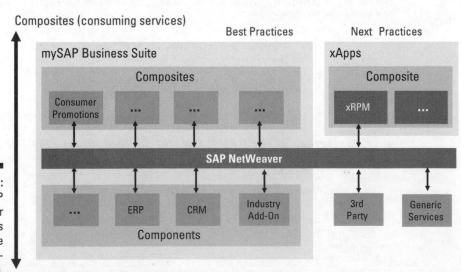

Figure 7-1:
How SAP
NetWeaver
supports
composite
applica-
tions.

Building Better Mousetraps

SAP added the tools you need to make composite applications practical and easy to build and package as SAP xApps to save your company money and to make your business run better. The real question is, do these SAP xApp™ mousetraps really work better?

The answer is yes, and the following sections describe exactly why.

Reusing what you've already invested in

Composite applications increase the return on your investment in applications because they take your existing applications and find all kinds of different uses for them. Frequently, this has the result of bringing the data or features of one application to a whole new population of users. It can also mean solving new problems at lower costs because you aren't starting from scratch, but from the functionality provided by your same old favorite programs. In either case, composite applications tap into the value from your installed base of applications.

Saving money up front and all along the way

Because composite applications are created through modeling rather than through a programming language, you can easily modify them without affecting the underlying components that you're repurposing.

Most of a composite application is controlled through *business content,* which is basically a description of what you want to get done. This means you can adapt solutions to the needs of your company's infrastructure and reduce deployment costs because you're not getting in there and tinkering with hard-coded interfaces. When SAP delivers new ways to upgrade or extend a composite application, you don't have to upgrade your current applications or existing composite applications. You can introduce new functions more cheaply and without messing up what's already in place.

Increasing flexibility

The whole idea of a custom application is that it fits your unique requirements — sort of like getting a suit made to order, right? So, the process should be flexible. It is.

The same modeling approach to building applications allows you much more flexibility when customizing composite applications to meet your exact needs. Changing the structure of the models is much easier and less prone to error than changing or developing custom code in a programming language such as Java.

Taking one from vendor A, one from vendor B . . .

SAP NetWeaver has *mapping capabilities* that enable you to integrate applications using XML so that one application can to talk to another, all for a fraction of the cost of development and maintenance of traditional methods. Also, if you don't have to continually build from scratch, you don't have to worry about maintaining a lot of custom code.

SAP and its merry band of partners provide connectors to the most common non-SAP systems that you might need to integrate, even if they're not yet XML-enabled. Even legacy applications can be integrated with SAP solutions, just for the one-time cost of Web services enablement. Instead of replacing your existing applications, you can get a bigger bang out of your existing solutions.

Going to market, to market

Ever sit around waiting to get a system up and running because a vendor is bringing out a new version of its application next month (or so it promises)? Because composite applications are independent of the release cycles of the individual applications that lurk under them, they are faster to develop and deploy. This means that you don't have to wait around until the next version of an application comes out — you can just go ahead and build what you want, when you want it.

The same goes for SAP. If SAP sees a need, it can create a composite application for that need right away. You get current and timely solutions to critical situations that just can't wait around to get your attention.

Zeroing in on your industry

Do these things work whether you're in the toy manufacturing business or aerospace industry? Yes, and here's one big reason why.

SAP uses composite applications to develop solutions that address industry-specific business scenarios, using both generic and industry-specific components. For example, an intellectual property management solution is being developed to meet the specific requirements of the media industry. SAP or specialized independent solution vendors (ISVs) can provide similar applications.

So whether you build toy rockets or real ones, you're likely to find something to help your business take off (pun intended).

Automating it

Composite applications sit on top of both mySAP Business Suite and enterprise applications from other vendors, but also on top of SAP NetWeaver and all of its components. This means that problems that you couldn't solve with previous generations of technology just might be within your reach now.

SAP NetWeaver brings a lot to the table: advanced collaboration features, knowledge management, data warehousing and analysis, master data management, XML messaging, and more. SAP xApps already have automated processes that you could never effectively automate before, such as the end-to-end product definition process or mergers and acquisitions. You have far fewer limitations on what you can achieve than ever before.

Using Modeling to Build Composite Applications

Enterprise Services Architecture, which you hear about all through this book, is a new way of designing applications. SAP NetWeaver is a new set of tools for building applications. It makes sense to bring these two together, right?

In order to do that, SAP created a new *programming model,* which is a fundamental approach along with basic building blocks that programmers use to create programs. The new model bridges Enterprise Services Architecture and SAP NetWeaver so that programmers have a ready-made pattern for matching the way you design applications (Enterprise Services Architecture) with the way you build them (SAP NetWeaver). The way that this new programming model comes to life is through the SAP CAF, the tool for building composite applications that is covered in great detail in Chapter 16.

Figure 7-2 shows how, in creating a generic composite application, the functions of SAP NetWeaver and services from existing applications might be combined. Some services come from the SAP Enterprise Portal, others from SAP® Business Intelligence, SAP Master Data Management, and SAP®

Exchange Infrastructure. In addition, other services come from the other applications shown at the bottom of Figure 7-2. All of these work together to create a new application.

Using Web services based on both existing application services and enterprise services is a big part of this new model. But the complete model goes far beyond that. The ultimate goal of this new model is to lower the costs of developing and owning software. SAP uses this new model to build its products, and you can use the new model to extend and customize SAP products and to create custom applications of your own.

This programming model has its very own goals, which are to

- Increase the use of modeling in application development to create relationships between services so that your company can create applications automatically instead of programming them by hand. This speeds development and makes programs easier to change.

- Increase the number of reusable components in an application. One set of tools would be used to manage master data in all applications, for example. A tax engine might be created to perform tax calculations. Commonly used functions could be carried out with shared components and standard approaches.

- Make SAP NetWeaver and the tools it provides the foundation of all SAP products.

- Use the portal as the user interface for all products.

- Accelerate User Interface (UI) development by using *patterns* — reusable combinations of components and processes that appear over and over again when you're creating applications. Patterns are a great way to give programmers a head start.

- Employ business-process management tools to control and customize the behavior of programs. This means you get a clear separation between process control and business logic.

- Use one nice, consistent approach across all applications to such challenges as reporting, integrating desktop applications, and accessing data.

- Adopt a single approach to storing all different kinds of data that takes into account the different needs for transactional data, replicated master data, and unstructured data-like documents.

At its heart, this new programming model maximizes the amount of each program that is made up of reusable components, anticipates as many potential problems as possible, and provides a standard method for solving them. The result of such a model is a new kind of software that is far less costly to develop and far easier to change and maintain.

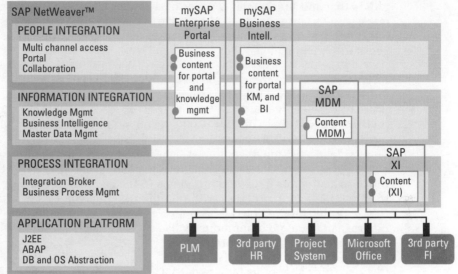

Figure 7-2:
The
structure of
a generic
composite
application.

So the bottom line is that composite applications change everything: the way existing applications are used, the way new applications are structured, and the way that programmers create applications.

The following sections dive into some real-world examples that show the power of this approach.

Taking Composite Application off the Rack

Say you're the CIO of a huge multinational firm that makes clothes and shoes at hundreds of factories worldwide with sales in many different countries. You face a situation that is making you bite your fingernails and lose sleep at night. Here it is in a nutshell: To make this company work, every month hundreds of purchase orders flow from the central office to all of the factories, worldwide. Each purchase order has an order for an item that may have hundreds of variations in size, color, and style (the ladies shorts in plain blue, size large; or how about yellow, size petite; or does that customer in China like it in the pinstripe fabric?).

The way the business works now is that, six months before the shoes and clothes are expected to show up on retailers' shelves, purchase orders go out to all the suppliers who will be making this stuff. Now get this: The purchase orders that specify how many shoes of each color, size, and style and how many jerseys and soccer shorts to make and with which team logos are sent out *before* any customer orders have been received. Each purchase order is a guess with multimillion-dollar stakes.

As customer orders come in, the company scrambles to adjust the purchase orders based on the demand for various types and sizes of products. The suppliers can then either agree to the changes or reject them if they don't have time in their schedules or they can't get enough raw materials or whatever.

This cycle of adjustment continues right up to the last minute for each purchase order, which in itself is enough to send any CIO to the loony bin. But the boss also wants to extend this chaos to the last minute in many cases by tracking the work in progress at the supplier, so that changes can be made on the fly, during production. While almost every company issues purchase orders, just about no other industry has such a complex relationship that relies on really close collaboration.

Okay, so think about this for a minute. The company uses mySAP ERP and many other SAP applications to plan and execute these purchase orders, but this complex process is not part of the normal functionality of SAP products. If you were really CIO of this apparel company, what would you do?

Well, the solution the real CIO of this company chose is to automate this functionality using a custom composite application that allows for collaboration as the purchase order flows down the line. Here's what he did:

- Purchase orders are created in mySAP ERP and then moved to the mySAP Supplier Relationship Management (mySAP SRM) system, which is used to manage the collaborative part of the purchase order process. my SAP SRM has many features for this sort of collaboration.

- Changes can be initiated by the supplier or by the company, but the purchase order doesn't get updated in the mySAP ERP system until the changes have been agreed to on all sides.

- The data in mySAP ERP is the basis of an ongoing and exacting planning process and has to be accurate and contain only changes that are confirmed (and not just proposed).

- The composite application has roles for the central office, the company liaison to suppliers, and the factory contact, providing a unified view of a complex business relationship, which leads to greater efficiency and fewer mistakes.

- The user interface for the application is Web-based, and just the minimum amount of data needed flows through the system. Only portions of the purchase order from the mySAP ERP object are moved back and forth to mySAP Supplier Relationship Management (SAP SRM), making the application more efficient and reducing the chances of introducing errors.

Nifty, huh? Like all composite applications, this solution builds on the existing infrastructure and adds vital functionality in a fraction of the time and cost that other approaches require.

SAP xApps: Delivering on the Innovation Promise

Now imagine you're a hard-working product manager at SAP who is trying to create a solution that companies will line up to buy. Wouldn't the composite application approach have all the advantages for the product manager that it did for the CIO in the previous example?

The answer is yes, and that's what SAP xApps are all about: Delivering products that are actually composite applications. Now because SAP xApps have all of mySAP Business Suite and all of SAP NetWeaver as a starting point, they can go where other applications fear to tread and do things that were not possible with technology and applications in years past. For this reason, SAP xApps are frequently focused on making a product that addresses an innovative process.

Best practices are proven business processes, and automating them is the focus of mySAP Business Suite applications. *Next practices* are innovations that are on the cutting edge.

The marriage of SAP xApps with its focus on next practices and mySAP Business Suite with its focus on best practices is a blissful union. It lets you manage the innovation cycle while reducing associated costs and risks. Here's how:

- Early adopters can take advantage of SAP xApps to drive innovation with the assurance that they are not creating an integration headache down the road or placing existing systems at risk.

- Late adopters get the advantage of a continuously expanding and comprehensive mySAP Business Suite as next practices mature into garden-variety best practices.

Another thing to remember is that out of the box, SAP xApps contain only the composite application itself (which includes SAP NetWeaver and the SAP CAF) and not the underlying software components that are required to run the SAP xApp. For example, SAP xApp Resource and Program Management (SAP xRPM) requires a skills-management system from SAP or another provider, but SAP xRPM does not contain the related HR components. These must come from SAP or some other vendor's HR application. SAP xApps don't care what vendor provides the underlying functionality, as long as it's there.

SAP xApps bring benefits galore

It doesn't take a brain surgeon to figure out that if you can buy a solution out of a box, rather than spending tons of time building your own application, it's a good thing. But just in case you're justifying the purchase of SAP xApps to your boss and you have to throw reasons at him or her, go ahead and quote these three key benefits you get from SAP xApps:

✔ SAP xApps give you innovation at a lower cost. By providing packaged innovation through composite applications, SAP liberates you from your reliance on niche products or extensive modifications of existing applications. This approach lowers initial development and life cycle maintenance costs.

✔ SAP xApps allow you to base your development on the very same platform SAP uses — the SAP CAF. That means you get support from SAP or its partners. This translates into both low initial cost of development and easy integration with SAP or non-SAP applications, and it keeps your IT costs in check.

✔ Because SAP xApps are built on SAP CAF, this speeds the development of both mainstream composite applications and SAP xApps by SAP industry business units, solution groups, and partners. Because SAP xApps aren't tied to the release cycles of underlying components, you can continue to introduce new functionality while using a more differentiated, less disruptive, and less expensive upgrade strategy.

SAP xPD: An SAP xApp wunderkind

An example of a great way to use an SAP xApp is in the area of product innovation management, which is beyond the present scope of mySAP Business Suite. SAP xApp Product Definition (SAP xPD), which combines existing processes such as product specification and sourcing with collaboration and knowledge management, enables any product manager to manage a portfolio of products from initial planning and creation to obsolescence.

SAP xPD, which you can purchase as a standalone product, provides a solution that would otherwise require you to do tons of custom development. Through SAP xPD, everyone involved in the product development scenario is guided through the process. Information and capabilities you get from underlying applications in human resources, finance, product life cycle management, and supplier relationship management work hand in hand with knowledge management and collaboration capabilities.

SAP xPD starts by helping you collect, categorize, and evaluate ideas. Then, the steeple chase begins: Through a product definition process based on hurdles or gates, xPD gradually collects more and more information from external sources and through direct connections to the ERP and internal product management systems. One of the goals is to keep a multidisciplinary team in touch so that obstacles and roadblocks that may appear down the road are discovered early in the process.

Now like high-tech exterminators, the best product definition processes ruthlessly kill bad ideas as fast as possible early on, and SAP xPD helps collect the information to do that. All the collaborative features and knowledge-management features of SAP NetWeaver are brought into play in this spree of squashing bad ideas.

Figure 7-3 shows the high-level structure of xPD, who the application serves, and the components and services it relies on.

SAP xPD is a packaged composite application that snaps on to an existing IT environment, driving a cross-functional business process

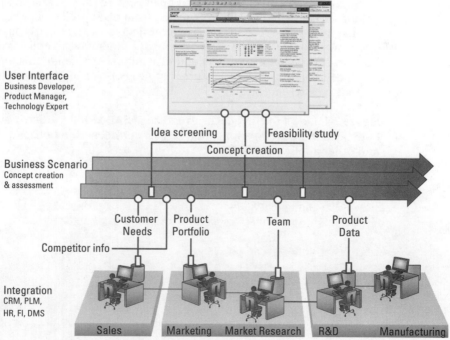

Figure 7-3: The architecture of SAP xPD.

SAP xRPM: A portfolio of projects

SAP xApp Resource and Program Management (SAP xRPM) is an SAP xApp dedicated to project management on a massive scale. Think about the pharmaceutical industry, for example. The whole future of a company depends on successful research, and as many as a thousand research projects may be underway at the same time. If only one or two more projects are successful each year, that can make a huge difference to a company. Many industries have these same large-scale product management problems, including IT management at any large company and high tech manufacturing.

The idea of SAP xRPM is to manage all of your projects like a portfolio of investments. Frequently, the status of projects and resource allocation or use isn't obvious. Most companies can't answer questions about where they've allocated the best resources and personnel, when people will roll off projects, or where they'll go. Providing more information about how well each project is meeting its goals allows the right resources to be allocated to the right projects.

As a composite application, SAP xRPM reaches into all of the existing systems, such as ERP, HR, and product management, to create a comprehensive database that includes what's expected from each project and how well it's meeting its goals. From a summary of project information, it's possible to drill down into the details and then use SAP NetWeaver's collaborative features to coordinate with others and take action. With all of this information at hand, companies can make sure that projects are aligned with their current or emerging strategy.

Figure 7-4 shows the high-level structure of SAP xRPM. Notice how the different steps of the xRPM application rely on services from both SAP NetWeaver and other applications.

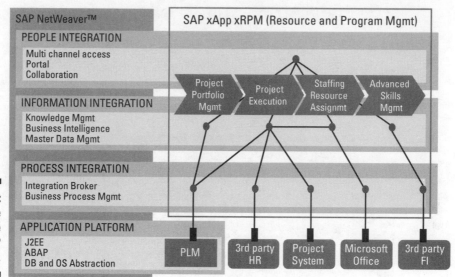

Figure 7-4:
The
architecture
of SAP
xRPM.

The Future of Composite Applications

Composite applications are the better mousetrap of application development in the present and future for every part of SAP. As the SAP CAF matures more and more, people developing front-line applications are likely to migrate to it. At some point, the composite application approach will run through every mySAP Business Suite application and be used for virtually all custom development.

The modeling approach also provides you with the flexibility of a contortionist at the lowest possible cost. SAP will continue to produce more specialized versions of its products that are tailored to the needs of specific industries. More partners will participate in the development of SAP solutions, and lucky you — you get to reap the benefits.

Part II
The Cast of Components

"We can monitor our entire operation from one central location. We know what the 'Wax Lips' people are doing; we know what the 'Whoopee Cushion' people are doing; we know what the 'Fly-in-the-Ice Cube' people are doing. But we don't know what the 'Plastic Vomit' people are doing. We don't want to know what the 'Plastic Vomit' people are doing."

In this part . . .

Well, the leg bone's connected to the thigh bone, the thigh bone's connected to the hip bone . . . or in this case: The SAP® Enterprise Portal bone's connected to the SAP® Web Application Server bone, that bone's connected to the SAP Business Intelligence bone, and so on.

This part will do something similar to that silly song. In it we'll methodically walk you through every SAP NetWeaver™ component, explain what it does, and explain how it works with the other components to help your business. Will the explanations be simple? Thankfully, yes. Reading this part will put you in the elite collection of people who actually understand what every part of SAP NetWeaver does.

Now that this book has been published, that group is growing rather rapidly, but you can still feel proud you were smart enough to join the ranks of the SAP NetWeaver educated.

Chapter 8

SAP Enterprise Portal: Something for Everyone

*W*hat is SAP Enterprise Portal (SAP EP)? Good question. But like figuring out the meaning of life, the answer is not simple. The portal is so powerful and covers so much ground that no one image or analogy can encompass it.

As this chapter explains in detail, the portal is really about integrating users to applications, at all levels, and bringing many things into one, neat, organized place.

So, What's a Portal?

A *portal* is kind of all things to all people. It's an instrument panel that presents key performance metrics, a control panel that can bring together functionality from many different applications so a user can get work done, a card catalog, an encyclopedia, a classification system, and a file cabinet. A portal can be a meeting room in which people share thoughts using instant messaging, discussion forums, shared directories, Web presentation, and e-mail lists. It can be a one-stop shop for customers to place orders, track shipping, and get updated product information. Through a portal, suppliers can plan production runs based on customer demand, streamline deliveries, and expedite invoicing.

Interface explained

In technology, the word *interface* has one definition and two meanings. The definition is the connecting point between two elements of a system. This means a couple of different things in computing. One meaning is that an interface is the place where one thing plugs into another thing, such as where your keyboard plugs into your computer, or how data is passed from one program to another. Another meaning is the appearance and visual interaction methods of a program from the user's viewpoint. In a diagram that illustrates computing as a pancake stack, the interface, also called the *presentation layer*, is the top. Practically, this means the graphical user interface (GUI) — otherwise known as "what you see on the screen" — is where you, the user, plug your thinking into the computer.

The interface is what people are talking about when they say, "It's where the rubber meets the road." A five-hundred pound engine under the hood exists solely to put power behind the few inches of rubber that are in contact with the asphalt. In the same way, the SAP EP brings all the power of SAP NetWeaver and every SAP application to the user's browser.

And that's just from the user's perspective. For programmers, the portal can be a powerful development tool allowing engineers to combine resources and applications to create new composite applications. A portal can also work behind the scenes, mapping information between different systems, integrating data from a variety of sources into a coherent snapshot to help build targeted business processes quickly and make them inexpensive to maintain. And this is just the beginning of the portal's capabilities.

In the final analysis, however, you can best understand the portal as simply the visual interface between a user and all the underlying applications and information an enterprise has put together to address business needs. The operation of SAP EP is like all the work that goes on behind the scenes of a Broadway musical, while the portal interface is like the public display of the show itself.

The Purpose of the Portal

At its most basic level, the purpose of a portal is simple: to organize complex assortments of information and tools in an accessible way. As the name indicates, a portal is a kind of doorway. SAP EP is both a doorway to SAP's underlying applications and a doorway to all the business information — in all its many forms and from all types of sources — contained within your company. SAP EP is the layer that interacts with the user, coordinates that interaction, and channels it to SAP NetWeaver components, mySAP™ Business Suite solutions, and other applications. Then it displays the results.

Today's business environment is complex and constantly changing. It thrives on the free flow of information, and technology can sometimes be a bottle-neck in that flow. While conventional business applications are primarily organized around tightly defined business functions — accounting, market-ing, human resources, purchasing, and so on — portals bring together diverse parts of a business. By combining different sources of information and applications in one location, the portal streamlines the users' real-world activities, allowing people to get the job done more quickly and easily.

Using a portal, you can view an order from the Sales department's system, check it against the customer's financial info in the Accounting department, and send it on its merry way to Shipping. If the customer calls about the order, all the information — from when the order was placed to who signed for the delivery — can be instantly accessed. The SAP Enterprise Portal has a much greater scope than any single application and can optimize processes throughout the company.

The Portal's Job in SAP NetWeaver

SAP's *raison d'être* (that is, why they started the thing in the first place) is that the more control you have over your business data, the more control you have over your business. However, in a company of any size, no one, not even the CEO, needs all the information all the time, no matter how impor-tant the data might be. Instead, users need exactly the data necessary to make their jobs easier and their decisions more informed. And this informa-tion needs to be organized and presented in a useful way. For example, when you're driving toward a busy intersection, you don't need a detailed map of the neighborhood traffic patterns; you need a simple guide for what to do, such as a stoplight.

The stoplight provides unambiguous information that allows you to make a quick decision. Like the driver of a car, the CEO, CFO, and CIO of a global company need unambiguous information on which to base their decisions — but each needs a completely different organization of data to do his or her job. And this is true throughout the company, from sales rep to shipping clerk. At each step of the way, portals simplify and personalize information and functionality.

Does this mean that each employee needs a portal designer as a sidekick? Although that would be great for the portal designer employment outlook, it isn't really necessary to get the job done. Instead, portals are designed to be *role-based,* so that each user only sees information that makes sense for him or her. Further, all employees can tailor their own portals from a well-defined set of options based on their roles in the business. While traditional business applications are usually function based — accounting software, for example — portals pull data and tools from as many sources as necessary to create a view that allows you to treat the portal as if were just one application built just to help you with your specific job.

The portal can, of course, just simply present the functionality of SAP's underlying applications, but it also it has a bag of tricks all its own. It can deliver the functionality of multiple programs on a single screen. It can guide you through a business process from beginning to end, providing help along the way and keeping track of where you are in the process.

You'll be happy to hear that SAP EP is a very generous soul, and it offers a variety of options to tweak its interface so that you can have maximum control over exactly what it displays. SAP also provides out-of-the-box portal templates that capture those business processes and implement best practices in various areas, such as sales or purchasing. You can modify these templates in many different ways at the company level, at the department level, and even at the individual employee level to create a uniquely personalized portal for each and every employee.

The portal also is a sophisticated tool for communication, offering instant messaging, shared folders, threaded discussion boards, blogs, and e-mail lists. Best of all, most of the features can be added, subtracted, maintained, and utilized by the users themselves, without IT department assistance.

Figure 8-1 shows which SAP NetWeaver capabilities the SAP EP provides.

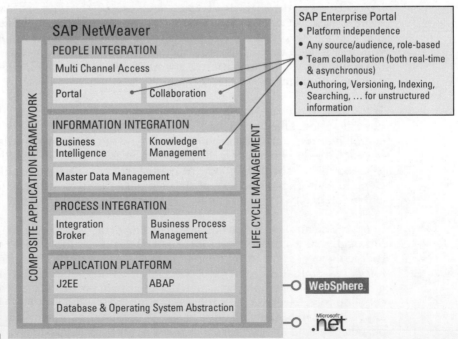

Figure 8-1: An overview of the capabilities of SAP EP.

How the Portal Helps Your Business

A portal is like one of those handy gadgets they advertise on TV that slices, dices, and does just about everything else you need it to. How do you get your arms around this thing? This section offers some examples of how the portal is commonly used to bring it all into focus..

Help yourself: Employee self service

Imagine you're a new employee on your first day of work. The company that hired you needs to know a whole lot about you, and you need to know bunches about the company.

In the past (and perhaps still in the present), you'd be given an unreadable employee manual and a huge stack of forms to fill out — health insurance forms, direct deposit forms, 401(k) forms, and forms authorizing the company to give you more forms. On every form, you have to write your name, address, and probably your employee number or social security number.

And why, exactly, do you have to write this information over and over? So that someone down in the bowels of the HR department can enter all the info into a bunch of different programs. Wouldn't it be great if you could enter the information once with no paper forms involved? Whenever someone in HR needs the information, he or she knows right where to find it. And wouldn't it be great if, when you moved into a new home, you could update your address and home phone number once instead of filling out all the forms again?

And say, under the current paper-based system, that while you're filling out your insurance forms, you wonder if your health benefits cover writer's cramp. Can you look up "writer's cramp" in your employee manual? Wouldn't it be great if all the information about employee benefits was in a searchable database (try "carpal tunnel syndrome")?

If just this one business process were moved onto a portal (see an example of one in Figure 8-2), it would save hours of duplicated effort and employee time and reduce the work load on the HR department. And that is money in the bank.

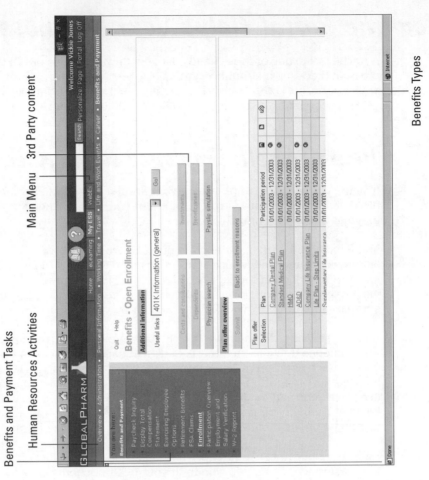

Figure 8-2:
The employee self-service user interface.

Help your boss: Manager self service

Next, say you're a hiring manager processing a new employee. You have to make sure she gets signed up for benefits, gets on the payroll, and has a desk and an e-mail address.

This means HR forms, accounting forms, and IT forms to deal with. Right now, you might have to fill out paper forms and submit them to different departments, where different people enter essentially the same information into their own system. This is what you call labor intensive.

And what are the odds that all the forms are filled out correctly or that three people will enter the information in exactly the same way? If something is wrong, how do you track down where the error occurred?

Using SAP EP, you can create a comprehensive personnel record for the manager that shows the details of the employee's salary history compared to company averages, work background, and vacation time by accessing multiple databases and programs — all with a single logon and password, as shown in Figure 8-3. You can also create a completely different view for the employee, pulling data from the same sources, but displaying it so that it makes sense from a different perspective. Why two views of the same info? Well, although the manager needs information on work history, the employee is more interested in seeing a current benefits listing. Different roles, different needs.

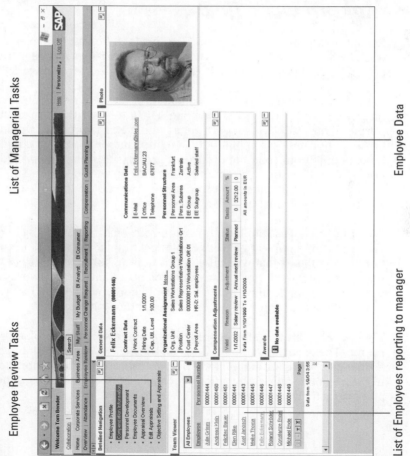

Figure 8-3:
The manager self-service user interface.

List of Managerial Tasks

Employee Data

Employee Review Tasks

List of Employees reporting to manager

What about the IT department that has to build the portal? Doesn't the time spent eat up the cost savings? Actually, implementing a portal is a net win for IT as well, because the portal can use the HR and Accounting departments' systems that the company already owns. By extending the life of the existing systems, the IT department saves money and spares programmers the training they would need to learn how to program and maintain a completely new application. By building existing systems into a portal, IT can incrementally add new systems, features, and functionality, while seamlessly phasing out outdated systems.

Making work flow

Remember how characters in *Star Trek* beamed down to the planet (there was always a planet) using a transporter? SAP EP does a similar trick by bringing people virtually across time and space so they can work together.

For example, say that you're a manufacturer and you're having an issue with quality control on the production line. The green whatsits are coming out purple. What to do? One way to get a handle on the problem would be to set up an ad hoc multidisciplinary team to look into it. The team could be made up of people from your manufacturing group, suppliers who provide key components, and employees from the Quality Assurance department. You could even get some customers involved in your attempt to identify, troubleshoot, and resolve your quality control issue.

Now that you've assembled your team, your next step is to give them a method to communicate effectively, in real time, using an online collaboration tool. (At least that would be our next step, but then we're geeks. Some people might spend the first day thinking up a name for the work group.) The question is, what kind of tool? If you could combine the best features from a bunch of existing applications, what would that look like?

The SAP EP pulls this kind of stuff together in a snap in its collaboration rooms. These virtual rooms contain all the best communication features such as instant messaging and bulletin boards, and the best collaboration tools from enterprise-level applications such as e-mail, newsgroups, scheduling, and contact management.

If your company is a global company (and today even small- and medium-size businesses often have international employees, partners, and customers), you probably need people in different time zones to be able to leave messages for each other, share documents, and view charts and diagrams. You need an interface that the participants can use in their local languages. And remember, not all team members are necessarily employees, so the team will need some control over who can cross corporate boundaries.

With SAP EP collaboration tools, you can use any or all of these functionalities. Your team can organize itself as the members see fit, using tools that are appropriate for the job at hand. At any point and from any location, the team can decide who needs to be invited to join, who's no longer welcome, and what type of information individual team members can contribute. The team has access to all the resources of the portal, but most importantly, they can do it on their own terms without the need for IT to build or maintain anything.

Knowledge is power

In this information age many companies are realizing that their most valuable asset is the information stored in their systems, documents, and employees' brains. As people move in and out of jobs in your company, they carry with them valuable information about how to do their jobs. In many cases, when they move from job to job, this valuable information moves with them because there is no place for it to be stored and no process for extracting it either from their brains (mad scientists need not apply) or their databases. You can use SAP® Knowledge Management features to help extract and locate information that might otherwise go unused.

In spite of themselves, most companies end up in the publishing business, producing brochures, white papers, spec sheets, price lists, forms, and proposals on paper. Other publications exist on hard drives as presentations, spreadsheets, and word-processing documents, or on servers as esoteric Web pages. Plus, of course, there is the immense amount of e-mail that any good-sized company produces every day.

The knowledge-management features of SAP EP can turn this unruly collection of documents into something you can actually access and use through a user interface, as shown in Figure 8-4.

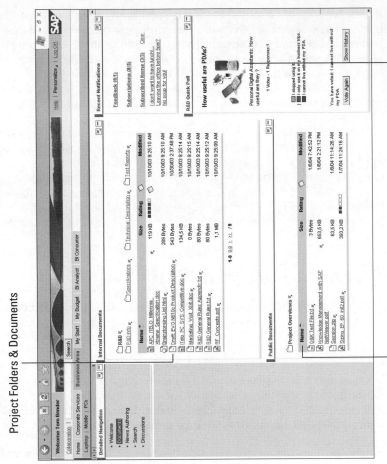

Figure 8-4:
SAP EP
knowledge
management
features.

Project Folders & Documents

Internal Survey

Public Documents

The Parts of the Portal

Okay, quick review: SAP EP is a tool for creating role-based user interfaces that brings together functions from many applications into one place under a consistent look and feel. But exactly how do you create a portal?

The main method you use to create these interfaces is layout templates that combine HTML, scripting languages, and special portal components called iViews. *iViews* (sometimes called *portlets* by other companies) are mini programs that communicate with the underlying applications, moving information from one program to another, combining it with other data, and/or displaying it on the page.

Although companies can custom design iViews, for convenience SAP has already built over 2,000 iViews and over 80 industry-specific packages for everything from the chemical industry to government, aerospace, and the financial sector.

So, what exactly are the bits and pieces of SAP EP you might work with? Well, we tell you in this section, breaking them down by who is likely to use them.

Parts for end users

SAP EP gives users the power to control what they see on an interface screen by moving the parts (the iViews) around and configuring what it is that they do. The iViews are smart enough to present these choices to the user and to work together to provide a delightful user experience. Here's how.

Personalization and customization

Personalization and customization are two features that set a portal apart from a regular old Web site. With a Web site a user can't make major changes, such as rearranging elements on the page, choosing additional content, and removing things that aren't useful. With a portal, a user can make those changes.

When portal designers speak of these kinds of modifications (which is every single day), they use *personalization* to mean the kind of modifications the individual user makes and *customization* to mean the kind of modification a company or programmer makes. Think of it this way: Adding a polished wooden knob on the shift stick of a car is a nice visual touch for the driver, so it's a personalization. Adding a new CD player or an ejector seat to the car adds to or changes functionality, so it's a customization.

Viewing things with iViews

No matter what you'd like to display on a portal layout, iViews are small pre-designed content modules that save you a lot of effort creating an interface from scratch. Need a weather map of New England on your portal? Add an iView. Need a table of all New England regional managers' quarterly sales? Add an iView. Need out-of-the-box integration between SAP EP and the Documentum Enterprise Content Management platform for interacting with both content and content management services, allowing end users to search, browse, create, edit, view, and deliver content through portal interfaces? Add an iView. (Okay, okay; we got that last one from the iView catalog.)

iView eventing

Unlike your lazy dog, iViews don't just sit there. They talk. They talk to other iViews, to the programs they fetch information from, and to the portal. When you're looking at an iView of all New England regional managers' quarterly sales and you click on Bob Smith's name, the iView sends you to a detail page — and notifies the iViews on that page that they should display Bob Smith's info.

This process is called *eventing*. By clicking on Bob's name, you are creating an event, which is communicated to other iViews that can react to it even though the user is not directly interacting with them. Eventing is really important when you are using the portal to coordinate the activity of iViews that may be interacting with many different applications. The iViews can manage interaction with multiple systems automatically, in context, triggered by eventing.

Ad hoc what?

Most people spend their days doing familiar tasks. A sales person spends the day selling, a programmer spends the day programming, a writer spends the day getting coffee and hitting the Delete key. But sometimes special projects come up and you need to figure out how to do them while you're in the middle of doing them.

The *ad hoc workflow* capability of SAP EP is a flexible, collaborative to-do list used to define a business problem in explicit ways. It can then create and send alerts or updates through the portal to address changes in the process as they happen.

Say you've been assigned to represent your company at a trade show in Boston. You contact the regional sales managers to pull together information about past Boston trade shows — the cost, the leads generated, and what they did to get ready. You ask the managers to go off and gather the information, then come back and make some decisions about which vendors to use, who will staff the show, and how the budget will be split up.

Ad hoc workflow allows this list of tasks to be assembled and assigned, and keeps everyone in touch as the various tasks are accomplished. If a task needs to be skipped, changed, or reassigned, that's fine: After all, ad hoc workflow is designed to function in the real world, not a perfect world.

Showing up on a desktop near you

Anything a desktop productivity suite can do, SAP EP can do, simply by accessing the functionality of the desktop applications from within the context of your Web browser. Say you want to read your e-mail, check your calendar, or send an instant message. iViews are available for all of these purposes and more. But the portal takes the data one step further: Because it's Web based, it is not tied to any one machine and you can use the same familiar interface regardless of your location.

Parts for SAP knowledge management

The SAP knowledge management features of SAP EP help manage the world of unstructured documents. You can use knowledge management capabilities to index, classify, navigate, search, and publish that ungainly mess of documents in all of the shared directories of the company so it becomes a powerful knowledge base.

Classifying data, structured and not so

Classification is the system for organizing and identifying content so that users can find it later. Now, if you're going to publish and archive massive amounts of information, you need to identify the data in ways that reflect how people naturally think about the information so that they can easily search for and find a particular piece of data. This is especially important in dealing with *unstructured data,* meaning things like audio/visual files, HTML pages, word-processing files, spreadsheets, and presentations.

Classifying data using a variety of systems (called *taxonomies*) is important, because different users have different needs. For example, librarians classify books by the Library of Congress catalog card number and the Dewey Decimal System; readers, however, usually search for books by author, title, or subject.

The overall framework for a system of classification is called *taxonomy*. We're *sure* that you remember this from seventh grade science: the taxonomy of living things is Kingdom, Phylum, Class, Order, Family, Genus, and Species. The taxonomy of people is *Homo* (genus) *Sapiens* (species). The taxonomy for your business is up to you, although SAP does provide many different kinds of taxonomies as business content.

Searching and navigating

Massive amounts of data stored in many different locations won't do you a bit of good if you can't quickly find what you need. Search and navigation are the magic keys to distributed repositories of documents. They provide a consistent interface across all the possible sources for the data.

After you have your documents classified, you can easily search by metadata, category, or keyword. Navigation, however, is a little trickier. The goal of navigation is to present a way to sift through the information and find what you're looking for in a way that makes sense to you. This means that portal designers have to provide a navigation hierarchy that reflects the perspective of a target audience — and the navigation has to be explicit, visual, and easy to communicate.

The most common navigation system in computing is the Windows desktop. By adapting the metaphor of files and folders, users can quickly find their way through the underlying directory structure to the documents they need. Although underlying structure and protocols are different, Windows keeps the navigation the same when you're navigating in a workgroup situation. It is still all folders and files, no matter where on the network they live.

Portal developers have to design similar navigational structures, even when a page is generated by many different applications or a document draws on lots of sources for information.

Everybody wants to get published

In the business world, *publishing* might mean that you post a document to the server or save it to a data repository. SAP EP gives you a ton of control and plenty of options for how to do that.

You can assign roles and privileges to a document, deciding who can read it, who can download it, and who can update it. You can associate it with another page or with an iView so that it can be used regularly by others on the portal. You can even associate update alerts with the document to notify others when you make changes.

You can update all the mission-critical company data that goes through your hands throughout the portal simply by saving a document to the portal. Say you are in charge of keeping your region's sales figures up to date. You work on them in an Excel document, and when you're ready, simply post the spreadsheet to the portal. An iView on the CEO's portal page combines your figures with others' regional statistics and displays a daily sales pie chart on the page.

Parts for everybody working together

SAP EP not only brings iViews and documents together, it also brings people together and provides different ways to help them communicate, organize the work of a team, and generally keep track of what's going on.

Collaboration rooms

Now we get to the water cooler-like features of a portal. A *collaboration room* is a shared workspace — a single place on the portal where people can get together and exchange information about a specific task, activity, or job. If you're a project leader, you can quickly add a portal page to the collaboration room and tell your team members all about it. Within the room, you can do all the normal portal activities, such as adding iViews and posting documents, but you can also add instant messaging, discussion forums, Web application sharing, ad hoc workflows — anything that you like.

You can do all these things anywhere in the portal, but by specifying an area as the collaboration room, you can manage all the communications among team members more efficiently by assigning permissions and responsibilities to the area. Figure 8-5 shows a typical collaboration room.

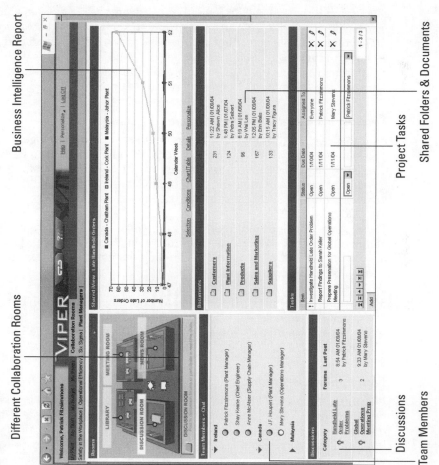

Figure 8-5:
Collaboration rooms.

Discussion forums

We like to think of *discussion forums* (often called *threaded discussions* or *bulletin boards*) as the tried and true workhorses of online communication; they allow project teams to post opinions, review comments, and add observations as time goes by. Discussion forums are a great way to gather opinions on a subject. And because they don't occur in real time (meaning people don't all have to be online at the same time to exchange information), they allow everyone to weigh in, no matter what time zone they're in.

Discussion forums also offer a number of advantages over e-mail and instant messaging. Primarily, they are a great way to keep track of how a conversation evolves. People can chime in when the mood strikes them and you can go back and review posted messages at any time. You can answer a question or offer instructions to people who are at different stages in a task and they can refer to your posting when they reach that point.

Chat rooms and instant messaging

Instant messaging (IM) and *chat rooms* enable users to exchange text messages in real time within a private window. You may have used IM services offered by AOL, MSN, and other online providers. Because instant messaging has picked up a lot of momentum in the business world as well, SAP EP offers its own version of secure instant messaging.

To get started with instant messaging, you make a list of users you want to communicate with. When someone from your list goes online, the instant messaging service alerts you. You can then open an IM window and send text messages to that contact in real time.

SAP instant messaging operates like any consumer IM service, but with one crucial difference — it is integrated with SAP portal authentication so that you can be sure that you are chatting with the CEO and not some CEO-wannabe.

Web application sharing

Web application sharing (sometimes called *Web conferencing*) is a kind of remote control for computers that goes beyond simply being able to see who else showed up for an online meeting. Multiple presenters in different locations can lead a live remote presentation — and as they type or draw on a whiteboard screen, all of their mouse movements and keystrokes are visible to the audience. In a collaborative session, remote colleagues can use the whiteboard to capture ideas or edit a shared document on the spot. Most people use this sort of capability through a third-party service on the Internet. SAP EP offers its own version designed for use within your company's firewall.

The parts behind the scenes

All of this fancy functionality builds on a enormous amount of plumbing. Luckily, the developers of SAP EP are excellent plumbers. They have created a variety of components, some of them hidden from view, that provide the foundation for SAP EP functionality and make it easy to use and powerful.

Security and the single sign-on

They say that security is like an onion, meaning that it has many layers (and it can make you cry). Security measures include dozens of different types of protection, each with its own tools and issues. For example, security measures protect against the following:

- ✔ Invasion of privacy
- ✔ Identity theft
- ✔ Theft of proprietary information
- ✔ Viruses and worms
- ✔ Data corruption
- ✔ Unauthorized access
- ✔ Physical damage to the computing systems
- ✔ Corruption of underlying applications
- ✔ Nuisance attacks (a kind of Internet vandalism)

Defensive weapons in the fight include encryption, passwords, antivirus applications, firewalls, and backups.

One of the advantages of the SAP EP is that, rather than doing the equivalent of parading out the National Guard, all this protection takes place both seamlessly and invisibly. You can access data from dozens of applications in multiple locations without reconfiguring your computer's settings or entering your user name and password dozens of times. And you can do this without reinventing the wheel because the SAP EP leverages your company's existing security standards.

Administrative stuff

Administrative tools and capabilities might not be showy features that you brag to your friends about, but good administrative tools are essential to keeping an active portal running smoothly.

Things like adding new members, assigning permissions, granting access to new areas, and monitoring system performance are what keep the portal humming along smoothly. If your portal is going to evolve with your business, adding new functionality and integrating new applications is vital. One of the most important features of SAP EP is the way it allows administration of the portal to be delegated to someone who is closer to the people using the portal. For example, you can allow a project leader to create users and control their permissions so all of this work doesn't have to happen at a central location. This can help you in the never-ending battle against bottlenecks.

Flexible content management

Like somebody having to put six kids through college, the content management system in SAP EP has two jobs: It deals with both content administration and management of the content repository.

Spread out over multiple locations, the content repository can be comprised of unstructured content as diverse as video files and customer forms. Some data is privileged and can only be accessed in special circumstances. Other content in the repository also can change second by second — the rise and fall of stock prices, for example.

Many content management systems are capable of handling the first job — creating content, uploading, publishing, editing, organizing, or deleting. SAP EP's Content Management System was designed specifically to do the much more difficult task of administering the content repository.

Server unite!

Systems index their stored information using different keys. The Unification Server functions as a huge cross index. This system allows the portal to return relevant results when a user navigates across systems that store information in different formats.

For example, say you're managing a hectic software help desk. (Our condolences.) When you pull up information on a client, your iViews must pull the data from multiple applications that treat the data differently. One application sorts registration information by customer name, another system uses a unique ID, another is organized by software license number.

However, using the Unification Server, it's easy to create relationships between the data sources. In fact, in many cases, you can view the customer records of multiple applications on the screen and just drag and drop indexed records to create a relationship. The server then converts a customer name into a customer ID number, uses the ID number to find the license number, and uses the license number to see when the customer last called the help desk. It cannot, however, solve the customer complaint — that's up to you.

Creating Business Content for Portals

Knowing how much you love preassembled stuff, SAP and its partners offer a number of preassembled iView libraries for the quick integration of information, applications, and services into your portal. The two types of libraries are the business package and the workset.

> ✔ The **business package** is built around the most common tasks and most frequently requested information for a given industry or job title. There are business packages for aerospace and financial services, for example, as well as business packages for procurement specialists.
>
> ✔ The **workset** is a collection of iViews that is built around the most common tasks for a specific job (for example, handling compensation).

Here's a handy rundown to help you remember the differences: A business package is typically a collection of pages, while a workset is a collection of tasks on a single page. An iView, on the other hand, is a single task on a portion of a page.

Key components of business packages include:

✔ A role-based enterprise portal

✔ Pre-defined application integration to applications

✔ Collections of reports and queries

✔ Taxonomy of documents and files

✔ Integration of Web content

Your Portal Applications Toolkit

SAP EP has a development environment, the Portal Content Development Kit, and tight integration with other components of SAP NetWeaver to make it as easy as possible to create iViews and manipulate all the other powerful elements of the portal.

Exploring the Portal Content Development Kit

The Portal Content Development Kit (PDK) is a developer's dream toolkit that contains all the information and tools you need to create or modify your own iViews. The standard PDK is Java based. There are also PDKs that allow you to make use of existing programmer knowledge, such as IBM WebSphere or Microsoft .NET.

Each kit provides:

- ✔ Documentation
- ✔ Examples
- ✔ All required Java libraries (.jar files)
- ✔ Developer's Portal, which is a workset for portal content developers
- ✔ Eclipse-based wizards for iView creation

Using SAP NetWeaver Visual Composer

Not everyone can be a skilled programmer — some of us are lowly writers. But we mortal types also need to access portals, right? The simplest way to create interfaces for the SAP EP is through the SAP NetWeaver Visual Composer, which allows a business user (meaning non-programmer) to create user interfaces through an easy-to-use graphical modeling environment. The output of SAP NetWeaver Visual Composer can be a user interface for the SAP EP or a user interface that runs in other places.

Empowering users with Web Dynpro

Web Dynpro is a guide to designing user interfaces that allows users to create and modify pages in what portal designers call *model-driven development methodology.* Using Web Dynpro, you arrange a page by assembling it from configurable components in any way you wish. Web Dynpro automatically generates the code for the runtime platform of your choice — J2EE, ABAP, Microsoft .NET, or others. While SAP NetWeaver Visual Composer is designed to help business users create what they need, Web Dynpro is aimed at making programmers more productive and programs easier and cheaper to change.

Getting ambitious with SAP Composite Application Framework

The SAP Composite Application Framework (SAP CAF) takes the idea of Web Dynpro to a more ambitious place. Instead of building user interface pages from existing, adaptable components, SAP CAF allows the user to model the entire application in a graphic, drag-and-drop environment. SAP CAF extends the idea of modeling beyond the user interface to the entire breadth of the application, and in doing so creates a really productive environment for creating applications.

Integrating the Portal with the Rest of SAP NetWeaver

Because it is the universal user-interface layer, SAP EP is connected to every other SAP product. Here is a run down of how they all rely on SAP EP.

Close buddies with mySAP Business Suite

Although the SAP EP can use almost any underlying application, it was designed to be completely integrated with the mySAP Business Suite, that comprehensive family of business solutions that are essentially running Fortune 500 companies around the globe.

SAP EP has been designated as the user-interface layer of the future for all solutions in the mySAP Business Suite. Over the next few years, every one of SAP's applications will use SAP EP and the portal development environment to build their user interfaces. How's that for compadres?

Presenting SAP Business Intelligence

The SAP® Business Intelligence (SAP BI) application integrates all your corporate information and gives you an extremely powerful set of tools for examining the data: analytical processing, data mining, query design, reporting, and analysis. These allow you to create analysis reports, support decisions at every level, and present business intelligence applications through the portal.

Sitting atop SAP Web Application Server

The SAP EP, like all other SAP NetWeaver components, runs on the SAP® Web Application Server (SAP Web AS). The application server operates the underlying programs in the SAP runtime environment, and it functions as a Web server to display the portal in a browser.

SAP Exchange Infrastructure extends the reach

Using the messaging and adapters provided by SAP® Exchange Infrastructure (SAP XI), iViews and other parts of the SAP EP can reach out to bring in information from virtually any source, inside or outside your company.

The Future of the Portal

SAP EP has been designated as the user-interface layer of the future for all solutions in mySAP Business Suite and for the SAP xApps™ line of packaged composite applications. As time passes, every one of SAP's applications will use SAP EP to build its user interfaces.

Once upon a time, the user interface was a programmer's afterthought, second cousin to the things that applications could actually do. But as applications became more complex and users became more sophisticated, the interface was asked to carry more and more of the load. Innovations like eventing for iViews, integration with powerful applications, and a variety of other features have shown that the portal is capable of delivering the same perspective on business processes that users have grown accustomed to on the desktop.

The gap between what is possible for the client/server and what the completely accessible Web can deliver is shrinking every day. As the portal replicates the functions of the client/server application and the application accesses additional functionality through the Internet, users will demand a consistent interface to make using both easier. Eventually, users may not even be aware which they are accessing. It is easy to see that as the portal matures, this gap will disappear completely. The portal has just begun to flex its muscles, and it will offer improvements in types of *collaboration* (the ability to share information of every kind across every level of the organization).

Chapter 9

SAP Mobile Infrastructure: Information Hits the Road

In This Chapter

▶ Getting familiar with SAP® Mobile Infrastructure

▶ Discovering the parts of mobile infrastructure

▶ Finding out how developers create mobile applications

▶ Figuring out where SAP Mobile Infrastructure fits into the SAP NetWeaver™ puzzle

*W*hether you call it wireless or mobile technology, it's the coolest thing to happen to technology since the Internet. With mobile technology, you can use laptops, wireless phones, and PDAs to keep on track and in touch (for better or for worse). You can take your contact info and calendar anywhere. You can make a call or shoot off an e-mail from your hotel room or the airport departure lounge. When you get back to your desk, you'll still have a ton of e-mail and dozens of messages, but you already answered the most important ones, and you can happily ignore or file the rest.

Mobility has turned the moments waiting for elevators, riding in cabs, and waiting for planes into productive time. It has changed the pace of doing business to supersonic and allows your company to respond faster to change.

But think about it: That first stage only improves individual productivity. The underlying business processes — sales, procurement, supply chain management — remain unchanged. SAP Mobile Infrastructure (SAP MI) is the next generation of mobile technology that not only allows you to check your e-mail, but to connect to your company's backend systems from any and all mobile devices you can possibly cram into your briefcase. SAP MI enables smart phones, laptops, PDAs, and Tablet PCs to connect to your enterprise systems, supporting specialized applications designed for your particular industry or activity.

If mobile phones and PDAs can change the face of business, imagine what mobile access to Enterprise Resource Planning (ERP), Customer Relationship

Management (CRM), and Supply Chain Management (SCM) can do. In this chapter, we do just that.

Why SAP MI?

The world of mobile technology has expanded rapidly and chaotically. Laptops, cell phones, and PDAs have gotten cheaper and much more powerful. Various wireless protocols — Bluetooth, Wi-Fi, 802.11a, and 802.11g — have arisen, without any one becoming the clear standard. Wireless connectivity is still shaky or nonexistent in certain locations, and it's fraught with security and privacy concerns.

At a personal level, if your cell phone cuts out in the middle of a call or is broken up by another conversation, you can just call back. But, on a business level, if your data transfer cuts out or is garbled while transmitting a large customer order, it could cause serious problems. The question is, how can you safely do business no matter where you are — in your office, on a plane, or in a client's warehouse in Oshkosh?

The plus of open standards

SAP Solutions for Mobile Business has one purpose: To bring business processes to mobile devices in a seamless computing environment, a kind of universal mobile adapter. To provide a complete solution, SAP created mobile applications that work across multiple platforms and systems and developed an infrastructure for these applications using (surprise!) SAP NetWeaver as the foundation.

An important aspect of SAP MI is that it's based on open standards such as Java, XML, and SOAP. This means that the platform can run on all kinds of devices and networks, from laptops to smart phones, and from wireless LANs to Bluetooth.

But though they're built on open platforms, the mobile solutions in SAP MI are tightly integrated with their corresponding SAP solutions, as shown in Figure 9-1. Various mobile applications can add capabilities and extend the reach of every piece of the mySAP™ Business Suite, including

- ✔ mySAP ERP
- ✔ mySAP Customer Relationship Management (mySAP CRM)
- ✔ mySAP Supply Chain Management (mySAP SCM)
- ✔ mySAP Product Life Cycle Management (mySAP PLM)

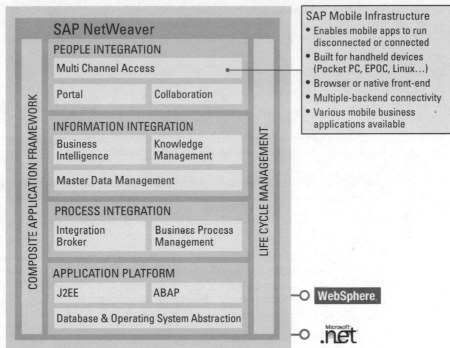

Figure 9-1:
SAP
Solutions for
Mobile
Business —
business in
motion.

SAP MI, powered by SAP NetWeaver, serves as the framework for all SAP's solutions for mobile business.

What goes on?

So you want to hear about this thing in action? Okay. Here's a typical business scenario: An equipment service worker shows up at your plant to fix your lathe. (You do have a lathe, don't you?) In the past, she would fill out a few forms that you would have to sign (for example, a work order, a time and materials report, and an order form for a new part). The forms would sit in the truck until the end of the day when she went back to the shop. Next, an administrator would try to make out the repair person's handwriting and manually enter the forms into the system. The following day, the administrator would file the part order with a supplier. You would then wait around with your broken lathe until the part arrived at the shop and the repair person came back and installed it.

Now, using mobile technology, the process is automated. Service people enter their time and materials on a mobile device, for example a Tablet PC. Parts used on the repair are automatically subtracted from the truck supplies' inventory. Orders for necessary parts are automatically placed with suppliers, who can immediately respond with delivery times. You can know, often before the service person leaves, when the part will be in and when the service person will be back to fix your lathe. (Won't your lathe manager be happy!)

What SAP MI does in SAP NetWeaver

What do you need to integrate mobile devices throughout your enterprise? In order to handle mobile functions effectively, you need

- ✔ A foundation for mobile computing that is as comprehensive as possible.

- ✔ That foundation must be fully incorporated into all of your back office applications and databases, no matter what they may be.

- ✔ A system that recognizes and adapts to all of your existing business processes, that also needs to be open and customizable, able to grow and change with business needs. That means it must also be flexible enough to deal with any devices or new business scenarios that may be added to the system now or in the future.

- ✔ Your mobile devices to fulfill their functions even when they aren't connected to the network (which is really, really important).

This is quite a challenge, trust us.

Getting under the hood

Using SAP NetWeaver as a foundation, SAP created a platform-independent, end-to-end framework that does all this stuff and more. SAP NetWeaver, a J2EE-compliant server, provides the components that allow you to connect server applications to backend SAP systems, such as SAP R/3® or to other third-party systems.

SAP MI is based on the open-industry standards Java, eXtensible Markup Language (XML), and Simple Object Access Protocol (SOAP). Using these standards, you can establish an open and secure communication channel where you authenticate clients and encrypt and compress data, and the delivery of that data is guaranteed.

As a complete solution, SAP NetWeaver and SAP MI are multiple specialists: They allow you to add multiple devices in multiple classes to multiple network infrastructures serving multiple business processes. (Multiplication like this really adds up.) Figure 9-2 shows the one-to-one mapping between SAP MI and the multichannel capabilities of SAP NetWeaver. Multichannel means that the applications created with SAP NetWeaver cannot only be used through a browser, but can also find their way to end users wherever they are through mobile devices. It's SAP MI that makes that possible.

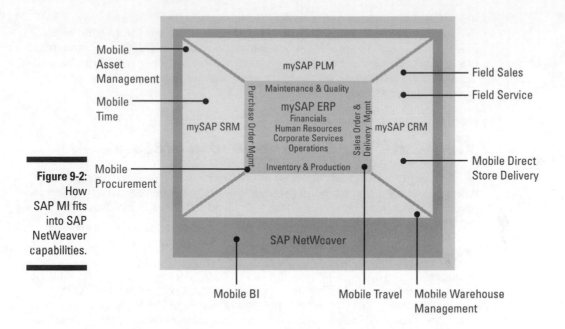

Figure 9-2: How SAP MI fits into SAP NetWeaver capabilities.

Open architecture

SAP MI's open platform architecture is the independent type. It's independent from any device, so it can support mobile hardware ranging from PDAs to laptops to phones. It's also network independent, working with wireless LANs, Bluetooth, and General Packet Radio Service (GPRS). And because the entire infrastructure is built on SAP NetWeaver, it has a number of additional advantages, including

- ✔ **A disconnected framework** that runs on the mobile device, so that the application can run without being constantly connected to the backend server.

- ✔ **A synchronization framework** from the device through any middleware to the backend, so that the information is monitored as it is transferred to and from the device to the backend, and nothing gets lost.

- ✔ **A development framework for applications** that gives you the ability to extend and customize applications directly within SAP NetWeaver Developer Studio.

- ✔ **A development framework for devices** that permits the development of basic structures and interaction patterns that go with whole families of devices.

And, best of all, SAP MI comes out of the box with a variety of pre-designed solutions based on employee roles (such as salesperson, human resources manager, or accounts receivable clerk). These are built around the kind of things every company needs to do (CRM, HR, SCM, BI, PLM, and so on). SAP MI also comes with completely pre-designed applications for specific industries, such as service providers; chemical, pharmaceutical, utility companies, and so on). This gives you standard, immediately useful applications, as well as lots of useful starting points for developing custom solutions for more-unique business needs.

How SAP MI helps your business

While most of us are tied (literally) at the hip to our mobile devices, the whole reason we carry around these devices is to up our personal productivity. As the following examples show, SAP MI adds to that convenience by adding the value of specific enterprise applications.

Keeping track of assets at Frankfurt Airport

Fraport AG, the owner and operator of Frankfurt Airport, had to streamline a key safety feature: the maintenance of fire shutters on the airport's 22,000 ventilation units. These shutters are vital because, in the event of a fire, they lock down the ventilation units, isolating the blaze and slowing the spread of the fire.

In November 2003, Fraport began to implement SAP Mobile Business for Asset Management. Using the new system, employees performing inspections use PDAs to read radio frequency identification (RFID) tags mounted on the shutters. Using radio frequencies, the inspector reads a shutter's bar code ID and the equipment number assigned to it by the mySAP ERP system. The employee then accesses the relevant information about the shutter, including the last date of inspection and any scheduled repairs. If the shutter is defective in any way, employees record this information on the PDA and a work order is automatically added to the airport's maintenance engineers' schedule.

Besides the obvious improvements in airport safety, Fraport also eliminated a substantial amount of paperwork and associated errors. The new mobile system uses a list of standardized error codes and procedures, reducing entry errors and decreasing the possibility that steps in maintenance procedures could be missed. Further, German law regarding the documentation of safety procedures are rather strict and require Fraport to archive maintenance records for ten years. The former, paper-based system cost over $100,000 to archive and administer. The new system costs a fraction of that.

Bell Canada, getting parts on the run

Bell Canada, the leading telecommunications company in Canada, outfitted 4,000 field technicians handling installation, maintenance, and repairs with SAP Mobile Business for Mobile Procurement. The system, installed and implemented in under four months, gives technicians access to over 55,000 parts in the company's rapidly changing catalog and provides an interface with Bell Canada's SAP R/3 backend.

Using the system, technicians search the catalog by part number, description, or key word, and they can view part pictures and cost information. When they find the part the customer needs, they load a shopping cart and specify the delivery location. Minutes later, the system gives them feedback on their order: Quantity available, delivery date, and ship-from location. If the product is out of stock, the system creates a purchase order and tells the technician an approximate delivery date.

Because the technicians spend most of their time out of the office, the system also permits them to work when they are out of reach of the network. When offline, their mobile devices (laptops or PDAs) offer them a smaller catalog that covers the parts they order most, and when they reconnect to the network, they can simply click a button and the SAP Mobile Business system transmits the shopping cart contents automatically while it updates the catalog.

This system makes sense because it puts technicians in the field instead of at their desktop computer or on the phone searching for parts, something that used to take hours every day. Technicians know when the parts are coming, so they'll be ready for their scheduled appointments. If there is a problem ordering a part, they find out about it immediately. Managers can also keep up-to-the-minute track of inventory levels and technician requests, something that used to only appear in monthly reports.

What were the technicians looking at? Figure 9-3 shows what a Hewlett-Packard iPAQ Pocket PC interface looks like for a sales order application, to give you an idea of how this can work.

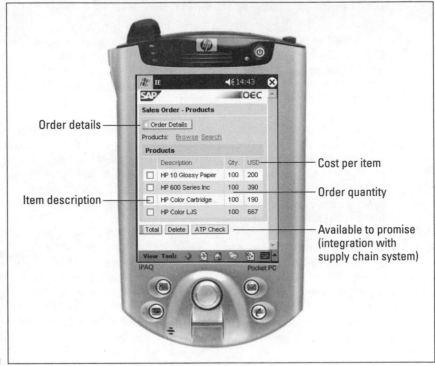

Order details

Item description

Cost per item

Order quantity

Available to promise (integration with supply chain system)

Figure 9-3:
A mobile sales order interface for the Pocket PC.

The Three Pieces of SAP MI

There are three pieces to the SAP MI puzzle. The first two components of SAP MI live apart, one on the mobile device (also called the *client*) and one on the server. On the client side, SAP MI includes its own business intelligence, data storage mechanisms, and Web server. This allows the device to work even if it's not connected to the network. When the client is connected, the synchronization and replication components connect with the server components to link and synch up with the backend system. At this point, the server-side components of SAP MI go to work to handle server-side synchronization and administrative-type duties.

The third element in SAP MI is the development environment, where you build or modify applications. This takes place separately from either the client or the server on the developer's workstation. In the following sections we take on the first two pieces, and after you understand how they work, we roam over to the development arena so you can see how applications and interfaces are created.

SAP MI at home on your mobile device

Mobile technology is, in large part, a matching game. You have to get the mobile thingie to connect to the backend whatsit. You have to make sure that the data entered in the device is synchronized properly with the enterprise systems. After all, it would be bad if you took a multimillion-dollar order but you weren't sure whether it actually made it into your backend system.

The SAP MI components that live on your mobile device, whether a PDA, laptop, or wireless coffee cup/cell phone combo, provide the platform for synchronization and data replication that ensure *data consistency*.

Making a connection

Okay, so like we said, the client system contains its own Web server, database layer, and business logic. It also includes a Java Virtual Machine (JVM) and provides an Application Programming Interface (API) for mobile applications. Because client-side applications are usually built in Java Server Pages (JSP) and Java is very Web savvy, the applications can use a browser for an interface. The browser connects to your mobile device's internal Web server, which runs the JSP application. Sometimes applications are built to run directly on what's called a *native user interface* (versions of Java that are optimized for PDAs, phones, or laptops).

Because SAP MI includes business logic right on your mobile device, no one has to wait for a network connection to get to work. Any activity — placing orders, signing for a delivery, viewing a catalog, or checking client info before an appointment — can take place whether the device is connected to the network. All data is synched with the backend systems at a later time, whenever possible. This makes the system perfect for workers who spend their days running around in the proverbial field, away from both wireless connections and office LANs. It also works when you're standing in the elevator or hotel shower.

The two tions: Synchronization and replication

A number of issues are involved in synching and replicating data when you move information back and forth from client to server:

✔ You absolutely have to guarantee that no data gets lost.

✔ You must ensure that the data is transmitted privately.

✔ You have to handle errors and conflicts that happen when two employees are working with the same information.

✔ You have to make sure that the information is seamlessly integrated into the backend system it's headed for.

On the client side, SAP MI handles these challenges by using (get ready for this, because it's a mouthful), secure, encrypted, and compressed data transfer via HyperText Transfer Protocol with Secure Sockets Layer (HTTPS) while employing standard connection types such as Global System for Mobile Communications (GSM), GPRS, local area network (LAN), wireless LAN, and cradles. All this just means it calls on technologies that protect data from prying eyes and makes sure that the connections you make don't disappear like a politician's promises after election day.

Server-side synchronization and replication components ensure that the data submitted by the mobile user finds its way to the right place.

Figure 9-4 puts this all together. It shows the way parts of SAP MI reside on both the mobile device and on the server. This provides the glue so the results of the interaction with the user on the mobile device can find its way to the application on the server, even when access to the device may be intermittent.

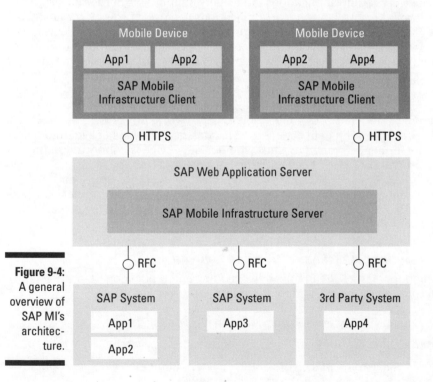

Figure 9-4:
A general overview of SAP MI's architecture.

Parts of SAP MI on the server

Now jump over to the server side of this mobile technology equation. This is kind of the Cinderella side, because the server side is the one that sits at home in your office, patiently waiting for those who are lucky enough to go out to the ball to check in from their mobile devices.

Synchronization and replication from the other end

The server and client tend to divvy things up between them. While the mobile device contains the rules about how, when, and where information goes (called *transaction logic*), the parts of SAP MI that live on the SAP NetWeaver server contain the logic you need to connect to all the underlying applications, from SAP's R/3, CRM, ERP, PLM, or SRM systems, to any other company's database or application.

You can use a variety of types of synchronization, depending on the needs of your system:

- **Asynchronous synchronization:** Think of a one-way airline ticket. Here data is sent one way — from the device to the server, or from the server to the device.

- **Synchronous synchronization:** This is a roundtrip kind of thing, where the mobile device sends data to the server and the server sends data back, or vice versa.

- **Smart synchronization:** The device and the server get together and decide which sends data and which receives it.

- **Generic synchronization:** All the information in the mobile device is completely replaced with new data. (You want to be careful with this one!)

- **Delta synchronization:** This is a subset of smart synchronization where the system checks what data has changed in the device and only submits that information to the server.

While this is relatively simple on the client side, on the server side a variety of tests and checks need to be performed to ensure the integrity of the data. The data must be validated before it can be added to a backend system to make sure it's the right kind of information. (After all, you wouldn't want just any information to move into your server's neighborhood, would you?) For example, if two service people are working with the same information and both make changes, systems are in place to call attention to what could be a data conflict.

This system of monitoring the synchronization and replication process, checking for errors and usage, and automatically creating functional scenarios for putting this technology to work for a specific application is fully integrated into SAP MI and SAP NetWeaver toolkits. You have all the necessary equipment you need to respond to whatever situation comes along.

Administrating the thing

Probably the toughest job SAP MI has is handling connections to the underlying applications and databases. Most of this is done through a built-in central administration and deployment tool.

A variety of independent tasks can be handled through the administrative console, including

- Monitoring of messages transmitted between mobile devices and the server components
- Error handling and problem analysis
- Monitoring and logging
- Purging data
- Reporting and overviews

To manage all these complex tasks, your IT administrator creates what's called a *deployment definition,* which is essentially a profile of either the role of the user or the device. The administrator picks and chooses from predesigned menus of devices and user roles, or builds a new definition from both (kind of like an a la carte menu thing). The deployment definition then controls what applications run on the device and how the data from the device is processed. This makes your life easier by speeding up and simplifying your administrative tasks, and it guarantees the overall stability and reliability of the applications that run on the device.

From the console, an IT administrator gets a bird's-eye view of a matrix of unique device IDs, applications running on the device, and the application's infrastructure deployed to each device. This also allows you to handle software patches and updates from one central location. If the deployment definition changes, the new data is automatically loaded on the appropriate device.

How Developers Do What They Do with SAP MI

As we promised earlier in this chapter, now that we've covered how SAP MI works between the client and server, we help you get a handle on how a developer would build this thing. Developing applications for mobile devices involves the SAP Mobile Development Kit, a neat little package to warm the cockles of any developer's heart.

SAP MI in a kit

The SAP Mobile Development Kit, part of SAP MI, contains all the tools, samples, code libraries, and documentation that you need to connect any of SAP's applications to a mobile device or build mobile-type stuff for third-party applications.

The Mobile Development Kit is not a design-time tool like Web Dynpro. It does not require SAP R/3 applications or SAP NetWeaver to be running for you to develop working applications. So what is it? This little kit contains plug-ins for SAP NetWeaver Developer Studio that accelerate the test and deployment cycle of integrated solutions into the overall SAP standard processes and solutions.

Polyhedrons for mobile types

The easiest way to picture SAP MI is as a series of three-dimensional polyhedrons. Okay, maybe that's not the easiest way. But the heading got your attention, didn't it?

To understand SAP Solutions for Mobile Business, start with a simple one-dimensional list of the types of solutions offered by the underlying SAP applications, which include the following:

- ✔ **Role-based solutions:** Solutions based on your job description (for example, programmer, sales manager, accountant).
- ✔ **Process-based solutions:** Business-process solutions such as CRM, HR, SCM, BI, PLM, and so on.
- ✔ **Industry-based solutions:** Solutions based on the kind of business you do, such as being a service provider, retail business, chemical, pharmaceutical, or utility company, and so on.

These are the kind of out-of-the-box SAP solutions based on industry best practices that you can combine, mix, match, use as is, or customize to fit your unique needs. Out-of-the-box integration allows you to get up and running quickly, which saves you a bunch of money.

The mobile in mobile infrastructure

Now, on top of this already powerful and sophisticated level of technology, SAP mobile business plops a further set of integrated components that are designed specifically for mobile computing:

- SAP Mobile Asset Management
- SAP Mobile Service
- SAP Mobile Sales
- SAP Mobile Procurement
- SAP Mobile Time and Travel

The following subsections take a look at each component.

SAP Mobile Asset Management

As our accountant keeps telling us, you gotta have assets. In fact, all large companies have a tremendous catalog of assets that need to be tracked, maintained, replaced, and so on. Most companies also have an extensive staff to do this job. Field technicians, plant engineers, auditors, and warehouse personnel busily log assets, record their location, and perform updates and compliance checks. This data is often kept on paper, in inspection logs and inventory catalogs, making it difficult to search for specific information.

With Mobile Asset Management, employees can stop the paper chase and keep all this information in a backend system. Inventory can be continuously updated, asset status can be checked instantly, and employees have a complete picture of all the information relating to the assets, including location of every item, the jobs that need to be done, and users who need to be involved.

SAP Mobile Service

If your company is a smart company, you know that customer service isn't just the responsibility of the Sales and Customer Service departments. Every employee who comes into contact with customers needs to be able to answer customer questions, check a variety of information, and record customer requests. That's where SAP Mobile Service comes in. It gives onsite technicians access to the entire CRM system. This means they can access service information, such as previous visits, status of repairs, other employees' contacts with the customer, billing status, and more. The field staff can log any and all interactions with the customer as well, giving the Sales and Customer Service departments additional, in-the-trenches information about the customer.

SAP Mobile Sales

A sales person's life is not an easy one. All that travel, all those orders to juggle, all that bad coffee at client sites. On top of that, they have to access and report data all the time.

Many sales people are already glued to their PDAs to keep track of contact information and appointments, but SAP Mobile Sales goes much further, giving sales staff access to the entire resources of the CRM system back at the home office. Tools such as opportunity, lead and account management, and credit lookup assist sales people in their initial contacts with the customer. A range of marketing materials and interactive sales tools help them make the sales call; and catalogs, inventory lookup, pricing, and order reporting all help the sales person go for the all-important close.

SAP Mobile Procurement

The big payoff — the order is in and your commission is assured. But somebody has to get the stuff out to the customer. When servicing clients, field employees often need to order parts or equipment. SAP Mobile Procurement allows you to search online supply catalogs, check inventories, compare features and pricing, process orders, and get client and management approvals. The most commonly used features and current catalog items can be kept on the mobile device, so even when you're outside the network, you can take those orders and synch the data when you return to the office.

SAP Mobile Time and Travel

Ah, the expense report. Great when the expense check shows up, a horror when you're filling it out. All those receipts, all those notations about mileage and client entertainment. (Yes, they were legitimate, every one of them.)

Any employee who travels needs to keep track of expense items and trip details. SAP Mobile Time and Travel plugs you directly into the travel expense management and cross-application time sheet (CATS) capabilities of the corresponding applications, as well as the various HR functions that your company uses to track payroll.

How SAP MI Plays with Other SAP NetWeaver Kids

SAP MI only becomes valuable when it brings some needed application out into the field. To do this SAP MI works closely with SAP NetWeaver and the mySAP Business Suite solutions.

The future of SAP MI

Mobility takes applications out of the office and allows them to be used anywhere your company does business. The future lies in extending the mySAP Business Suite to every platform and device that your business needs to realize the full benefits of mobile.

As the number and types of mobile devices grow (and they will), speedy development also becomes a key to your growth. SAP is currently creating a workbench framework for development that can be operated as a central WYSIWYG (What You See Is What You Get, pronounced *wizzy-wig*) development studio so that you can develop mobile applications that run across any device and that leverage any of SAP's mobile capabilities in a simple way.

mySAP Business Suite solutions

Although you can use SAP MI to bring any server-side application or database to a mobile device, SAP MI was not designed to lead a lonely life. It was specifically designed to serve as the mobile component of a series of tightly integrated applications that brings all the processes of your enterprise to the doorstep of mobile technology. SAP MI, SAP NetWeaver, and the mySAP Business Suite collectively form a triple play of technology that can handle almost any enterprise challenge you throw at it.

Every one of the applications in the mySAP Business Suite operates at a global enterprise level. That means that you can mix, match, and customize the functionality of SAP NetWeaver and SAP MI. You can choose whether to deploy them within your company walls via wireless LAN, or outside the walls in the big, wide world via wide-area mobile data networks.

SAP® Business Intelligence

Using SAP MI with SAP® Business Intelligence allows you to create mobile-friendly versions of queries and reports, so that employees in the field have access to the same kind of data their desk-bound cohorts have in the office. Because mobile devices often have a screen size limitation, it's possible to adjust report layouts or only deliver the most important information in Wireless Markup Language (WML) code form, allowing everyday humans to actually read the data on a smart phone screen.

Chapter 10

SAP Gives Business Intelligence

*E*verybody from the mail clerk to the CEO is making business decisions today. Of course a good business decision is usually based on data, and not just any old kind of data. You need good, consistent data all around your organization. Otherwise, the CEO (or mail clerk) could decide to close the most lucrative plant and invest all the company's money in swamp land in Florida.

The mission of SAP Business Intelligence (SAP BI) is to create a single container in which all the data necessary for making good decisions is stored, analyzed, and served up to the right people at the right time. In the ideal situation, when a decision needs to be made, the relevant, organized, timely information is available in an easy-to-use form. Informed decisions should help you avoid the sticky problem of building a new plant in a swamp.

SAP Business Intelligence is one of the largest umbrellas for functionality in SAP® NetWeaver™, and your brain may hurt a bit as we go through all the moving parts. But be of good cheer: We explain nice and clearly how it all fits together.

First, What Is SAP BI?

At the center of SAP BI is a data warehouse, which is an unfortunate term because it gives the impression of trucks arriving with pallets of data that are then stowed away on a shelf. Before that metaphor starts to stick, here's a better one.

SAP BI as a whole is like the cockpit of a super airplane. The enterprise is the plane and SAP BI is the onboard computer, collecting data like speed, gas airflow, fuel level, and weather conditions. That data is promptly sorted, analyzed, and displayed so that both the pilot and navigator have the information they need in the form they need — whether a diagnostic readout or a speedometer — to make the right decision in real time. Knowing your speed is useful. Realizing you're about to hit a major storm pattern is critical.

Collecting and sorting the raw data for decisions is the job of the data warehouse. Resting on top of it in SAP BI are analytical and reporting engines that transform that data into useful information.

What's It Do?

So, if the enterprise is an airliner zooming around the corporate sky, what does the instrument panel show? Where is the information coming from? How can it be simplified so that you can use it to fly the plane?

Of course we could leave you to the mercy of several-thousand pages of documentation that explain the millions of lines of code in all of the different programs that make up SAP BI. This seems a bit lazy on our part, though, so instead we read that material for you, whittled it down to the big picture of SAP BI, and go through each part.

The job of SAP BI in SAP NetWeaver

The role that SAP BI plays in SAP NetWeaver is that of a central, integrated repository for information from distributed and heterogeneous sources. Hmmm . . . that's accurate, but a bit dry. We can do better.

In your enterprise, just as in your home, data is stored all over the place, from the box of tax papers in the basement to the recipe file in the kitchen. In your enterprise, the good old Enterprise Resource Planning (ERP) system has its data, the friendly Customer Relationship Management (CRM) system has its data, and a grandfatherly legacy system that has been running for 20 years on a mainframe has even more data. Add to that your Web site data, your co-workers' spreadsheets of data, and even that department down the hall that nobody's quite sure what it does might have some data. To find out about the big picture, say customer or sales activity, the data from all these applications must be brought together.

But wait. What if the data is quarterly sales in ERP but monthly sales in CRM? What if different customer ID numbers or overlapping sales regions are used in different databases? What if one system keeps its data in dollars and other uses euros? How can all this be brought together and analyzed? SAP BI.

SAP BI is the database hub, the universal translator, the statistician, and report writer for SAP NetWeaver. When people think of systems that use data warehouses, they frequently think of reams of reports cranked out in batch mode. That sort of thing is still useful and SAP BI can do a great job of it, but at its best SAP BI is more like an airliner computer, transforming raw data into more useful information by integrating it into the context of the enterprise and historical insights. That's how SAP BI prevents the CEO in the pilot's seat from hitting a major air pocket.

Figure 10-1 shows how SAP BI sits squarely in the information integration area of SAP NetWeaver capabilities.

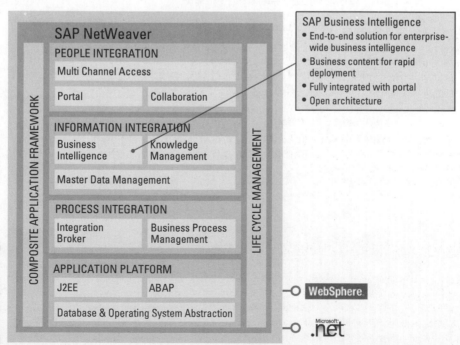

Figure 10-1: SAP BI's role in SAP NetWeaver capabilities.

SAP BI and your business

So, SAP BI helps people in your business who need data. Now who could that be . . . everyone in the company?

From handling a customer inquiry about an order to running a huge pharmaceutical research division with a thousand different research projects, pretty much every industry and every job in every company can make use of SAP Business Intelligence.

You can basically break down into three groups who benefits from SAP BI:

- ✏ **Authors and analysts** who need advanced analysis tools as well as the ability to ask questions on an ongoing basis. For these folks, everything must be easy to use.

- ✏ **Executives and knowledge workers** who need personalized information tailored to the context of their jobs and presented by an intuitive user interface. They want a playbook for how to analyze data and the ability to do their own in-depth analysis.

- ✏ **Information consumers** who need a snapshot of a particular data set to perform their operational tasks and who can do without more advanced, interactive analysis features.

Of course, then there are your customers, partners, and suppliers — everyone who uses quantitative information to make or enhance their decisions. SAP BI is about aligning strategy with execution — about getting the right information to the right user at the right time in the right format to make the right decision. Right?

Example 1: Decision support

You and your co-workers drew straws to decide who would sign off on next year's promotions and marketing budget. You lost. Now you need to figure out what changes you have to make to be more responsive to customer demands. And to do that, you first need to pull together as much information as you can to create the most complete picture possible of this year's sales and what difference (if any) your marketing efforts made.

Some of your company's key customer and supplier information resides within the SAP system. Some of it lives on in the legacy mainframe that was already in place when you started with the company. And still more data is arriving through the company Web site every day in the form of a steadily growing stream of orders. However, you aren't sure who's ordering what.

You can't favor the data from one source over the other — the person in Singapore making purchases via your Web site at 3 a.m. may not be your average customer, believe it or not — so what you need to do is combine the streams of data arriving from each portion of your enterprise to get the bigger picture. By integrating information from the Web site — Who buys online? How often and how much? What time of day? — with seasonal and historical data from legacy systems, SAP BI can both provide an historical picture of your sales and provide trending information and upsell guidance with just the right level of detail.

What if you're the CEO and you need the biggest picture available? What if you want to know who your best customers are, who your best suppliers are, and how they intersect? Within SAP BI, you can integrate the data coming from your suppliers' systems, your retail channels, and even your own HR system. After matching and integrating all three, trends and patterns emerge. Do the best suppliers line up with the best customers? Are the suppliers delivering the best mix of products for your needs?

By combining data from multiple systems in different parts of your business, a holistic view of your company and its process gradually swims into view. For example, take a look at Figure 10-2, which shows what a user interface might look like that provides an integrated environment for sales analytics. With delivery of information like this, SAP BI grants you the power to spot where and how you can adjust your process to make the entire enterprise run more efficiently.

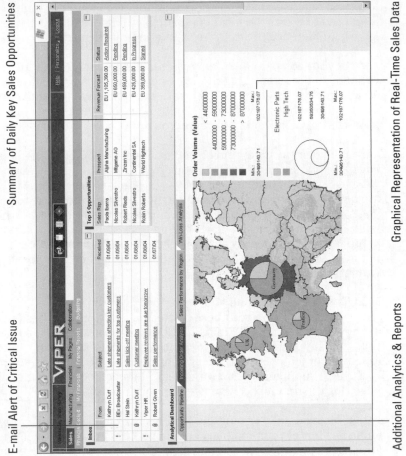

Figure 10-2:
User
interface
for sales
analytics.

What about the cost of all this? As Figure 10-3 shows, the investment to enhance the information for a large number of employees need not be huge. It's possible to provide a small amount of information simply and cheaply in a way that will improve the performance of a huge number of people.

Example 2: Corporate Performance Management

CEOs, as a rule, don't need minute-by-minute updates about their companies' best suppliers — they'd rather be playing golf with each other. Churning out massive, alarmingly comprehensive portraits of the business might strike the quiet types in the CFO's office as fun, but most executives would find this overwhelming and would rather have just the information they need to take action, preferably delivered to them in the simplest form possible at the very moment they need it. They need to know when alarm bells are ringing, not how well the alarm bells are working.

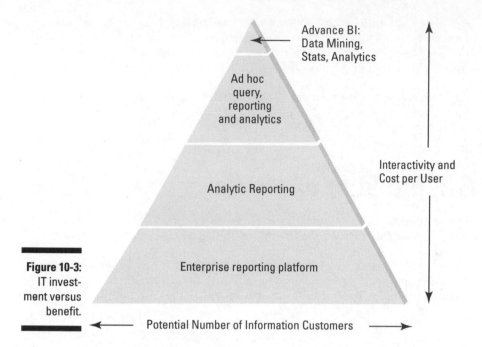

Advance BI:
Data Mining,
Stats, Analytics

Ad hoc
query,
reporting
and analytics

Analytic Reporting

Enterprise reporting platform

Interactivity and
Cost per User

Potential Number of Information Customers

Figure 10-3:
IT invest-
ment versus
benefit.

SAP BI has the ability to tailor its results to the level of detail and summary that its users need to do their jobs. In the CEO's case, that may be a single number representing total company performance or earnings per share, taking into account profitability, efficiency, revenue growth, churn, and so on, displayed in a corner of his or her computer screen. That might be the ulti-mate top-level view of the enterprise, but the principle can be applied to rating customers, employees, or other key metrics of a company's health. After data have been collected and integrated in the SAP BI data warehouse, the analytical process and end result can happen with whatever level of detail you need.

SAP BI: How It Works

One simple way to think about SAP BI is as a data warehouse, surrounded by tools to move information in and out, clean and summarize the information, and then analyze it to answer important questions.

Although the data warehouse aspect of SAP BI is vital and important, don't let it overwhelm your understanding of the product. As we mention earlier in this chapter, resist the urge to picture loading docks and teamsters when reading the words *data warehouse*. Unlike the brick-and-mortar variety, a data warehouse doesn't replace the databases used and produced by legacy systems, CRM, ERP, or any other three-letter abbreviation solutions. It rests on top of them, collecting streams of data from each system and reformatting them for use by analytics software. The original data isn't touched — the warehouse uses a duplicate, cleansed, consolidated data set.

So think of BI instead as a metadatabase that invisibly contains the databases your enterprise already has in place. With that in mind, you are now ready to get a tour of the parts of SAP BI.

SAP BI: The Sum of Its Parts

Figure 10-4 shows SAP BI in all its complex glory. As you can see, a lot is going on — data flowing from the information sources, through the data warehouse, into object models tailored to the different mySAP™ Business Suite solutions, and then for presentation through the SAP Enterprise Portal. The following sections walk through each part and show you how they do what they do to make this all come together.

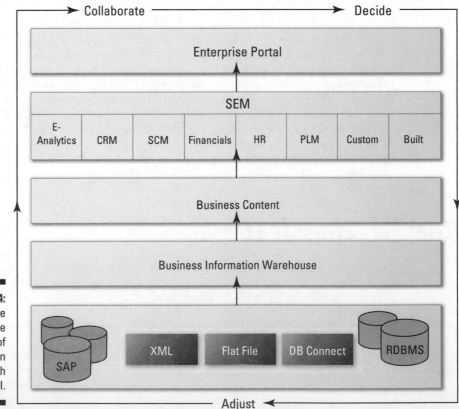

Figure 10-4: The structure and flow of information through SAP BI.

Parts for moving data around

The parts that we describe in this section are used for moving data from the source systems that contain it to the SAP BI data warehouse, and then organizing it, passing it out to others who need chunks of it, and preparing it for analysis.

Extraction, transformation, and loading clean up data's act

Okay, call us fickle: As much as we fought it before, it might be time to bring the warehouse metaphor into play. Picture the data arriving at the warehouse on pallets from the far-flung systems of the enterprise — SAP systems, suppliers' systems, the Web-based transaction engine, systems written in COBOL 30 years ago by programmers who are living in Florida retirement homes by now. Some of this data arrives on virtual palettes, some in electronic boxes, other in digital bags.

Before that data can be unloaded and stored in the warehouse, the SAP BI extraction, transformation, and loading routines communicate with these systems, extract the data, and clean it up to make it consistent.

Cleaning it up is the hard part here. The software has to scan the data in question for errors, redundancies, and irregularities. SAP BI then transforms the data into formats that you previously selected. For example, based on business rules that your organization chooses to implement, nine-digit ZIP codes may be reduced to five digits, or vice versa; dates, social security numbers, or other similar data are transformed to fit a standard designed to make delivery a smooth process.

Stashing things in a data warehouse

When the data arrives, it's sent first to the Persistent Storage Area (PSA), where it's copied and kept for backup purposes and to minimize the load on the systems providing the data, which can't handle the stress of doing their jobs and answering questions. So, if warehouses had waiting rooms, the PSA would be it. Upon arrival, the data takes a number, kicks back with a newspaper, and stays put until needed. Then, it undergoes another round of cleaning and is passed along to InfoObjects in the Operational Data Store (ODS).

In the ODS, SAP BI begins to thoroughly massage and aggregate the data according to your enterprise's wishes. Here, InfoObjects that represent the scope of a user's request are assembled. One InfoObject might represent a customer, another a sale, another sales data by region. All these would be populated by using corresponding data back in the PSA. Another object might require the same data for a global sales analysis or sales in Chicago last year. All these objects begin life in the ODS. More complex analyses are distilled into a form called InfoCubes, which live still further up the information chain.

InfoCubes are one of the most important types of containers in the SAP BI data warehouse, so take a moment to reflect on them. InfoCubes are structures that make it easy and fast to answer questions about data. Here's how InfoCubes work: The kinds of analysis and investigations that are likely to be done are anticipated and appropriate data is stored in a multi-dimensional way that makes answering questions very fast.

To do this, the InfoCube uses a special structure for storing data called a *star schema.* This is a structure where data is organized in interrelated database tables for simplified analysis. Those interrelated tables might store the same piece of data many times, but given the importance of being able to provide a fast, accurate, comprehensive answer and the fact that storage is cheap these days, that doesn't pose a problem.

Business modeling

Even after data has been scrubbed thoroughly clean, it's still just a collection of facts and figures until it's been subjected to the question and analysis that provide the information that users are looking for. *Business modeling* is the art and science of transforming vast seas of data into structures and models that make asking and (more importantly) answering questions as painless and as comprehensive as possible.

This occurs with InfoCubes. (The previous section explains InfoCubes.) By filling up these structures when the data is loaded, much of the work of crunching the analysis happens in advance. The goal of business modeling is to design these containers so that the widest possible range of questions can be rapidly answered.

In the context of SAP BI, business modeling refers to the process of building InfoCubes.

Process chains keep track of things

As data moves through the warehouse, being transformed from mere data into useful information, SAP BI keeps track of these transformations through something called process chains. These *process chains* document the changes at each step as data is cleansed and massaged from its native format into the preferred SAP BI structure. This provides a trail of transformations and mappings in case something goes wrong or processes need to be modified.

SAP BI attaches metadata to the information (see the later section "Metadata Repository") at each step on the trip through the data warehouse to allow you to track changes and allow real-time monitoring of the data.

After the data has finished analysis, process chains allow you to reverse-engineer the data or backtrack through a set of transformations to see how results were achieved, or whether mistakes were made.

Going downstream: Open Hub Service

Raw data is transformed and flows into the data warehouse, and it can just as easily flow out. Open Hub Service allows SAP BI users to selectively request that key business information be exported for use in downstream analytical or other applications outside the data warehouse.

If, for example, a company's Marketing department wants to pitch a new anti-aging cream to retirees living in Orlando (including any former COBOL programmers), it might ask the warehouse for a data subset including all customers over the age of 65 within 50 miles of Orlando.

The subject-specific data subset is sent to a data mart outside the warehouse where the Marketing department can conduct subsequent analysis on the subset — slice and dice it by age, household income, order size, and so on. The Open Hub Service extracts data from the data warehouse and pumps it into relational databases for use by all sorts of applications.

Parts for data analysis

So what good is data that just gets moved around a lot? No good. So we move on. The parts in this section focus on actually using the data in the data warehouse to answer your questions and perform advanced analysis.

The part where the questions get asked

While the data in the warehouse is transformed into InfoCubes to speed up asking questions, here is the part where the questions actually get asked.

Online Analytical Processing (OLAP) is the star of the SAP BI show, as far as users are concerned. OLAP is a collection of tools and mechanisms for analyzing and prodding the data with questions and getting useful results.

The OLAP partner, SAP BI Reporting function, is another user favorite because it's the part of the program responsible for presenting answers as visually appealing graphs and well-formatted reports. The Reporting feature can also be customized to pretty much any end product that you desire.

Hidden treasure: Data mining

Data miners, data shovels in hand, are big believers in serendipity. Their job is the pursuit of patterns, trends, and other hidden indicators buried inside the mountains of data stacked in warehouses like yours. They believe that patterns detected in past behaviour or attributes (a customer's spending habits, her home ZIP code, level of education, or the number of household cats, for example) can be accurate predictors of similar or desired future behavior.

Data mining, therefore, can be a powerful tool for decision-makers; it's not quite knowing the future before it happens but it enables a pretty good guess at identifying key predictive characteristics.

SAP BI includes a number of common, powerful tools and techniques for data mining, including Classification, Decision Tree Analysis, Clustering, Association Analysis, Approximation, Scoring, and a raft of other techniques that statisticians talk about to show off at cocktail parties.

Setting off alarm bells

The SAP BI alerting mechanism is what triggers the alarm bells when the CEO's magical indicator of company performance drops below 3.8, or when any other key performance indicator (KPI) is met or not met, based on your business's rules.

Alerts are usually generated by the final results of an OLAP analysis. They're not necessarily meant to signal a warning alarm — SAP BI could be asked to send an alert to a company's head of sales when a routine analysis produces higher-than-expected numbers in the third quarter.

Like reports, you can customize alerts to fit your preferred interface and level of analytical detail.

Metadata Repository

Data can't keep track of itself on its way through the warehouse. It's too busy being scrubbed, squeezed, and prodded to jot down notes on what happened, where it's going, and where it's been.

You need descriptive data to keep an eye on the herd flowing through to the warehouse: *metadata*. In this case, metadata is data that describes attributes of the data. (Yes, you could create meta-metadata to keep an eye on the metadata, but wouldn't that be like putting your spring jacket on over your winter coat?)

Metadata includes everything that happens to your data upon and after arrival in the data warehouse including the transformations it's undergone; when, how, and with what parameters those transformations occurred; and where it came from.

That metadata requires its own repository inside SAP BI, and the Metadata Repository is it. (Catchy name, huh?) Not only is a central repository for metadata necessary for efficient processing — the more metadata your data has, the more complex a question you can ask it — but it's also vital in this day and age of increased scrutiny and regulation to have a metadatabase vouching for your data's integrity at each step of the way.

Performance is key

Key performance indicators (KPIs) are important at many companies because they indicate how the company keeps score of its success or lack thereof. KPIs are set with great care because as soon as you start keeping score, most people try to get the highest score possible without always thinking about the bigger picture of the business. One way to think of SAP BI is as a massive system for defining, calculating, and managing KPIs. Because they're so central to the way that companies think about themselves, they're frequently used in conjunction with alerts.

Planning with data

We pause here for a moment so that you have the chance to ask yourself what you were planning to do with the answers printed in a pretty report after SAP BI finishes poking and prodding your data with questions. If you don't have a good answer, don't worry — SAP BI has a few suggestions about that, too.

The SAP BI Planning Framework is a set of features that are designed to guide and define enterprise planning for your Finance, Marketing, Sales, or even Operations departments. The framework is a playbook and environment for running different types of planning processes. Your company may prefer the top-down approach of "Here's the target number, now make it work, or else!" Or maybe your managers plan from the bottom up — submitting their budgets and then waiting to hear from the CFO about whether the numbers add up.

Either way (or with any other approach, actually), the planning framework delivered within SAP BI enables you to define and plan corporate objectives, knitting together input from multiple tiers of the enterprise along the way.

Parts for publishing

After you've gotten the answers that you sought, use this following set of parts to get information to those who need it when they need it.

SAP BW Business Explorer

It's time to switch metaphors again. Considering how much more exciting Daytona is than your standard-issue widget factory, a visit to the NASCAR circuit appears to be in order.

Imagine that the data warehouse is actually roaring under the hood. While raw data is fuel that's injected into the engine, the results are output to the dashboard (user interface) and to the crew (business people) in the pits (cubicles).

This is a particularly apt metaphor for discussing OLAP and SAP BW Business Explorer (SAP BW BEx, for short). That's because after data in the warehouse is squeezed into InfoCubes, it's analyzed with OLAP, but all this takes place underneath the hood. BEx is the user interface.

BEx leverages the OLAP suite of analysis tools to query data, receive answers, and then continue drilling down into the data by using interactive analysis. BEx enables you to define the queries and specific analysis and reports that you or your users might be interested in seeing.

Business Explorer Broadcaster

BEx Broadcaster is a new capability in SAP BI that provides access to analysis and reporting, such as BEx. But unlike BEx, which requires users to get off the couch and start asking well-thought-out questions, BEx Broadcaster automatically publishes reports of predefined OLAP queries at predefined, user-specified intervals. Ask the question once, tell BEx Broadcaster how often you'd like it asked again, and then it takes care of the rest.

At the end of every quarter, for example, BEx Broadcaster might be triggered to run a detailed analysis of gross profits and issue reports in a specific format that's automatically sent (via e-mail or what have you) to a preset list of executives in the CFO's office.

BEx Broadcaster expands SAP BI publishing abilities to aggressively produce reports whenever important trigger points or other conditions are met — whether the triggers are based on the calendar or the internal conditions of your business.

Open interfaces

SAP BI is the friendly type and it plays well with others. SAP BI supports a number of open interfaces and standard application programming interfaces (APIs) for use by third-party tools, including OLE DB for OLAP, OLAP BAPIs, and XML for Analysis. The ability to allow you to ask questions no matter what setup you have opens a huge number of possibilities for including SAP BI functionality in other programs.

Parts for specific industries and functions

Like all of SAP's products, SAP BI is tailored to the needs of many industries in the following different ways.

Business Content: A handy shortcut

If SAP BI is analogous to an airplane cockpit in a box, Business Content is a sample set of blueprints to get your flight analysis and reporting started.

SAP BI ships with a large collection of already defined, industry- and function-specific components designed to run as soon as it's out of the box. Based on the best practices of each industry, SAP's Business Content options are essentially toolkits filled with predefined data structures, query types, data cleansers and extractors, and other building blocks of a solid, if a bit generic, SAP BI implementation.

Analytical Applications

If Business Content can be likened to the airplane cockpit blueprint, the SAP BI preloaded Analytical Applications can be likened to an automatic computer that can build that cockpit for you based on the blueprint. It can't fly the plane for you but it has already calculated every successful take off and landing and has a few strategies that it wants to recommend.

The Analytical Applications are similar: They're preloaded applications containing best practice analytical models. One application might contain all the common calculations that are needed for a company in the retail industry. Another application might contain best analytical techniques common to any business — calculating the lifetime value of a customer, for example.

Creating Analytic Applications with SAP BI

Analytic applications combine all the different parts of SAP BI for a particular purpose. In creating such environments, all of the parts of SAP BI come together to turn data into meaningful information that can help you make the right choice or plan effectively. Here is a mini primer for creating such applications.

Start with Business Content

SAP has spent decades developing literally thousands of predefined elements of its Business Content portfolio, spanning all major industries. You may think your company is special (and it probably is), but SAP has built some predefined Business Content which might fit your needs as is or with only slight customization. In any case, you don't have to start from scratch.

Business Content defines standard InfoObjects, ODS objects, and InfoCubes that can dramatically speed up development. (Figure 10-5 shows how many objects are defined at each stage as data flows through SAP BI.) It's like starting to build an airplane from pre-built parts instead of starting with raw aluminum. When installing an SAP BI system and linking it to other SAP applications, a shared library of industry-specific Business Content radically simplifies the task of passing data back and forth from ERP software, a point of purchase, or mobile device, and the data warehouse.

A set of Business Content tailored to the airline industry, for example, would include data fields, such as dollar-per-passenger-mile, that are standardized across all SAP software components. They're also jumping-off points for creating customized data objects for your company's particular needs.

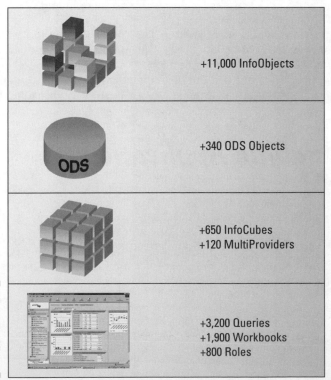

Figure 10-5:
SAP BW 3.2
Business
Content
add-ons.

+11,000 InfoObjects

+340 ODS Objects

+650 InfoCubes
+120 MultiProviders

+3,200 Queries
+1,900 Workbooks
+800 Roles

Neat tools for building applications

Unlike most applications, the SAP BI development tools are tightly integrated into the application itself. Imagine opening the hood of your car to find a toolkit and handy how-to illustrations nestled next to the engine.

Every level of SAP BI — the data warehouse, analytical engines, and reporting mechanisms — contains its own tools for customization that reside parallel to the components themselves. No standalone development environment exists, but administrative and development interfaces do exist to build, extend, and modify each component. One environment is for creating new ODS objects and one is for building InfoCubes. One interface is for creating new data-cleansing routines and another for outlining new OLAP procedures. They're all there, just not in one big development environment.

SAP BI and All the Other Parts of SAP NetWeaver

SAP BI is the master unifying repository and analytical environment for SAP NetWeaver. Here's how this capability is used by the other components.

SAP® Enterprise Portal

The ultimate in user-interface technology, the SAP® Enterprise Portal (EP) is perhaps the most powerful and fluid interface to SAP BI.

Within a single window, reports can be published as *iViews*. iViews are special content modules that reside in SAP EP and can be connected to applications outside or inside the portal, to documents on the user's desktop, to collaborative tools, and so on.

SAP EP is also *role based,* meaning that you can easily customize it to match your users' particular position inside the enterprise. From an SAP BI perspective, this means that reports can be aggregated and published on a need-to-know basis that the user has previously defined.

After these capabilities are combined, say, with the BEx Broadcaster, you might easily imagine a scenario where a business analyst is busy playing Minesweeper. Suddenly, the BEx Broadcaster issues a report in the form of a loud alarm. Still within the portal, the writer quickly instant messages colleagues about the alarm, and then checks for a link to a document with step-by-step procedures for solving the problem that the alarm announced.

Two elements of SAP EP are worth an even closer look — SAP Knowledge Management and Information Broadcasting.

Integration with SAP Knowledge Management

If you think of the data in your company as a huge attic full of information, the SAP® Knowledge Management (SAP KM) feature of SAP EP is the fastest way to search and manage that attic.

Although SAP BI is masterful at handling *structured data* (data organized in databases), SAP KM and its Repository Manager evolved to handle unstructured ones — Word documents, e-mails, and digital scribblings of any kind. The Repository Manager can also display in the portal window any documents residing in the data warehouse.

Users that need to rifle through the information without predefined analysis can harness the SAP KM array of indexing, searching, and rating tools. The real power of SAP BI with SAP KM is that unstructured data (the contents of your attic) can be used to provide contextual insights and relevance to your structured, SAP BI information.

Information Broadcasting

Similar to BEx Broadcaster and in fact enhancing it, the SAP EP Information Broadcasting feature has the ability to automatically push reports straight to the user via previously defined conditions (such as a time of year, when certain business conditions are met, and so on).

Following users wherever they go with SAP® Mobile Infrastructure

The world out there today is very mobile. Not every employee is sitting at a desk tapping into SAP BI happily through a workstation. Employees who prefer to work from the comfort of the beach can receive reports on wireless computing devices, thanks to SAP Mobile® Infrastructure.

You can easily connect SAP BI components to enable the broadcasting or analysis of reports to mobile devices.

Collecting data

Real-time analysis is never quite real time enough, somehow. With SAP® Exchange Infrastructure (SAP XI), you get an entire framework built atop XML for the automated collection and delivery of data to SAP BI. This delivery service moves as fast as your hardware allows.

Thanks to the SAP XI use of a well-defined open standard like XML, it's able to pull data not only from your own company's systems, but potentially from suppliers' and partners' systems as well. Adding that data ups the possibility of getting useful conclusions from the analyses you make.

SAP® Master Data Management

While SAP BI is busy crunching data, SAP® Master Data Management (SAP MDM) ensures that the data that's being provided from across the enterprise is consistent, and so is its metadata.

The reverse is also true: SAP MDM can be used by SAP BI to harmonize its results with the original, far-flung sources of data.

SAP® Web Application Server

SAP BI loves open standards, which is why SAP® Web Application Server (SAP Web AS) is its foundation and guarantees its operating system and database independence. By accepting queries and issuing reports through Web-based services built using SAP Web AS, IT departments don't have to think twice about the platforms that the data warehouse is running on.

The Future of the SAP Business Intelligence

The core of SAP BI is set. The data warehouse is already the indispensable hub for data flowing through the enterprise, and it's a key component of SAP NetWeaver.

Although the fundamentals of SAP BI will keep their current focus, and more and more Business Content and Analytical Applications will be added, the current mandate is to shift its use from reactive to proactive. Rather than wait passively for InfoCubes to be created and new queries logged, future generations of SAP BI will become more automated. This means that SAP BI will react to change and real-time conditions and work with other SAP NetWeaver components to deliver reports before users even know that they need them.

The other frontier to keep an eye on is the corporate firewall. The life of the enterprise doesn't end at the fringes of a company's network. The urge to create ever more complete portraits of an enterprise's performance will lead to more efficient methods of collecting data from vendors and customers and then melding that data with your company's own.

Chapter 11

Mastering SAP Master Data Management

In This Chapter

▶ Understanding the concept of master data

▶ Examining master data management examples and scenarios

▶ Exploring the way SAP® Master Data Management works

*W*e all live such hectic lives these days that it's hard to keep track of all that needs to be done. You're likely to have a work calendar on your desktop computer in the office and a paper calendar on the refrigerator at home with scribbled notes to yourself. Maybe you have a soccer league calendar for your kids, a yoga class schedule for yourself, and a school calendar to keep you from bundling the kids off to wait for the school bus when it's actually a legal holiday.

Keeping track of all this is frequently a tough job. Wouldn't it be nice to somehow create a master calendar, collecting all the information in one spot?

That's the job of SAP Master Data Management (SAP MDM), a universal data management system that can both accept information from all the different calendars in your data's life and also distribute information to them. SAP MDM can harvest data from all your individual databases, clean it up on the way to placing the items on the universal database, store relationships between items in different databases, distribute items from the universal database to all the individual databases, and control exactly who can change what in each database.

And to fit your lifestyle, SAP MDM doesn't force a central repository of master data on you as a way of keeping track of everything. You can pick and choose from several different styles of managing the problem of distributed data.

This chapter tells you all about the problem of managing distributed master data, why it's important to solve those problems, and how SAP MDM gets the job done.

SAP Master Data Management's Purpose in Life

SAP MDM is a unique product in SAP NetWeaver™ because it solves a problem that rears its ugly head only after the first wave of success for enterprise applications. That's because when SAP techie types talk about *master data,* they mean data that lives between the transactions managed by enterprise data.

Say an Enterprise Resource Planning (ERP) system is managing an invoice. The name of the store may be used in another invoice, the customer name and address will certainly be used again, and tomorrow the name of the salesperson will show up on other invoices. But if you look in the center part of most invoices, the unique transactional data stares right at you. *Transactional data* in this case is the list of products being purchased in this one transaction, along with the prices and tax calculations. This data is not going to be used again after this invoice has been processed.

So how does this relate to managing master data? Well, when enterprise applications first arrived, it really wasn't a big deal. Usually one ERP system at the central office had all the master data and all the transactional data. Of course the data had to be correct, but keeping it correct in one system was hardly a challenge. Ho hum.

The problem of master data arose when bigger companies started using enterprise applications and multiple ERP systems were running at the same company. How could the same master data in all the systems be kept synchronized? In Chapter 4 of this book, we describe how Application Linking and Embedding solves this very problem. Well, SAP MDM is designed to solve the same problem on a larger scale. Now, with not only many ERP systems, but many CRM, SCM, PLM systems as well as legacy systems, the challenge of maintaining accurate master data grows exponentially.

Master data mistakes can cost you

Because of the scope of master data, mistakes in the master data are more costly than mistakes in transactional data. Master data lives on from transaction to transaction. When bad master data is attached to many transactions, the resulting problems can be very expensive to fix because the mistakes flow deeper and deeper into a system. Well-organized master data is also key to allowing systems in one company talk to systems from another company. Mapping data between companies is a large problem that if solved can produce large savings.

Not convinced? Consider this: The Data Warehousing Institute studied the cost of data quality problems and determined in 2002 that bad data cost U.S. businesses, oh, about *$600 billion a year!* Now, not all this bad data is master data, but, Land O'Goshen, that's a pretty penny. SAP MDM can keep some of that money from running out your door.

SAP® Master Data Management goes to work for SAP NetWeaver

The role of SAP MDM in SAP NetWeaver is way more than just that of a special purpose repository. You see, this product not only helps collect master data from all over the place, but with the soul of a data janitor it also helps clean up that data. It finds duplicate data and stores relationships between master data in records across systems. It also distributes master data back to source systems.

Who owns the data in a corporation is a contentious issue that many a middle manager has perished over, and SAP MDM doesn't decide it for you. But after that issue is decided by your powers that be, SAP MDM helps the data owner maintain and make sure that whoever needs up-to-date information has it.

SAP MDM will also become more important as the transformation of the mySAP™ Business Suite, which we describe in Chapter 7, happens. As each of the mySAP Business Suite solutions becomes more service oriented, having a central master data repository becomes increasingly attractive and easy. SAP MDM will be in place, waiting to do the job.

SAP MDM to the rescue

Perhaps the fastest way to understand SAP MDM is to look at how the product makes a difference in the real world. Here are three examples.

Supplier analysis and consolidation

Say you own a big oil company and you have 90,000 employees who spend more than $50 billion a year worldwide. You could buy anything you wanted — even the New York Jets. (Well, maybe the New England Patriots would be a better deal.)

Having that huge budget is great, except that it's actually a quite difficult task to figure out where all the money goes. You may have five or six large operating units with hundreds of divisions, all spending bucks like sailors on leave. Each unit needs supplies that vary from oil-drilling equipment to paper clips.

The data that keeps track of all this spending is in hundreds of systems as well, and each system uses its own method of tracking purchases.

Finding out where the money is going is a job for SAP Master Data Manager and its *content consolidation* technique. Using SAP Master Data Manager facilities for analyzing and locating duplicate records, your company can first take a look at the data and identify locations where the same products are being bought under different names, categories, or ID numbers. Then the different flavors of vendors can be identified (you know, vanilla, chocolate, oil rigs). You may just find out that the company is actually buying printer cartridges from the German division of the same supplier that you use in the United States. At the end of this consolidation project it is possible to find out what the money is being spent on and how much is spent with each vendor for each type of supply.

This information helps in two ways. First, using it you can identify *maverick buying,* in which divisions purchase items on their own without using the supply contracts that have built-in discounts. Second, knowing how much you spend with a vendor can help give you the power to negotiate bigger and better discounts.

Keep in mind that SAP MDM can do all this without requiring that you do a massive data cleanup. It allows for a gradual cleanup along the way. A better understanding and a consolidation of the data can also lay the groundwork for more advanced uses of SAP MDM that build on the cleaned and consolidated data.

Executing a merger: Stage one

When company A buys company B, one of the first tasks facing company A is to figure out where the overlap is. For example, three groups of customers exist: customers who do business with company A only; customers who do business with company B only; and customers who do business with both companies. After a merger has been announced, the faster you sort out which part of which company goes with which customer, the better. Otherwise, you may have sales staff from company A and company B calling on the same customer or even competing for the same business without anyone catching on. Also, be sure that you quickly introduce company A's products to company B's customers, and vice versa.

One way to handle this is to wait until both companies are running on the same systems. However, in most mergers of any size, that usually takes years. SAP MDM provides a much better solution that goes like this:

1. SAP MDM performs a consolidation so that all customers are identified in all the systems at company A and company B.

2. SAP MDM harmonizes the data in all the systems.

Harmonization in this case has nothing to do with reading music. (After all, data doesn't make a sound — unless you count the screams of your employees when a database crashes.) *Data harmonization* means that the records in one system are supplemented with the records from all the other systems. The idea is that if the Customer Relationship Management (CRM) system in company A is populated with a list of all the exclusive customers from company B, and the customers of both companies are marked as such, you can avoid potential data confusion. With SAP MDM, all this is done much faster than you could by consolidating systems using other methods.

Merger mayhem: Stage two

So a year goes by, the dust settles on the merger, and everything is fine. The combined company is delivering better results than the two separate entities, the stock price is up, sales are up, and everyone is smiling and taking home nice fat bonuses. (Sounds kind of like 1999, doesn't it?)

However, even though you've consolidated some data, the systems are all still different. The IT department prepares an estimate for the cost of bringing all the CRM systems onto one system. The CEO looks at the estimate and hits the roof. Both of the CRM systems are less than three years old. The CEO doesn't want to shelve either one so soon. Isn't there a way that both systems can work together, using the same master data?

The Parts of SAP MDM

You probably guessed that the answer to the question at the end of the previous section is *yes* and that the solution involves SAP MDM. (See how smart reading *For Dummies* books makes you?) The way that the two CRM systems can use the same set of master data involves something called central master data management.

Central master data management moves responsibility for master data from the CRM system to SAP Master Data Management. What happens is that the ability to add or change master data is turned off in the CRM system. When a new customer record or any other master data needs to be added, an interface to the central repository of master data in SAP MDM is used. The new record is created and is distributed back to the CRM system. Under this approach, data quality is centrally managed and the possibility for introducing errors or duplicates is dramatically reduced.

The CEO is also kept happy because, instead of having to replace the two different CRM systems to get everyone on the same page using the same data, SAP MDM does the job for you.

The three examples in the "SAP MDM to the rescue" section show the three fundamental techniques used by SAP MDM: content consolidation, harmonization, and central management. SAP MDM is a general-purpose tool that has functions that can be used for many purposes. But more than most parts of SAP NetWeaver, SAP MDM has a game plan for implementation that involves three distinct stages.

SAP MDM deployment: It's an incremental thing

The idea behind implementation scenarios for SAP MDM is that one follows another. Content consolidation helps a company understand how its data is stored and find the important hidden relationships. Master data harmonization helps create a clean copy of the data everywhere so that each system has all the data it needs from all of the other systems. Central master data management creates one repository for master data that can be used by all the systems at a company.

To really understand SAP MDM, take a close look at the scenarios for implementation and then examine the parts that are used to make all that master data move around in just the right way. Figure 11-1 shows this progression. So, how does this work in action? Read on . . . .

Content consolidation

We start by looking at content consolidation (because it comes first). In a way, content consolidation is about cleaning up the mess that lurks in every company's data. One of the key principles of SAP MDM is that it's unreasonable to require any sort of big bang cleanup and system reengineering as part of the process of getting a handle on your data. Such an approach doesn't make sense given the realities of IT, where nobody has time to stop and clean data because they're all busy putting out IT fires.

Instead, cleaning up master data that may be stored in many different systems distributed around the globe is more of a gradual process. Here's how it works:

1. The parts of master data needed for matching and cleaning from all of the distributed systems are loaded into SAP MDM. The data is subjected to a variety of matching algorithms to identify duplicate data.

2. After the duplicate data is found, an ID-mapping table is created so that duplicates can be identified later on during reporting, analysis, or other processing.

3. The ID-mapping table can be loaded into the SAP Business Intelligence system for further analysis by combining it with the transactional data such as the global spend analysis described earlier.

Figure 11-2 illustrates this three-step process.

So now you're probably scratching your head and asking, if SAP MDM finds all this duplicate data, why doesn't SAP MDM just get rid of it? Good question. The answer is that this approach allows all the analyses to be performed and the problems with the data found, but the correction of that data can happen gradually. But because the ID-mapping table has been created, the data can be used and analyzed as if it were already corrected.

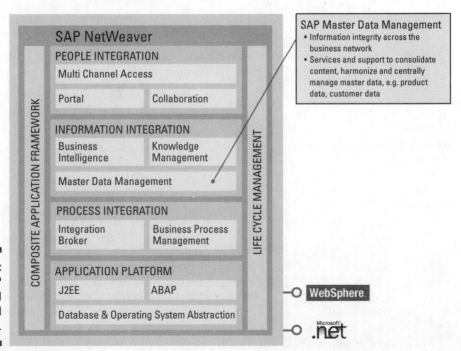

Figure 11-1:
The SAP MDM incremental approach.

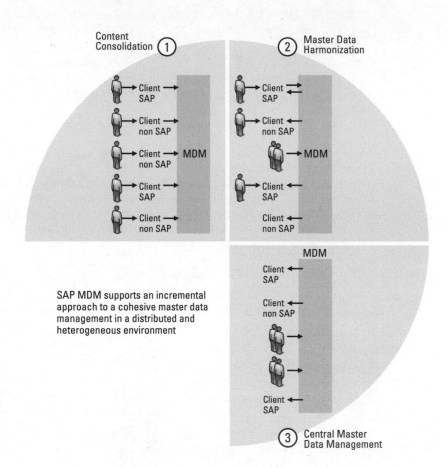

SAP MDM supports an incremental
approach to a cohesive master data
management in a distributed and
heterogeneous environment

Figure 11-2:
Content
consoli-
dation.

Master data harmonization

So, the data has been cleaned up. Great! But what's next? The next step,
which builds on content consolidation, is master data harmonization. In this
phase of using SAP MDM, the cleaned data starts to move around in the following ways:

- Data can be created centrally and then distributed to many different
  systems.

- Data can be changed locally in a distributed system and then the change
  can be automatically distributed to a central repository or to other
  systems.

✔ Data quality can be checked as data flows through the system.

✔ Master data received from a central repository can be extended in the local repository.

✔ A set of workflow steps can be applied to changes and updates to data to require approval for various kinds of changes. This means a data administrator can propose a change for the data owner to approve.

Figure 11-3 illustrates this process.

Central master data management

The clean data is bouncing around your company like a rubber ball. What now? When it's cleaned up, data is happily moving back and forth between a central repository and distributed systems, the next step is to run everything from the central repository.

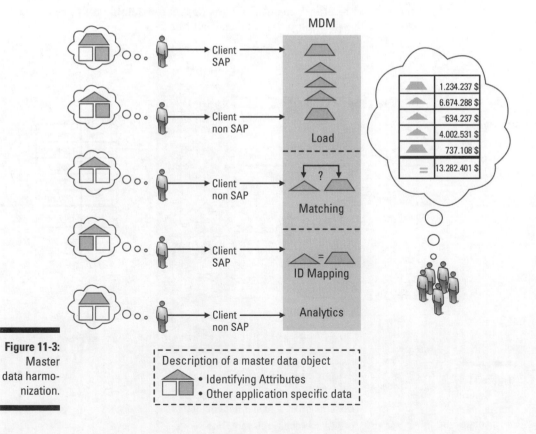

Figure 11-3: Master data harmonization.

In this scenario, you turn off the ability to change master data in the local systems. So, if a CRM system wants to add a new customer, for example, it can't. Instead, a user must enter the new customer through some interface to the central repository. Here duplicates are checked for and workflow steps pending approval can be applied. After the creation of a record has been approved, the new customer record is distributed to all of the eager distributed systems that may want to use it.

This structure allows for one point of control, which can go a long way to reducing costly data errors.

The ID-mapping table that you create in the "Content consolidation" section can still be used to map back from the central record to the instances of the central record in the distributed repositories.

Figure 11-4 illustrates the central master data management scenario.

Now that you understand these scenarios in greater detail, you're ready to make sense of the plumbing that makes it all happen.

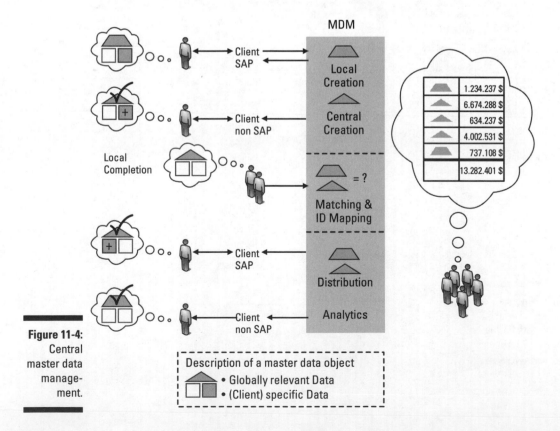

Figure 11-4: Central master data management.

How it all works

Because it came to the game a little later than some other components of SAP NetWeaver, SAP MDM wasn't built from scratch. This means that it takes better advantage of other SAP NetWeaver components that came before.

The general structure of the SAP MDM product is shown in Figure 11-5.

Note how the Content Integrator, Master Data Server, and Master Data Management Adapters interact with SAP Exchange Infrastructure, SAP Enterprise Portal, and SAP Business Intelligence. Take a closer look at how this works, starting with SAP Exchange Infrastructure.

Simplicity itself: SAP Exchange Infrastructure

This is an easy one. SAP Exchange Infrastructure is the SAP NetWeaver component that's dedicated to moving data around reliably, transforming it from one form to another, and coordinating data flow by using advanced business process management capabilities. What could be clearer? What could make more sense?

Moving on . . . .

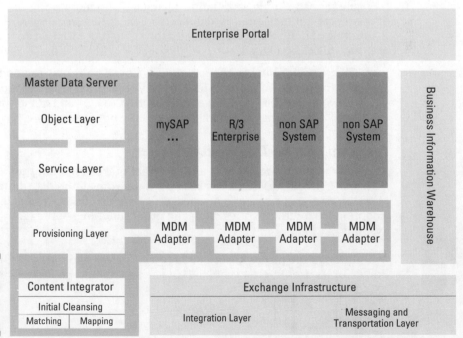

Figure 11-5: SAP MDM building blocks.

Weeding out the bad stuff: Content Integrator

After SAP Exchange Infrastructure moves data from the distributed systems into SAP MDM, the Content Integrator takes over and starts to automatically find duplicates, bad data, and any other meaningful relationships based on rules that you specify. As Content Integrator finds duplicates, it creates ID mappings. Content Integrator also has a powerful data search mechanism to help administrators look for data during the cleaning process.

Master Data Server

Data is all well and good, but you may be wondering how to make use of it. As the Scarecrow said to Dorothy, if it only had a brain! Luckily, the Master Data Server is the brain and memory of SAP MDM.

The cleaned data arrives in the Master Data Server, which then uses three layers to store and manipulate it:

- The **Object Layer** is a flexible repository for master data. For example, if ten customer records exist in all the distributed systems, the Object Layer has to have a place to store every field from all of them. The Object Layer comes out of the box with pre-defined objects for common data types.

- The **Service Layer** is like a toolbox for manipulating and managing master data. Tools for creating, changing, and monitoring the status of objects, running queries, defining and executing workflows, and collaborating about data cleansing all exist to help SAP MDM make the world safe for clean data.

- The **Provisioning Layer** masterminds how data is distributed by using SAP Exchange Infrastructure. This layer performs such functions as allowing distributed systems to subscribe to certain data in the central repository so that any changes there flow out to them.

Everything's normal: SAP MDM Adapter

You know what an *adapter* is — a thingie that makes one thing get along with another. SAP MDM Adapter accepts data from all the distributed heterogeneous source systems and normalizes it into a standard format. SAP MDM Adapter also interacts with search and other functions of the distributed systems.

In addition to the pieces described here, SAP MDM also uses SAP Enterprise Portal for its user interface and SAP Business Intelligence for data analysis.

Taking SAP MDM Out of the Box

SAP MDM comes with a full set of user interfaces that you can use to configure the product's behavior and provide each role the environment that it needs to do a particular job. Interfaces exist for administrators to configure the system, for data specialists to manipulate rules controlling the system, and for users who deal with data cleansing and reporting.

SAP MDM also provides Web services so that other programs can invoke functions to search for data or make other requests.

SAP MDM Plays Well with Others

Ever versatile, SAP MDM can manage master data stored in any of the mySAP™ Business Suite products. As SAP products gradually become structured along the lines of Enterprise Services Architecture, our crystal ball says that SAP MDM could become the master repository of master data for all mySAP Business Suite solutions. You heard it here, first.

The Future of SAP MDM

Have you noticed that brainy types like those at SAP sometimes see into the future? For example, SAP built SAP MDM because it believed that managing master data would rise in importance as IT architecture gets more distributed and more complex. The rise of Web services and the rapid adoption of Radio Frequency ID (RFID) tags have proven that point. Web services leads to a world of more distributed functionality, challenging architects to decide where they will manage master data. In addition, the SAP Auto-ID Infrastructure, which creates a nervous system for using RFID tags, will require a master mapping of RFID numbers to product codes.

Where is all this leading? To the growth of SAP MDM as a universal repository. If there is any application that uses or modifies master data, SAP MDM will be aware of it and become the master data manager for all SAP applications and your entire enterprise.

Chapter 12

Exchanging Data

· ·

· ·

SAP Exchange Infrastructure (SAP XI) is one of the most powerful and widely used parts of SAP NetWeaver™. At first glance, it seems pretty simple: SAP XI allows one application to send data to another application.

However, actually doing this job the right way is much harder that just sending a message from one place to another and back again. To solve this problem in a way that makes life easier for developers and provides all of the functions that applications need, SAP has added all sorts of powerful toolkits inside SAP XI.

In a way, SAP XI is a toolkit's toolkit. As this chapter explains, SAP XI is also essential to helping SAP NetWeaver fulfill its potential.

What SAP XI Is All About

So how does this magical exchange of data happen? Start with the message itself. In SAP XI, the message is usually in XML (eXtensible Markup Language), a flexible format for storing data that can handle almost any kind of structure in a simple way. SAP XI

✔ Has a way to define XML messages.

✔ Stores the descriptions of messages in a repository and keeps track of where they should be sent in a directory.

✔ Has the ability to map the fields of one message to another. SAP XI can then route the messages from one place to another or to many others.

✔ Contains a special toolkit for building adapters that allows any program to send and receive messages.

SAP XI has a powerful toolkit for Business Process Management (BPM), which allows messages to become part of complex processes. This can help many applications communicate with each other the way that they have to when one business integrates its systems with another.

SAP XI: The Data Highway

SAP XI, like other software, is simply a set of tools. But SAP XI acts like a superhighway: Whenever an application needs to send or receive a message, SAP XI is the road that carries it. SAP XI has on-ramps and off-ramps, and rules that make sure every message is received and read correctly when it reaches its destination.

Now on to brass tacks. The purpose of SAP XI is to connect applications with each other. The problem is that frequently each application has its own format for data. So SAP XI is also like a translator in that it specializes in converting formats between applications from SAP or any other vendors so that they can successfully exchange messages. In terms of SAP NetWeaver capabilities, Figure 12-1 shows how SAP XI fits in as the product focused on information and process integration.

Why not lots of little translators?

Now, you might ask, why is this translator a separate set of applications? Why not just include it in each application that needs it? Our answer is, why add essentially the same code to each SAP application? Also, because each application would have to be able to seamlessly talk to the others, each code base would need to be identically maintained. If they weren't, there would be a greater possibility for conflict.

Another reason is basic code economics. Adding this code to each application would increase the size of each application. The extraneous code might slow down an application while it's supposed to be doing something else, as well. It's just not an efficient way of doing things.

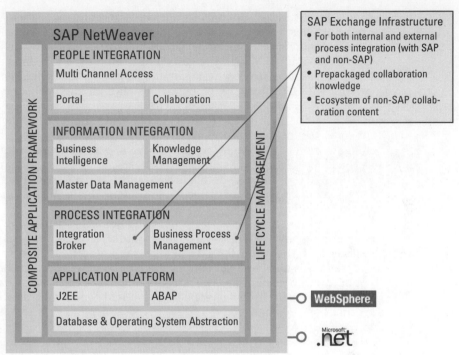

Figure 12-1:
The capabilities of SAP XI.

The need for a hub

In this translation of information, what you want is the complex logic of managing the conversation to be in the middle, in some sort of integration hub that transfers messages back and forth. SAP XI is that middle hub that's designed to manage the complexity of the conversations.

Processing business stuff

As you can imagine, SAP XI does a lot more than simply translate messages. What else does SAP XI do? Another part of SAP XI, the BPM component lets messages play a role in moving complex processes from step to step. The integration builder, a development environment, helps build both messages and processes.

When your company needs to orchestrate a more complex exchange of messages, the BPM tool acts as a conductor of multiple applications. Say that you send a message that requests a particular customer record. The BPM handles it. The BPM tool also might handle more complicated tasks involving time or location questions that can only be answered at remote facilities. A company, for example, has remote offices in London, New York, and Tokyo. But instead of sending queries from the home office to all three remote locations simultaneously, using the BPM tool, you can orchestrate this whole thing and send a particular message to a processing branch in London if it's before noon, to New York if it's afternoon, or to Tokyo if it's after midnight.

So take a look at another example: A credit check. Your company may have built some sort of credit score on customers or suppliers through the years. But, in addition to that, your company might subscribe to a third-party service that keeps a record of suppliers' financials. In this case, at your direction, the BPM tool can take both a private score and a public score and combine them into a composite score, improving the usefulness of the message's content.

Say your company is a large online store that has several different warehouses around the world. SAP XI's BPM tool could route the message to all of the warehouses and have each one of them bid on the job of packing and shipping a customer's order. The moment one of the warehouses responds positively within acceptable parameters, it could send a message back that the order has been fulfilled.

Figure 12-2 shows the role that SAP XI plays in both of these examples.

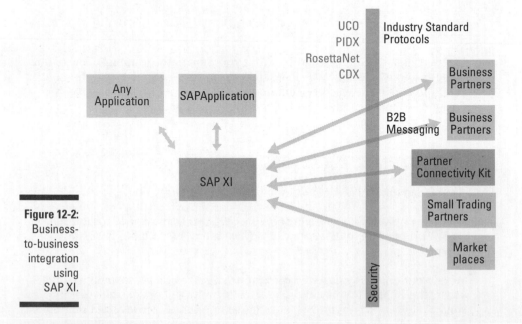

Figure 12-2:
Business-to-business integration using SAP XI.

How Does SAP XI Fit into SAP NetWeaver?

Before SAP XI was invented, some of the mySAP™ Business Suite solutions came up with their own way of exchanging data. The mySAP Customer Relationship Management (CRM) application's communications were handled by an application called CRM Middleware, for example. In SAP NetWeaver, SAP XI is in charge of all process integration and automated system-to-system communications.

While tools such as CRM Middleware are optimized to meet the needs of mySAP CRM, and for that reason will be in use for a long time, SAP XI is a more general-purpose tool. Applications created after SAP XI appeared, such as mySAP Supplier Relationship Management, use SAP XI to talk to other applications. The same is true for many other SAP applications: For example, if SAP® Business Intelligence (SAP BI) needs to talk to the SAP® Web Application Server, or if the SAP® Enterprise Portal needs to talk to SAP BI, they use SAP XI to communicate. In each case, you can use SAP XI to get the conversation going using all of the latest advanced features for message mapping and business process management.

SAP XI: Your Business's Best Friend

Technology like SAP XI can be hard to visualize with all that integration, automation, and translation going on. So perhaps the easiest way for you to get a handle on what SAP XI can do is review a few more examples in the hopes that one or more of them clicks with your business needs or your industry.

Example 1: Cheaper integration through an integration hub

Say you have an ERP and a CRM system. Why would you need to connect them? Perhaps because you need to coordinate the planning in the Supply Chain Management (SCM) system with customer orders.

Take the path of a purchase order in a fulfillment system, for instance. The actual procurement information, such as the identity of the customer who places the order, might come from the CRM system. This information needs to be passed between multiple application systems in a distributed system landscape. Connecting every system to every other system with point-to-point connections means an exponential growth in the number of interfaces. On top of many different kinds of systems, there may be many copies of each type of system (many CRMs and many ERPs), making the situation still more complex. (Mergers are frequently the evil cause of such insidious duplication.)

The classic stovepipe integration connects ERP right to CRM. But if you add a CRM system, now you have to connect ERP to both CRM systems, and as soon as you have two ERPs, you have to connect two ERPs to two CRMS systems, and so on. Pretty soon, the interconnections become an unworkable web.

The classic example of reducing integration costs is by using a hub, rather than tying together application systems in a spider web fashion. SAP XI replaces many point-to-point connections with a single connection for each application to such an integration hub. Then if you change something in the landscape, you don't affect the connection from the application to the hub. Each system retains its independence, whatever happens in the rest of the system landscape, because each system relies on the hub — the integration broker — to take the message to the appropriate application. Thus, you maintain one interface, and your customer order is good to go.

Example 2: Business-to-business automation

A common use of the central hub's features is when SAP XI replaces a "fire and forget" purchase order with a monitored interaction. Say you need to send a business partner a purchase order, but because that's a "fire and forget" kind of communication, it's as if you're sending an e-mail — you may know the partner will get the e-mail, but you don't know when he'll read it or respond to it.

But with SAP XI, you can use the BPM tool to control timing. You can send a partner a purchase order, but instead of wondering when she will respond, you can have an agreement with her that within 24 hours if you don't get an answer, you will automatically send the order to another partner. This ensures that processes aren't unreasonably delayed while an order sits unattended. This policy encourages the partner to create a process to accept, reject, or change the order within 24 hours. Because you are using SAP XI, you know that your processes will keep moving.

Example 3: Building relationships with suppliers

Another example involves a manufacturer using *Electronic Data Interchange* (EDI) technology to automate a relationship with a supplier. EDI is an ancestor of XML messaging systems developed using the technology of the mainframe era. The manufacturer could send an EDI purchase order to the supplier and know it was going to get there, but not know much else because there was no way of keeping track of the order.

BPM allows the manufacturer to fire off a purchase order, keep a timer going in the BPM layer, and initiate another action if the right message doesn't come back — such as "I've got that part for you" — within 24 hours. Or if the wrong message comes back — "I don't have that part for you" — that purchase order is then fired off to a secondary supplier.

The Various and Sundry Parts of SAP XI

SAP XI is a complex nest of functionality with many abstract layers to manage message processing and distribution. Here's another way to think of it: SAP XI separates the difficult jobs it has to perform into design-time and runtime components, and then uses as much indirection and abstraction as possible to make the system flexible and easy to change. SAP XI also provides tools that you can use to define message formats, map one format to another, define processes, and allow those processes to interact with the outside world through messages.

If you're still confused about what SAP XI does, you're not alone. It's hard for someone who doesn't have a Ph.D. in computer science to understand why all those layers are there. We try to simplify things so that any non-geek can understand what's going on inside SAP XI.

SAP XI has the following components:

- ✔ Integration builder
- ✔ Integration repository
- ✔ Integration directory
- ✔ System landscape directory
- ✔ Integration server
- ✔ Central monitoring

Figure 12-3 shows all the moving parts of SAP XI that come into play as it connects applications together. In the sections that follow, we go through these parts one by one.

Integration builder

The *integration builder* is a comprehensive development environment used at design time. Integration builder is essentially a tool used to define messages and processes, map one format to another, configure the way they'll be used with other systems, and store all sorts of related information. The definitions are stored in the integration repository and configuration information is stored in the integration directory.

Integration builder builds stuff. This is the component of SAP XI that defines the structure of a message for the integration server to send.

But, it's important to understand that integration builder does more than build messages. It's also involved in BPM. The integration builder may be building an XML schema for you or helping you define a message based on a schema, but it also has tools that help you define a process too, called a *process modeler*. A process modeler is where design time comes in.

So, what about that design time thing, you ask? In order to understand that, you need to understand the difference between design time and configuration time. So, read on . . .

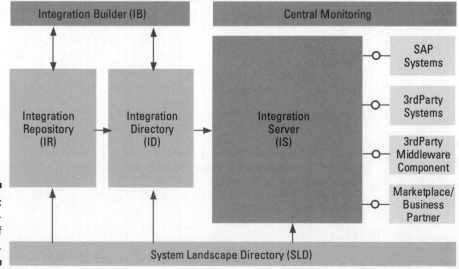

Figure 12-3:
The architecture of SAP XI.

Design time in the process editor

During design time, you drag out every editor in the integration builder to help you define a business process. This is done in a graphical tool inside integration builder, where you

- ✔ Define messages with an interface editor
- ✔ Create rules using the condition editor
- ✔ Map from one message format to another with the mapping editor
- ✔ Try to define the overall business process with the process editor
- ✔ Knit everything together with the scenario editor

This process provides a complete blueprint of the part of your business that SAP XI is helping with. In configuration time, you take this blueprint and connect it to the real world to work in a specific situation.

Figure 12-4 shows how each of these editors controls a different part of the integration repository.

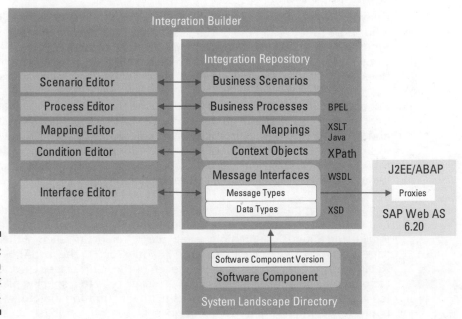

Figure 12-4:
Integration builder at design time.

At design time, integration builder's integration features come into play. Here's where it does the specific mapping between two applications systems, a sending application and a receiving application. The integration directory has a central repository for all interfaces that are involved, a library of the application-specific XML structure. To create mappings between messages, we drag and drop into the graphical mapping tool so that a business analyst or an IT person can then define the relationship between the sending and the receiving system.

For example, a purchase order from SAP and a purchase order from another vendor, though they're both formatted as XML, are not exactly the same because the message structures are different. Integration builder allows you to drag and drop icons to show the relationships between the sending system and the receiving system. It's a very graphically driven environment that requires no knowledge of code and handles many tasks automatically. For example, it has a built-in library function that transforms dates and values. A classic example for the latter is when you have to deal with two names for the same item. In one application system, you might call a pen "ballpoint pen 1," but in the receiving application, the product identification might be "123-15."

Configuration time

Okay, so at design time you have this electronic drawing board that blueprints a business process and the business interaction. At *configuration time* you determine what information you need to actually route messages. What's the trigger? How does the system determine if something's right or wrong? How does the system know if it's supposed to branch to another process chain?

Put another way, at design time you describe the players on the team, who's quarterback and what the quarterback does; who's the defensive lineman and what the defensive lineman does. At configuration time, you tell the system what play to run. The description of the roles would be at design time, and the description of the plays to execute come at configuration time, including when you're going to run each play.

Say you're mapping orders for office supplies. At design time, you define the fact that you have three mythical office supply stores Staple City, Paper Clip World, and Super Duper Supply as receivers. You define each of their message formats. Then you map from the SAP message in the mySAP Supplier Relationship Management system to each of those message types. At configuration time, you actually connect the message type to a specific place where it's going to be sent on the Internet using the integration directory. Then you connect that information to a set of rules. In order to establish these rules, you've got a set of criteria — whether you want the low price or the best discount or whatever for each request — that helps you figure out where to send the message.

But that's not all you do at configuration time. For example, you might ask: How do I know that one particular message is associated with a particular process? That's handled at configuration time, too.

For example, some of those messages are coming back from your exemplary office supplier, Super Duper Supply, and the bulk of those are positive. In other words, "Order received; I'm going to fill it tomorrow." There might be a few orders that can't be filled that you want to send out to the secondary supplier. For all of your messages, the system has to know where to route them. Integration builder creates routing information such as which fields of the message will be used to help determine where a message should go. Then it stores that information in the integration directory. The integration directory is also where you set some of the more technical parameters of the system's communication, such as the protocol — HTTP, for example — or whether it's using an adapter, that sort of thing.

Integration builder has configuration wizards that walk you through the configuration process and configuration editors that allow you to set the information manually.

Figure 12-5 shows the kind of information that the configuration editor of the integration builder controls in the integration directory.

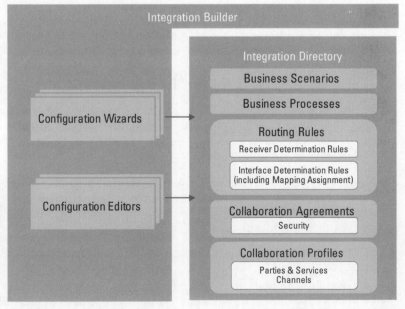

Figure 12-5:
Integration builder at configuration time.

Integration repository

SAP XI hangs onto a lot of data that describes the structure of messages and processes. Such data that describes other data is called *metadata*. The *integration repository* is where SAP XI keeps the metadata that describes data types, messages, processes, and the mappings and connections between them. The metadata might describe an application interface, or a purchase order, or a process for checking a client's credit, for example.

If you were to examine the files in the integration repository, you'd find XML schemas that define the structure of XML messages and special languages to describe processes. Not only are there places where you can add XML schemas for your own messages, you can also take advantage of any or all of the ones currently in use. If the mySAP CRM system has the ability to send out XML messages, if mySAP ERP has XML messages, or if they're part of important industry standards, they're described in the integration repository.

The integration repository comes with message formats used by all the mySAP Business Suite solutions, with message formats for standards such as Rosetta Net, and with process templates that provide a head start on implementing common business processes.

SAP XI's integration repository is involved at design time, configuration time, and run time. What exactly lies in this particular repository? In the integration repository are what SAP calls objects. These *objects,* put simply, are data types. The idea is to create a centralized access point for these objects, so that you can reuse them and locate existing information easily.

The three basic data types stored in the integration repository are

- ✔ SAP message
- ✔ Industry-standard message
- ✔ Business process templates

For example, imagine a data type called "address." In your company, addresses are used not just in purchase orders, but also in ship-to notifications. You benefit from using — or reusing, as the case may be — the same data type in multiple messages.

Any reusable data types are stored as objects in the repository. As you combine multiple data types into groups, you create message types. These message types are shipped with SAP applications — this is part of the content — so you don't have to go through and create it. SAP can even take a message type from an SAP application and map it to a second data type, such as an industry-standard format.

The integration repository offers what SAP calls *business process templates* as its third data type. Almost every industry has an XML standard, and SAP created these templates to follow those standards and to ease the job of creating whatever blueprint of your business processes you need to make. They're not preset, canned business processes, because SAP doesn't know exactly what your company is up to. But it is possible to make an educated guess as to what your various steps might be, because many business transactions are very similar, like a pattern in purchasing or customer order processing. For example, there might be a business process template for sending and acknowledging a purchase order. There might be another business process template for an inquiry about inventory availability, and so on.

Integration directory

The *integration directory* is where the messages types and processes described in the integration repository are connected to the real world. When a message comes from a partner, gets checked by a process, and then is sent to an internal system, the metadata that describes all of these connections is stored in the integration directory. Your business partners' system landscape and applications, naming conventions, IP addresses, and routing rules for why the purchase order is sent to supplier A instead of supplier B, are all stored in integration directory. In essence, the integration directory describes who you're talking to, how you're talking to them, and the rules for talking to them.

Just like snowflakes, no two businesses are exactly alike. A company that implements and installs SAP XI has its own business rules. Integration directory captures those unique rules in the form of data. For example, one bunch of data might describe the difference among various suppliers, and the conditions that come to bear to place an order with one or the other.

In addition, the integration directory also contains addresses — but these aren't your typical street addresses and postal codes. No, these are the specific locations where messages are headed.

Those of you versed in these kinds of systems may be wondering at this moment: How's that different from system landscape directory? (If you're not, don't worry; that just means you have a life beyond technology.) The answer is that the system landscape directory is similar to the integration directory, but instead of describing messages and processes, it describes the systems that are sending the messages around.

System landscape directory

The *system landscape directory* is simply a directory of technical information about the programs and computers being connected by SAP XI. It contains very low-level information, such as IP addresses, software release dates, version numbers of an application, and so on.

System landscape directory is in fact used to store the most technical parts of the infrastructure; integration directory is concerned with the logical parts of the infrastructure. The idea is this: The details of a system can be defined in the system landscape directory the same way that the DNS system of the Internet allows an IP address to be assigned to a domain name. The IP address may change, but everyone can still find a site by using the domain name. The integration directory can store information like IP addresses directly. However, if the integration directory uses an entry in the system landscape directory to refer to a system instead of including a direct reference, the information describing that system can be changed without having to change the integration directory information at all.

In the system landscape directory, you'll find all the technical information specific to your company that's required to link one computer sending and receiving messages to another. You can see specifically which components have been installed and the versions and vendors of the software. This is important because the message types and interfaces might be different in various versions. In order for the system to know how to handle content and what to automatically put into the integration repository, it uses system landscape directory. You need to know the version of the application, what server it is running on, and the IP address. All of this and more is captured and contained in the system landscape directory.

You might use this information to select specific message types. You can have multiple system landscapes for your Quality Assurance, Development, and Production departments, for example. SAP XI is smart enough to adapt when you move information from one system landscape to another — from the development to the QA process, for instance. When that happens, SAP XI takes the configuration information and moves it over.

SAP XI is programmed to always go to the system landscape directory to find where messages should go. For example, when the applications goes from development to QA, the software essentially says, "Let me ask the system landscape directory where the messages should go."

Integration server

The *integration server* is the brain, where it all comes together at runtime. When you send a message, the message goes through the integration server. The processing of the message will be based upon the information that is configured in the integration directory, but all the thinking is done by the integration server using all the information in the integration repository and the integration directory.

The integration server is the engine responsible for routing a message. The integration server doesn't really have components; it's more of a pipeline where a couple of steps take place, such as logical routing, technical routing, mapping, and the calling of adapters.

So how does the integration server work? Well, when an application sends off a message, at the time it sends the message, the application doesn't know who the receiver of the message is. So it just sends the message to the hub — SAP XI. The hub's task is to determine what receiving system should get the message. So in the hub's integration server, or what SAP calls the *pipeline,* four things could happen:

1. The integration server does the logical routing. This is where it determines, based upon the configuration information from the integration directory, the logical receiver of the message. This could be the vendor Super Duper Supplies, for example.

2. After the integration server determines the receiver, it determines what application system at the receiver should get this particular message.

3. The integration server determines the technical endpoint — the URL or the IP address of that particular receiver. When the integration server knows which system is to receive the message (because it has the mapping information), it also knows what mapping applies for that particular receiving system.

4. If no mapping is needed, the integration server can skip this last step. But if it needs to map this message from another vendor's CRM to SAP's message format, then the integration server executes instructions to take one XML schema and transform it into the receiving system's expected schema. It's in this last step that the integration server calls the appropriate adapter required to communicate with the receiving system. Or, if the same software is running on the receiving system's application server, the integration server determines that it can communicate natively.

Figure 12-6 provides a clear summary of this pipeline and how the information in the integration directory supports it.

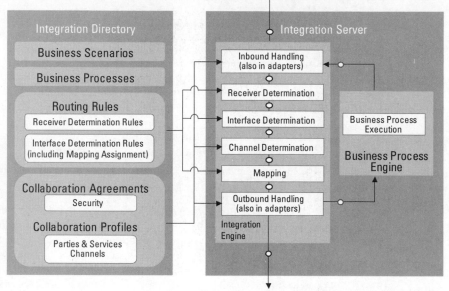

Central monitoring

Exactly as the name suggests, *central monitoring* monitors and assesses whether the messages are successfully flowing between systems. This centralized access point gives you a view of the whole integration scenario and presents the constraints, technical end-to-end monitoring, and everything you need so that you can see the path that messages take.

Did a message run into problems? If there's a problem, you click on an error message and drill down for more information. Central monitoring has the equivalent of gauges on the dashboard of a car, showing oil pressure, voltage generated, coolant temperature — the health of the entire system. Are messages flowing? Is every part of the infrastructure sending and receiving messages? Or is some part of the system under stress and in need of attention?

An engine for business process

If you earmark a message to go to the business process engine to provide information to help move a process along, at some point in the pipeline the message gets detoured there. (Of course, this doesn't apply when SAP XI is just passing messages that are not related to a process from one application to another.) When a message comes in, the *business process engine* primarily does two things. One, it looks for a set of things that match, called *correlation identifiers* — is there a unit purchase order number within this document, or some other attribute to look at to recognize if there's a response? Two, the business process engine runs the message through the actual process engine, which controls what's supposed to happen to it.

When the business process engine needs to send a message to another system, it uses the integration directory and the pipeline to look up the other system and send the message. The business process engine doesn't connect to the other system itself; it utilizes the existing infrastructure in the integration engine to do that. When the messages come back to the integration engine from the business process engine, the correlation handling determines if the message should be sent to another system or to the next step in the process.

You see, each step of the business process uses the integration engine to figure out how to get to the next step. And that step could either be inside or outside the business process engine. If the next step is inside the business process engine, the integration engine uses the integration repository to determine this, and then just sends the message along. The destination can be another system, too, in which case the integration engine sends the message there. The idea is that the business process engine doesn't know how near or far the end is, or even how far the next step is. The business process doesn't have to know — it just knows that there is a next step and that the integration engine is going to send the message on its way there.

It's a law

The graphical tool involved in the model development process builds its code in a language called *BPEL4WS*, or Business Process Execution Language for Web Services. BPEL4WS is a standard jointly created by BEA Systems, IBM, Microsoft, SAP AG, and Siebel Systems. (These are some pretty heavy hitters.) This language is used to specify business process behavior based on Web services. Processes in BPEL4WS are built on top of XML, XML schema, WSDL, and UDDI, and call on export and import functionality by using Web service interfaces exclusively.

What that means to you is that if you've already got a tool in your company that supports this standard, and you've already created a blueprint for what your business process looks like, you can simply export those processes from your existing tool and into the SAP tool. You don't have to go about redesigning it in the SAP tool. Also, of course, you can export the ones that you create so that the investments that you take in creating these models are future-proof: You can simply export to some other tool or share them with your business partner or subsidiary. Of course, this also gives SAP an opportunity to shift its models as well.

Speaking with the adapter framework

In order to understand the *adapter framework,* think of it as a rather large toolkit that applications use to talk to SAP XI. Certain libraries available in Java, and a certain architecture called the Java Connector Architecture, are all about building adapters so that one application can talk to another. The adapter architecture makes sure that whatever program you're in, whether COBOL or any other language, you can find a way to talk to SAP XI.

SAP also uses the adapter framework for its own development adapters, so SAP XI has a set of technical adapters that can talk to Java Database Connectivity (JDBC) databases, intelligent messaging service message queues, flat file, or File Transfer Protocol, for example.

Any time the SAP XI needs to talk to something outside of itself, it uses the adapter framework to communicate, as well. For example, if you have a small supplier with a small, non-XML system that doesn't have the resources to integrate with SAP XI, you can give the supplier a connectivity kit to create its own adapter.

Parts for managing processes

Okay, unless this is the first thing you've read in this book, you probably realize that process is king around SAP. So take a gander at the process editor, which allows you to graphically create, configure, and manage processes. The process editor is an environment that has a set of objects that you use for modeling a particular business process. The various application systems that you already have in your system landscape are available to the process editor — you can easily drag messages from a particular sending or receiving application and connect them to processes.

Say you want to use the process editor to model an order process for an online book store. The movement of products will have a unique flow between the warehouses and then to the customer, subject to a variety of important decisions.

In the first step, after an order comes in from the Web site, you have to figure out where this order message should go — the order should go to one particular warehouse, the one that has all the books the customer requested, because that warehouse the only place the entire order can be shipped from.

But what if there are items in the order that the warehouse doesn't have? The system has to decide whether another warehouse can fulfill the whole order, or if the order has to ship from more than one warehouse. All these sorts of details and situations are handled by the process model.

The message's journey, as seen through the eyes of the model, is a flow chart of yes or no questions. Is any part of the order for reference books? If it's yes, then go look in warehouse A; if no, move on to warehouse B. This process is likely to have multiple steps.

You'll be glad to hear that you're in charge of this whole thing. You can do whatever you want in creating the process: You can set timers, send alerts, or have process steps wait for several different messages to arrive before they proceed. You can send out messages to multiple locations and wait for a response from the first one or all of them.

How Developers Create Applications with SAP XI

Like most SAP NetWeaver components, SAP XI is increasingly using modeling as a way to allow developers to create applications. And as always, business content plays a major role in giving your implementations a head start.

A fine romance: Integration builder and adapter framework

The integration builder is the primary tool you use to build SAP XI applications. The adapter framework then uses Java Connector Architecture to connect systems to SAP XI.

There's something interesting about how the modeling of data types, messages, and processes allows you to take a different approach to creating applications. SAP XI offers *outside-in development*, which allows you to model application-specific interfaces with a code generator more easily than you could from scratch. The idea is that you tell SAP XI the messages you want to connect and which applications you want to connect them to. Then, the system creates the adapter for the application and the information in the integration repository and integration directory. This allows the system to process the message.

Using the integration builder, you generate what SAP calls a *proxy,* which is a programming stub, a program that has a fill-in-the-blanks sort of structure that can be enhanced to do what you need. You can then use the stub to implement the business application. For example, you can go into the integration builder and create an application interface that acts as a proxy for a purchase order, with its various data types such as address and purchase-order line items. The generated stub can essentially model the look and feel of a particular type of message.

What this process does is speed up application development. Customers and SAP application developers alike don't have to think about how to go about constructing an XML message and guaranteeing the message delivery. They can instead concentrate on adding the work of their particular application to the generated code.

There's more than one way to build an adapter to talk to SAP XI. Instead of building the adapter, you can build the message you want the theoretical adapter to generate, and then generate the code to include the message in the application. This method bypasses the requirement to make an adapter, avoiding a layer of indirection. Unlike with an adapter, your message is generated and sent directly by the sending program.

By the way, this is the way all new SAP applications will be built. Although it makes things a little more efficient, it also makes them less abstract. Using this method, the burden on programmers and the introduction of errors are greatly reduced.

Instant business content

Don't you just love instant? Instant messaging, instant brownie mixes (just add water). In the same spirit, instead of making you write your own business content, SAP XI comes prebuilt — just add your own business need.

The five basic types of business content in the system are

- Message types and scenarios for SAP applications
- Business packages for industry standards
- Business process orchestration for exchanges
- Process templates
- Mapping templates

In the case of mySAP SRM 4.0, you get application-interface descriptions and the scenarios for how a message can flow between the SAP system and the applications of a partner's SRM. The idea is to speed up the implementation process. You simply add the information that is specific to you as a customer — the routing between the applications is already set up.

Some of the content is built to work with industry standards, some of it only works within a pure SAP environment. Business process orchestration for various exchanges is part of the former. It comes with timers that are set between two communicating business partners. The most common usage of this is to execute functions or resend messages based on time. In other words, if a message doesn't get a reply, do something about it automatically.

Other business content includes the process and mapping templates that also help you to get up to speed quicker. One of the most difficult challenges in an integration project is to create mapping. It takes a lot of time and usually costs a lot of money. SAP XI comes with this mapping content (as long as you only need it for an SAP application) built in.

SAP XI and other SAP NetWeaver Components

So how does SAP XI get along with the other kids in SAP NetWeaver sandbox? Just as SAP Enterprise Portal is destined to be the user-interface layer for all mySAP Business Suite solutions and SAP NetWeaver, SAP XI is destined to be the way that you pass messages back and forth and manage certain types of business processes.

Already, SAP XI is playing that role for some mySAP Business Suite solutions. mySAP SRM, for example, uses SAP XI to connect to other applications. And as time goes by, more mySAP Business Suite solutions will make more use of SAP XI.

SAP XI plays an important role moving information around between SAP NetWeaver components. SAP Master Data Management uses SAP XI to transport the master data it is managing across distributed systems. SAP Business Intelligence, SAP® Web Application Server, and SAP® Enterprise Portal all make similar use of SAP XI as they need to.

Looking into the Future of SAP XI

Right now, SAP XI handles messages going back and forth between SAP and non-SAP applications. As time goes on, SAP XI should do more of what it is doing now — getting deeper into mySAP Business Suite, handling more message types, offering more business content to jump-start the solution to even more problems, automating many B2B relationships, and describing more processes. After SAP XI fulfills this vision to the fullest extent, what's next?

In the future, the emphasis will be less on the various components and more on SAP NetWeaver as a complete solution, creating services that allow you to model your business and have the flexibility you need, according to the principles of Enterprise Services Architecture. As this model grows, SAP NetWeaver becomes more and more of a foundation layer; instead of worrying about the technical plumbing; you'll deal with the business services built on top of SAP NetWeaver.

Chapter 13

SAP Web Application Server: The Cornerstone of SAP NetWeaver

SAP Web Application Server (SAP Web AS) is to SAP® NetWeaver™ what Groucho Marx was to the Marx Brothers. (Where would the others have been without him?) If the other the SAP NetWeaver components can be considered general purpose tools for building business applications, you can think of SAP Web AS as a flexible and configurable engine for powering engines that run applications.

While many people don't associate SAP with deep infrastructure like application servers, the fact of the matter is that SAP has been building application servers longer than any other company — the SAP Basis layer at the foundation of SAP's first few generations of applications was an application server. If you count SAP Basis and SAP Web AS (shipped with all of the thousands of mySAP™ Business Suite solutions), SAP probably has more application servers running out there than any other company.

This chapter dives deep into the anatomy of SAP NetWeaver to take a close look at the SAP Web AS and its collection of components. These components provide the building blocks and key plumbing for all the products we discuss in previous chapters.

How Important Is SAP Web AS?

It's hard to overestimate the importance of SAP Web AS. In many ways, SAP Web AS is truly the foundation of SAP NetWeaver. All of the mySAP Business

Suite solutions run on SAP Web AS. Every one of the other SAP NetWeaver components need SAP Web AS, either because they run on it or they draw on some of its capabilities.

In Chapter 1 we discuss the stack. Our discussion so far has dealt with the top of that stack, which contains the user interfaces and business, process, and integration logic. In this chapter you move to the bottom of the stack and look at the nuts and bolts that the SAP Web AS provides to make SAP NetWeaver possible.

This is not a chapter for the timid. You go right under the hood and start taking the caps off distributors and getting your hands dirty. If you are the kind of person who likes being close to the greasy technological metal, or even likes watching somebody else working on it, this chapter is for you. But even if you're less interested in details, it's still likely that our nuts and bolts tour will be illuminating.

The Heart and Soul of Web AS

In Chapter 4 we make a big deal about abstraction and about how the original SAP versions of various sorts of toolkits grew and were rebuilt over the years to become SAP NetWeaver. One of the most famous and widely used parts of SAP's previous generation of technology is the BASIS layer, which was the first foundation at SAP for platform independence. BASIS allowed the same SAP applications to run on IBM mainframes, Microsoft servers, and Unix servers. BASIS also provided all sorts of useful tools that made it a lot easier to write the kind of applications that SAP is famous for.

Well, in those days, the world of IT was a younger, wilder place. Dinosaurs like IBMMainframeasaurous roamed the world. Networks were rare and proprietary, and the bright light of standards did not warm the primordial ooze.

These days, the world of technology has grown older and more stable. As a result, things that were created by SAP in BASIS are now defined by standards. Java, for example, has become a standard platform-independent language and has associated with it all sorts of related standards for connecting to databases, writing adapters, or writing code for mobile devices. Web services are becoming another important standard. Of course, HTML and XML are hugely important standards as well.

So, given this background, it is possible to revisit the job of SAP Web AS, which is to

✔ Provide a platform-independent foundation for writing applications for business.

✔ Provide a runtime environment for executing business applications.

✔ Provide as much help as possible in the form of toolkits and utilities to help make scalable and reliable applications easy to develop and cheap to operate and upgrade.

✔ Meet these goals by using as many widely accepted standards as possible.

Figure 13-1 shows an interesting view of how BASIS gradually morphed into SAP Web AS.

All the things that BASIS did, SAP Web AS also does, including supporting the ABAP language. SAP Web AS breaks new ground, however, by supporting the Java language, as well as the Web Dynpro environment for creating Web applications, user interfaces, and Web services.

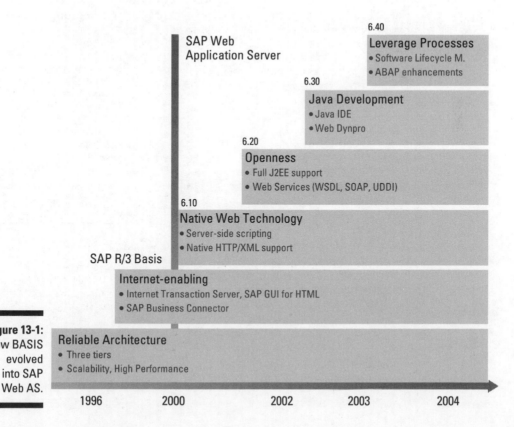

Figure 13-1: How BASIS evolved into SAP Web AS.

SAP Web AS reporting for duty

When you take a look at Figure 13-2, you can see that it is no accident that SAP Web AS sits near the bottom of this group. As we've said, almost all of SAP NetWeaver rests on the capabilities provided by SAP Web AS.

The job of SAP Web AS in SAP NetWeaver is to provide all of the support that applications need to do their jobs. One way to think of SAP Web AS is as a collection of functions that every application needs. Need to create Web services or HTML pages? Need to access a database? Want to run programs written in Java and ABAP? Do you need a structured workflow environment for your program to interact with the outside world through SAP® Exchange Infrastructure, Web services, or some other proprietary method? SAP Web AS has got all these covered. SAP Web AS even accelerates the development of applications through its Web Dynpro environment for creation of utilities through modeling and through a variety of other utilities for interacting with smart forms, managing alerts, archiving records, and so on.

So, SAP Web AS is a great big toolbox, an accelerator of development, and a runtime environment where everything works.

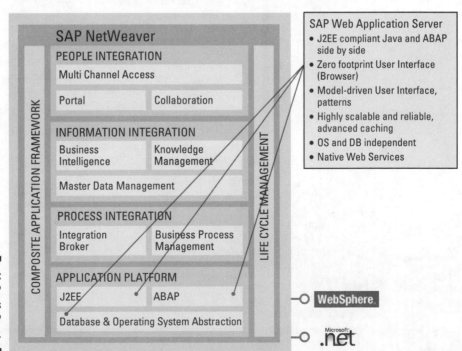

Figure 13-2:
How SAP Web AS fits into SAP NetWeaver.

But really, who cares but the most deeply technical among us? Besides being a central part of SAP NetWeaver, what can SAP Web AS do to help your business? Well, the answer is that SAP Web AS plays a vital role in completing the last bit of a solution that lies just outside the reach of all of the preconfigured business content that makes SAP applications work for a particular purpose.

SAP Web AS helps your business

Before diving into the details of all of the SAP Web AS moving parts (and there are many of them), here are some examples that show the kind of things you can use the SAP Web AS to do.

As a general general-purpose toolkit for toolkits, SAP Web AS can sometimes be hard to understand and explain. In the following examples, we try to bring some of this complexity to life in a real-world situation.

Example 1: Extending R/3 on demand

So, there you are at the end of a successful implementation of an SAP R/3® system. Your CEO is lavishing praise on the IT department for meeting the deadline under budget and delivering all of the promised functionality. (Hey, it could happen.)

But, as usual, during the implementation, the powers that be got a much better understanding of the requirements — the CEO suddenly realized that if the comprehensive financial picture of the business that SAP R/3 provides is used to enhance the information used in the corporate planning application, the senior executive team will have to guess a lot less about how to run the business.

The problem, however, is that the planning application is a hodge podge of spreadsheets and proprietary forecasting tools. It will eventually be re-implemented in SAP® Business Intelligence, but that won't happen for more than a year.

This is a problem made for SAP Web AS. The first thing that you do is create Web services using ABAP to access BAPI available from SAP R/3 to provide the corporate planning application with access to the required financial information. The CFO realizes that if this information is supplemented with the currency hedging currently in place, the corporate planning application can then show a risk-adjusted view of the future. SAP Web AS then uses Java to talk through a proprietary XML protocol to the portfolio management systems of the investment bank doing the hedging. SAP Web AS provides another Web service so that the corporate planning application can use this information. This has the added benefit of creating a layer that allows the interface to the portfolio information to be changed or even switched to a new investment bank without changing the applications that use this information.

(Okay, we warned you that this is a get-your-technological-hands-dirty chapter. If you don't need to understand the techie example, the point is just to appreciate the beauty of the improvements to the business processes that were achieved by using SAP Web AS.)

This simple technique of using SAP Web AS to handle difficult or nonstandard integration problems is classic. Choosing either ABAP or Java (depending on the job), you then can provide information from SAP R/3 or other mySAP Business Suite solutions through Web services to the people and applications that need that information. This will create enormous value for many SAP customers.

Example 2: Automating B2B with SAP Exchange Infrastructure

While many problems that face businesses today have an off-the-shelf solution, sometimes the most significant problems are one of a kind. This is frequently the case in business-to-business (B2B) automation, where legacy systems, special conditions, and the need for extra security often come into play.

In this situation, SAP Web AS shines in combination with SAP SAP XI. Each product plays an important role and is nicely enhanced by the other.

The typical B2B application starts out with the prepackaged ability SAP XI has to understand the data formats of all mySAP Business Suite solutions, such as the sales order in mySAP Customer Relationship Management or the purchase order in mySAP Enterprise Resource Planning. Then, through its adapter framework, SAP XI connects to and creates a flow of messages between non-SAP applications inside and outside the company (for example, messages exchanged between retailers and manufacturers to automatically generate orders when inventory drops to a certain level). Finally, SAP XI uses its business-process management capability to control the flow of messages. This solves the needs of many of your typical of B2B integrations.

But, of course, there is always an application such as mySAP Supply Chain Management that might need a special adapter to interact with the shop floor of a manufacturer, or the business process management needs a complex service to help with processing one of the messages because of an intricate business relationship. Or maybe the entire integration needs more of a user interface than SAP XI can provide. This is when SAP Web AS steps in and helps fill in the gaps.

The Bits and Pieces of Web AS

The documentation for every part of the SAP Web AS is only about a gazillion pages. Fortunately, we are not going to even come close to covering every aspect of the SAP Web AS in this chapter. (Count your blessings.) Instead, we talk about the major pieces so that you have an idea of the way this fine machine has been put together.

How it works

You can think of SAP Web AS as a pipeline. Here's what goes on in this particular pipeline:

✔ Incoming requests can come from HTML pages built using Web Dynpro, from Web services, from XML messages, and from all sorts of other places.

✔ SAP Web AS accepts the information from these requests and passes the information on to programs written in ABAP or Java that are running inside SAP Web AS. These programs can then process the data with the help of all sorts of toolkits that support workflow, archival, and other common business functions.

✔ Then SAP Web AS stores and retrieves information from a database using Open SQL. This allows you to write programs that support all the major databases just once.

✔ Parts of SAP Web AS are available for managing the life cycle of an application, from installation through configuration and upgrades.

The way that all of these parts fit together is shown in Figure 13-3. This figure shows the user interface portions of the pipeline at the top interacting with the rest of the parts that communicate with the outside world, do the work of the application, and move data back and forth from databases.

So, exactly what can each part can do? Read on to find out.

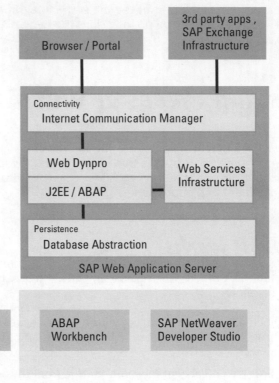

Figure 13-3:
All the
moving
parts of SAP
Web AS.

Speaking the language

Haven't you always wanted to be multilingual? Well, SAP Web AS is. In fact, most application servers support Java, some support other languages, but it is rare to find an application server that supports two programming languages. SAP Web AS supports both Java and ABAP so that SAP applications can have the best of both worlds.

Jiving with J2EE

Sounds like a music group, doesn't it? Actually, J2EE stands for Java 2 Enterprise Edition, and it's the formal name for the standard that defines the Java language and surrounding platform created by Sun Microsystems. Sun owns Java, but created it as an *open-standard application,* meaning that all the information about how to create and use Java technology is publicly available and is wide open for comment by any Tom, Dick, or Mary who cares to.

SAP Web AS supports the latest version of the Java language and many of the related standards. That means that programs written in Java according to the J2EE specification can run on the SAP Web AS.

Using J2EE as a foundation, standards for supporting mobile devices, for building adapters to other programs, for creating scalable objects for business, and for creating objects that are linked to database tables have been defined. SAP Web AS, conveniently, supports the most important ones.

SAP also has excellent tools for building Java programs and managing the life cycle of programs through development, which are covered in detail in Chapter 14.

Bopping with ABAP

No, you're thinking of ABBA, that band from the 1970s. This is ABAP, a language that SAP created to build its business applications. So much ABAP code is in place, in so many applications, running at thousands of large companies, that it really is not much of an exaggeration to say that ABAP runs the world, even though few people know it. Now you do.

SAP has invested billions of dollars in developing ABAP code, which it has used over the past 25 years to create a huge portion of the mySAP Business Suite.

Now, some people may wonder, now that Java exists, why should anybody care about ABAP? The answer is that new technology doesn't always displace old technology, especially when the old technology is great at serving a specific purpose. Radio still exists and does interesting things even after the invention of television, right? In the same way, ABAP is still an excellent choice as a language for creating business applications. SAP is committed to improving ABAP and keeps coming out with more and better features in each release, such as object-oriented features and a continually improving development and debugging environment.

ABAP and its development tools are actually so good at managing development performed by large teams of people that SAP had to supplement what was available in Java to bring the world of Java up to the ABAP standard. The Java Development Infrastructure, which we mention in this chapter and explain more fully in Chapter 14, adds to Java mechanisms for keeping track of relationships of components and automatically rebuilding software.

Here's a part for users

Don't forget the folks who use this stuff. SAP Web AS has many different parts for supporting interaction with users, both indirectly and directly. SAP Web AS can be used to create Web services that support user interfaces in the SAP® Enterprise Portal. All sorts of other mechanisms can end up interacting with users. The most important one, however, is a modeling environment for creating user interfaces called Web Dynpro.

Web Dynpro is a way to build the presentation layer including sophisticated user interfaces by modeling, rather than by writing code in a programming language such as Java. *Modeling* means that the developer describes what the user interface should look like by connecting elements that represent a user interface in a graphical modeling tool. Then, from the description of the relationships between the elements, most of the code is generated automatically in the programming language that makes the user interface work.

This approach to creating user interfaces means much less work for developers and also makes the user interfaces easier to change and less prone to bugs. SAP Web AS contains the runtime environment for Web Dynpro. (The development environment is discussed in Chapter 14.)

Parts to make applications logical

Toolkits exist at every layer of the SAP Web AS to do a number of things, from helping an application server talk to the world to modeling interfaces.

Business Workflow: Modeling processes for enhanced flexibility

Business Workflow is an engine that allows workflows to be modeled and executed. It's similar to the way that Web Dynpro allows user interfaces to be modeled, in that the developer has a graphical environment to describe a process that controls the execution of a program.

Business services: Special tools for special jobs

This one's a specialist. From Adobe Smart Forms which collects information offline, to systems for managing alerts, archiving data, managing records, and many other functions. SAP Web AS has lots of toolkits to help developers do very specialized things.

One part for integration and communication

SAP Web AS has tight integration with SAP XI, which uses SAP Web AS for its runtime. SAP Web AS also has the ability to communicate through special connectors with programs running on application servers from IBM and Microsoft.

The Internet Communication Manager is the collection of services that allows SAP Web AS to talk to the outside world through Web pages. In other words, the Internet Communication Manager is the Web server part of SAP Web AS that knows how to talk in the HTTP protocol, which is used to pass

HTML Web pages back and forth to browsers. It's also the protocol used for Web services.

Parts for storing and retrieving data

Java has layers such as Java Database Connectivity (JDBC) that are supposed to hide the details of databases from the programmers to save them grief. But SAP has discovered over the past 30 years what it really takes to write database-independent applications. Open SQL is the way they do it. It allows you to write code once and have it run on any relational database system supported by SAP, which means all the usual suspects: Oracle, DB2, SQL Server, and MaxDB.

Parts that make a life cycle manageable

SAP Web AS comes with the Java Development Infrastructure, which helps keep track of the way that components are related to each other. It also automatically rebuilds a program as needed and helps package programs for distribution. If life cycle management is your thing, you'll be happy to know that these features are covered more extensively in Chapter 14.

How Developers Develop with SAP Web AS

The SAP NetWeaver Developer Studio, Web Dynpro, SAP Visual Composer, and the SAP Composite Application Framework, all covered in Part III, are used together to create applications for SAP Web AS.

SAP NetWeaver Developer Studio is the most traditional form of integrated development environment (IDE) and the rest are modeling environments.

How SAP Web AS Works with Other SAP NetWeaver Components

SAP Web AS is closely related to mySAP Business Suite and to SAP NetWeaver. For both, SAP Web AS acts as the run time environment and provides that last bit of integration glue when needed.

SAP Web AS is the ultimate way to bridge the gap between *almost* what you want and what you *really* want.

The Future of SAP Web AS

SAP Web AS will grow and grow as more new toolkits are created that are common to different sorts of applications. SAP is committed to leading the pack in implementing new standards as they are accepted by the IT community, so SAP Web AS will probably absorb features of applications that are most commonly used. As modeling becomes more and more a part of development, it's likely that SAP Web AS will no longer need to have code generated for it. Some day, perhaps the models will become directly executable.

Don't Drown in All This Technology

Don't worry about all this techie stuff; be happy! Almost nobody in the world has a detailed understanding of all of the layers just mentioned. (Well, maybe a few people in an SAP office somewhere who haven't seen the light of day in 30 years.)

The reason all of these toolkits exist is so normal humans can actually stand on the shoulders of others and use their drudge work to do incredible things. All of this stuff really makes sense.

Part III
A Nifty Development Toolkit

"It only takes me nine different systems to create the one program we need."

In this part . . .

SAP® NetWeaver™ comes with a set of the most power-ful software development tools ever assembled. This part shows you the beloved SAP integrated development environment and then builds and builds on it with many different tools for something called model-driven develop-ment of enterprise applications. Model-driven is simply the neatest thing to happen to development since sliced bread (which you once used to make all those late-night sandwiches for developers burning the midnight oil — not anymore).

What SAP has essentially done is unlock the toolkit it's used to build applications for the past 30 years, polished everything up so that the rest of us can use it, and made it part of SAP NetWeaver. While only the digital grease monkey may understand some of the details, everyone should read this part to understand the tremendous poten-tial that awaits companies that use these tools for integra-tion and creating their own customized applications.

Chapter 14

SAP NetWeaver Developer Studio

The SAP NetWeaver Developer Studio is one of the most important parts of SAP NetWeaver and one that SAP had to bend some technology rules to create. That's nothing new for SAP, which has had to build its own tools to create its cutting-edge applications for years.

That sound you hear in the background, you know the siren sounding over and over again in the distance, is the geek alert. This chapter is about technology for technologists. However, even for the slightly curious, it will be enlightening.

Now, you might be tempted to think of SAP NetWeaver Developer Studio as the editor that SAP created for Java language programs. That's not exactly right because it's just part of what the SAP NetWeaver Developer Studio can do. The best way to think about SAP NetWeaver Developer Studio is as an integrated development environment (that does indeed have an editor for Java language programs), a modeling environment for user interfaces (Web Dynpro), and a tool to keep track of all of the parts of a large-scale program that is being developed by many people (the Java Development Infrastructure). In this chapter we cover Web Dynpro, the Java Development Infrastructure, and many more things that will bring a smile to any geek's face.

Why SAP NetWeaver Developer Studio?

It's true that SAP created the SAP NetWeaver Developer Studio because the programmers at SAP needed an environment in which to write Java programs, which were becoming an important way to create parts of the mySAP™ Business Suite and SAP NetWeaver a few years ago. Java has become an increasingly popular language for SAP's customers, who use it to create their own custom applications and to integrate solutions.

But the folks at SAP thought this thing through really well. They based SAP NetWeaver Developer Studio on the Eclipse Platform, which is a really cool toolkit for creating development tools. (You can't turn around in IT land without knocking over a development toolkit these days.) In the next sections, we tell you a little bit about Eclipse.

Giving it away

A little company from New York state named IBM created Eclipse, which just happens to be written in Java, to create its own development tools. At some point, these folks realized that it was in their best interests to encourage other companies to use Eclipse as well. So IBM decided to share the source code of Eclipse by releasing it as an open-source product, so that anybody who wanted to can take the source code, use it, and change it.

Well, IBM had spent more than $25 million or so to create Eclipse, and it turned out that the strategy worked. Many companies realized it would be better to use the foundation that Eclipse created than to reinvent the proverbial wheel and build their own development tools. (In case you're wondering, the development of Eclipse is now overseen by the logically named Eclipse Foundation, which includes IBM and many other companies, including SAP.)

Helping developers: Somebody's got to do it

So far, so good. SAP NetWeaver Developer Studio uses Eclipse to develop Java programs. But when you are developing Java programs that will eventually become enterprise applications, and when a large number of people are working on those programs, and when you want those people to be as productive as possible, well, let's just say that lots and lots of help is required.

Providing help to developers is not a new idea. Most software vendors offer some sort of integrated development environment (IDE) to make life easier. An *IDE* consists of a way to edit programs that checks for errors while you are editing and provides other sorts of help, such as keeping track of changes to all of the source code files and providing a way to quickly compile, execute, and debug the program.

SAP goes beyond garden-variety developer support in SAP NetWeaver Developer Studio in the following ways:

✔ Web Dynpro greatly increases the productivity of developers who are creating user interfaces by providing a *modeling environment,* which means developers write a lot less code, spend much less time fixing bugs, and can change and customize user interfaces much more inexpensively.

✔ The Java Dictionary keeps track of commonly used data types, such as addresses, social security numbers, or phone numbers, as well as database tables. This makes it easier to reuse code and keep track of what programs are using which data.

✔ The Java Development Infrastructure extends the notion of an IDE to keep track of the relationships between the large groupings of code called *components.* The source code and the relationships between them are kept in a design-time repository, and then the component build server knows exactly what to build when a change is made. (More on this later in the section, "A chunky component model for Java development.")

The purpose of SAP NetWeaver Developer Studio, then, is to improve the productivity of developers and the quality of the code they write. The following section gives some examples of how SAP NetWeaver Developer Studio is actually called to action on the IT battlefield.

Developer Studio in Action

You use SAP NetWeaver Developer Studio to write programs in Java, that much is clear. But why would you write these programs, and what do they do? The following sections give some examples to make it crystal clear.

Example 1: Java lives!

Given all the time we spend in this book talking about how business content helps control and customize mySAP Business Suite applications and SAP NetWeaver components, it would be fair to ask why anyone has to write Java programs anymore?

Frankly, people do it a lot less than they used to. However, Java coding is still the way to go when special needs pop up. For example, if you have to create a new application that can't be done any other way, or you have to integrate technology that wasn't really made for integration, Java is your best bet.

For example, say that your company has 500 different suppliers, and each supplier has his own Web site that gives prices on the various products available. Your company's portal team has used JavaScript to look up the prices for items on all 500 Web sites, but it takes forever to run this code on the browser. Perhaps the right way to solve this problem would be to use Java to write a custom Web service to perform the price lookup. The Web service could be written so that it works for a variety of suppliers, but more importantly so that it's accessible through open standards. That means that no one using the Web service needs to know details of what type of operating system it runs on or what database it uses. Because it is a Web service, the Java program could be used by all sorts of other programs in addition to the portal.

Or perhaps you want to use a legacy application written 30 years ago as a Web service. Wrapping legacy technology inside a Web service allows you to expose information in legacy systems that is available now through open standards that were not even a glimmer in some programmer's eye when the legacy system was new. You can leverage that data now in entirely new ways!

Example 2: Facing up to user interfaces

The goal of SAP NetWeaver Developer Studio is to help developers be productive in creating applications, not just in programming in Java. That's one of the reasons that SAP created Web Dynpro.

A huge percentage of the effort of creating any enterprise application goes into the creation and maintenance of the user interface. Realizing this, the folks making up the brain trust at SAP asked a simple question: How can we increase the productivity of developers when they're creating, maintaining, and updating user interfaces? Their answer is Web Dynpro, which is shown in Figure 14-1.

The way that Web Dynpro works is that all of the commonly used parts of a user interface (boxes, buttons, and so on) are described using metadata. Say that you're a developer and your boss has asked you to create a self-service application for employees to report time off to HR. With Web Dynpro, you use a graphical tool that allows you to create user-interface programs by dragging and dropping buttons and text boxes and the like onto a screen layout, as well as the defining relationships between them and data elements of the program.

Then, after you're done dragging and dropping, Web Dynpro uses the metadata description of what the user interface should do to automatically generate the Java code that actually creates the user interface.

Then when you need to change the user interface, it's more dragging and dropping, not more coding. This approach is a huge boost to productivity and also reduces errors, as well as giving the poor developer a break so he or she can actually go home at 5:00 p.m. now and then.

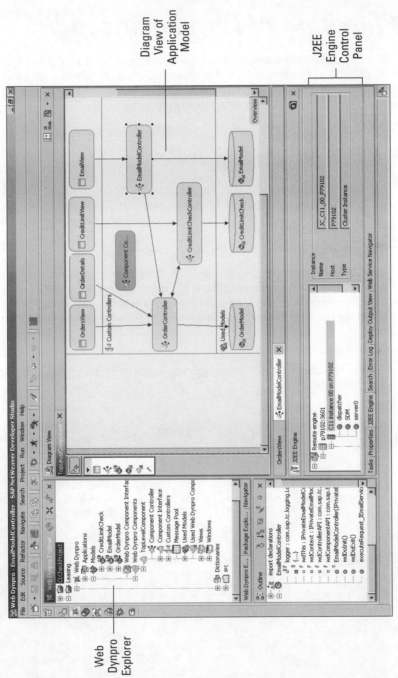

Figure 14-1:
A Web
Dynpro
screen for
modeling
of user
interfaces.

Diagram
View of
Application
Model

J2EE
Engine
Control
Panel

Web Dynpro
Explorer

The Plumbing of Developer Studio

Everything, from plumbing to software, is usually made up of parts. To explain the plumbing of SAP NetWeaver Developer Studio, we split the product into three parts: parts for writing code, parts for assembling applications, and parts for putting applications into production.

Parts for writing code

As we mention earlier in this chapter, the parts for writing code are all based on Eclipse. Figure 14-2 shows the way that the different parts of SAP NetWeaver Developer Studio sit on top of the Eclipse platform.

Total Eclipse

The Eclipse platform provides a huge amount of stuff for a head start in creating development environments. It includes tools and modules for creating special-purpose editors, interacting with source-code management systems, creating debuggers, and creating workspaces and saving their states.

J2EE

This is the part that allows programmers to use everything provided in the J2EE specification.

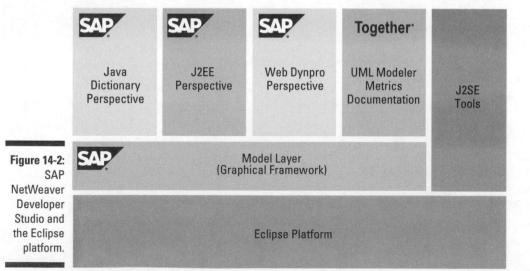

Figure 14-2: SAP NetWeaver Developer Studio and the Eclipse platform.

Java is used in a wide variety of applications, from things as small as a security card to give you access to your network, to applications that run on large servers. Java provides standards or parts to suit the need of the application. The main parts are

- ✔ J2EE or Enterprise Edition is the part of Java designed for server applications.
- ✔ J2SE or Standard Edition is the part of Java designed for desktop or client applications.
- ✔ J2ME or Mobile Edition is the part of Java designed for mobile applications.

Getting together . . .

Okay, Eclipse is great, and J2EE is really useful. But wait a minute, it gets better. SAP formed a partnership with a company called TogetherSoft (now acquired by Borland) to use its tools for the Unified Modeling Language (UML) in SAP NetWeaver Developer Studio. UML is one of the growing number of approaches to describing and creating applications through modeling, rather than by coding. Modeling is an important aspect of SAP NetWeaver Developer Studio.

Exploring the model layer

The model layer is a general-purpose toolkit that SAP created to support graphical, model-driven development. You know how in some programs there is a palette of different elements on one side of the screen and you can drag and drop them onto a canvas? The *model layer* is a bunch of tools to support that easy-to-use process. It helps create the visual elements, helps manage the dragging and dropping, and helps keep track of the metadata.

Looking it up in the Java Dictionary

The Java Dictionary is another one those elements that SAP has added to solve a big problem programmers face: not just editing code, but keeping track of how parts of applications are related, how code is rebuilt during development, and how it is packaged, distributed, and moved into production.

Here's how it works: Programmers define commonly used fields, such as a telephone number or first name, in the Java Dictionary. Then, when you write a program using a commonly used field, the program refers to the definition in the Java Dictionary. Entire tables of fields can be defined in this way.

This provides for many good things. First of all, if you want to change the length of the first name field, you can do it in one place, and it will be changed everywhere. Second, the Java Dictionary allows for support of different human languages. The label for the telephone number field can be stored in all sorts of different languages such as English, French, German, Japanese, or Chinese. When you use the Java Dictionary, support of multiple languages comes right along with it.

Additionally, the Dictionary provides an abstraction layer to the actual database. That means that if you need to switch your underlying relational database, having a Java Dictionary allows you to do that without affecting the applications you have written. Database independence!

J2SE

J2SE means Java Version 2 Standard Edition. It is the part of the Java specification related to the kind of programs that generally run on the client side. SAP NetWeaver Developer Studio has to be able to create and communicate with such programs.

Parts for assembling applications

You've plugged away at writing your code and you've got something working; then it comes time to figure out how to fit the part you are writing in with all the other parts that are being written by other people. SAP tackled all of the problems that come with keeping track of the relationships between the parts of large programs and coordinating the work of large groups by producing the enterprise applications it's famous for.

So, when SAP started to create its development tools for Java, the company found that many of the innovations that it had created for the world of ABAP just didn't exist in the world of Java. So to bring these benefits into the world of Java, SAP created the Java Development Infrastructure (JDI). (We explain more in the next section.)

Figure 14-3 provides a preview of how all of the parts of the JDI work together with the SAP NetWeaver Developer Studio to build programs, and then move them into production.

A chunky component model for Java development

JDI begins with the notion of components. Now the word *component* is used all over the place in this book and every other book on technology with about a thousand different meanings. For purposes of JDI, the *component model* means a way to group Java code into chunks and keep track of the relationships between the chunks. The idea is that if the JDI can keep track of which chunk of code refers to which other chunk of code, when one chunk of code changes, JDI knows what other chunks need to be rebuilt.

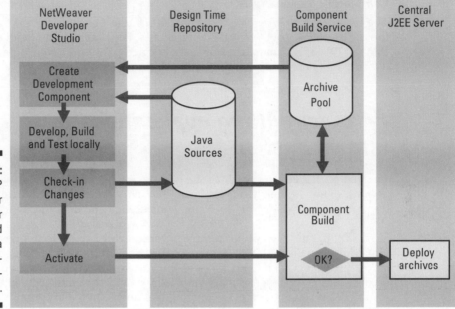

Figure 14-3: SAP NetWeaver Developer Studio and the Java Development Infrastructure.

So what, you say? Well, in most large Java projects, the way this problem is solved is through the ever-popular nightly build. Every night, all of the code that is checked in is rebuilt, and if it compiles, all of the tests are run, and if the tests pass, then everyone is happy. This is considered a best practice in the world of Java.

Well, the JDI and the component model say to heck with the nightly build. When you check in code, all the components that need to be rebuilt are rebuilt right then, and you find out right away if any compilation problems exist. Now there is a lot more to this, and many other cool things happen because of the component model as well, but this explanation gives you the general idea.

A better landscape with design-time repository

The *design-time repository* is the JDI's enhanced source-code management system that not only keeps track of changes to source code, but also maintains a record of the component relationships and of the different landscapes that you can create while developing code. (By *landscapes,* we mean the specific way in which certain servers, databases, or versions of software are used in development, while others are used for staging and production.)

The landscape information comes into play because there are differences between how code should be compiled if it is being run for testing on your desktop versus if it is intended for deployment to production. The design-time repository keeps track of these differences.

Component build service

The *component build service* is the part of JDI that does the rebuilding based on the dependencies between the components. For you programmers out there, think of this as a dynamic ant or make service. (For you non-programmers, *ant* and *make* are tools used to build programs.)

Parts for putting applications into production

The last part of JDI to explain is the *change management service,* which is all about moving the finished code from the development environment into production in a way that provides some consistency and accountability.

Most of the time, Java programs are put into products by someone copying new programs on to the file system of the production server. But, wait. Did all the files get copied? And who did the copying and when? And how can it be undone? The change management service has the answer to all these questions. It keeps track of everything you need when a program is deployed, makes sure it all gets moved into production, and keeps track of who did what and how it can be reversed (just in case). The change management service makes it really hard to make the typical mistakes that are made when deploying applications.

The Future of the SAP NetWeaver Developer Studio

Welcome to the future. It may come as no surprise at this point in this chapter to hear that the future of SAP NetWeaver Developer Studio is bound up in the brave new world of model-based programming. Less and less code is written by hand these days, and more and more is generated by modeling environments. Web Dynpro, part of SAP NetWeaver Developer Studio, is one of these modeling environments.

But no matter what the modeling environment, there almost certainly will always be a need to write code. What SAP NetWeaver Developer Studio will do in the future is speed the time to market or to production for any program by automating even more of the process and providing help in manipulating models. When code must be written, Developer Studio will make it as easy and error free as possible.

Chapter 15

Visual Composer: Going Codeless

· ·

· ·

*S*AP has made another step in the relentless march toward the switch to modeling (rather than coding) to create applications with the introduction of SAP NetWeaver Visual Composer.

Modeling means turning data sources, relationships, interface elements, and so on, into visual objects and icons that can be moved around a page. Assume you're a manager who wants a personal portal page that displays the monthly sales totals for each sales person on your team. In Visual Composer you'd simply drag a portal page icon onto your workspace (called the *storyboard*) from an interface elements list and fill it with content from the sales information database. You can build queries without knowing any query language simply by assembling icons and elements from various lists.

After all, why should you go through all that code stuff if you can, instead, just pick and choose the stuff a la carte? You shouldn't. This chapter tells you why.

So What Does This Composer Thing Compose?

Simply put, SAP NetWeaver Visual Composer enables you to happily drag and drop objects that represent data sources and interface elements to create content for a portal. Even if you're programming-phobic — say a business consultant, analyst, process expert, or writer of *For Dummies* books — you can use SAP NetWeaver Visual Composer to make a diagram of what you'd like a page to do. Then this clever application will not only present the content, but also make *iViews* (reusable and configurable portions of a page in a portal) that come ready to be deployed. In a nutshell, SAP NetWeaver Visual Composer is WYMIWYG — What You Model Is What You Get.

One of the chief benefits of this approach is that it dramatically reduces the amount of time that the IT department has to spend on content assembly and maintenance. This, instead, is left to the business experts. While these folks may not know the first thing about how to code, they completely understand the business process they're trying to model.

SAP NetWeaver Visual Composer is also a completely Web-based and platform-independent modeling tool. This means that a business consultant can sit next to a user in his office in Des Moines, access SAP NetWeaver Visual Composer from any browser, and build or customize content to reflect the customer's business needs on the spot. The application then generates code and acts as a debugger, tester, and documentation creator. Way cool.

Entire business processes, not just content, can be modeled in this way. Essentially, you can create multiple pages that track a process in depth by creating iViews and bundles of iViews on a similar theme (called *business packages*). No programming required.

Visual Composer: What's the Point?

The point of SAP NetWeaver Visual Composer is to create an environment that is people-focused, not just technology-focused. Visual Composer is very democratic, because it puts the tools for managing and creating content into the hands of all the people — power users, administrators, and content developers — not just the IT department.

Figure 15-1 lays this out quite clearly. At one extreme is the advanced tools for the seasoned developers. At the other end of the spectrum are the applications for the end users. Just short of SAP NetWeaver Visual Composer is the idea of iViews in the SAP® Enterprise Portal (SAP EP) that can be customized by business experts. Filling the gap between customizable iViews and advanced development tools is SAP NetWeaver Visual Composer, which is intended to meet the needs of power users and content experts who totally understand what applications need to do to help their businesses.

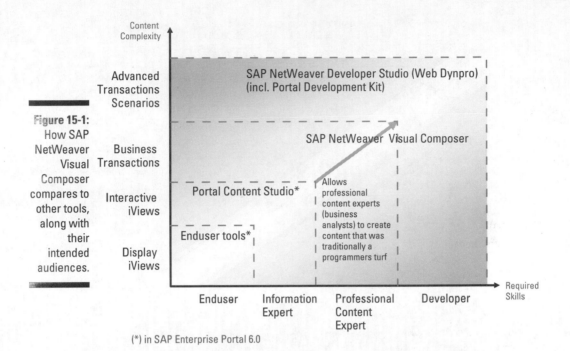

Content
Complexity

Advanced
Transactions
Scenarios

SAP NetWeaver Developer Studio (Web Dynpro)
(incl. Portal Development Kit)

SAP NetWeaver Visual Composer

Business
Transactions

Portal Content Studio*

Interactive
iViews

Allows
professional
content experts
(business
analysts) to create
content that was
traditionally a
programmers turf

Enduser tools*

Display
iViews

Enduser   Information   Professional   Developer
            Expert   Content
                           Expert

Required
Skills

Figure 15-1:
How SAP
NetWeaver
Visual
Composer
compares to
other tools,
along with
their
intended
audiences.

(*) in SAP Enterprise Portal 6.0

Think about how many people in your organization could use SAP NetWeaver Visual Composer in their browsers, designing and modifying applications from the office, on the road, or from home. Just imagine implementing a portal for a global business if you had to have your IT department hand-code each employee's pages. SAP NetWeaver Visual Composer permits a much cheaper and more rapid development of a company-wide portal by allowing you to delegate everything but the programming of the most sophisticated components to non-programmers.

Instead of looking at pages of programming language code, developers create the applications using visual tools. The screen shown in Figure 15-2 shows what the development environment looks like in SAP NetWeaver Visual Composer.

And SAP NetWeaver Visual Composer isn't just for the code-phobic. Hardcore coders can also use SAP NetWeaver Visual Composer to quickly pull together the elements they need to get started on building composite applications and use the visual tools to speed up development. And those in the know will be glad to hear that the application sets a common standard for content creation, based on industry and SAP standards.

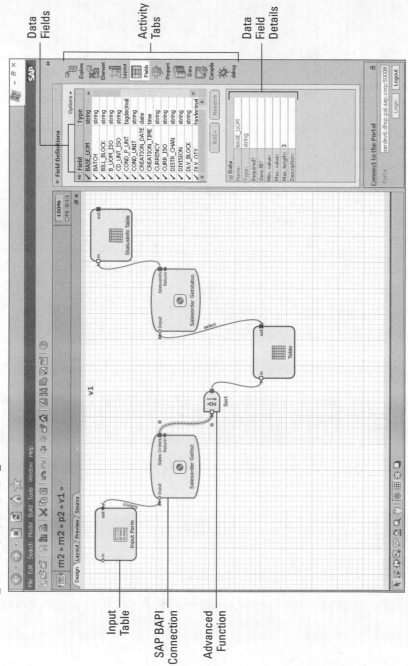

Figure 15-2:
The
developer's
view of SAP
NetWeaver
Visual
Composer.

Visual Composer's Cozy Cubicle in SAP NetWeaver

So where does Visual Composer reside in the SAP NetWeaver chain of command? Well, it is one of a number of complementary visual modeling tools that SAP has built to create a model-based environment. All these products have very cool modeling capabilities:

- ✔ **SAP NetWeaver Visual Composer:** The user-friendly modeling environment for business analysts.

- ✔ **Web Dynpro:** The modeling environment for creating user interfaces (UI) for developers.

- ✔ **SAP Composite Application Framework (SAP CAF):** The modeling environment for the entire application used to create composite applications and SAP xApps™ for developers.

- ✔ **SAP XI Workbench:** The modeling environment for SAP® Exchange Infrastructure (SAP XI) used by developers to create message structures and processes.

- ✔ **Web Application Designer:** The modeling environment for SAP® Business Intelligence (SAP BI) used to create applications for reporting and analysis.

Each of these applications is dedicated to helping developers do their jobs by applying *metadata* (data about data) information about an *object* (data set, database, interface element, and so on) that serves as a surrogate when describing relationships between abstract entities. This stuff is used to generate code based on the metadata descriptions, which allows the applications to create and configure data, services, and other applications through modeling.

Content on demand

Visual Composer is a bit of a chameleon: It's a powerful application that has different uses for different users. For example, with SAP NetWeaver Visual Composer

- ✔ Content experts or administrators who are charged with the overall administration of a portal can assign roles, manage content, and assemble role-based iViews for deployment.

✔ Business experts can design sophisticated packages based on the underlying services, or when necessary, do 80 percent of the modeling, then turn it over to a developer.

✔ Developers working in SAP NetWeaver Developer Studio can take a model laid out in SAP NetWeaver Visual Composer, make the final code enhancements, and deploy it back to the business expert.

Content expert self service

Not tired of imagining yourself as another person? Okay, say that you're an expert financial analyst. A portal has been implemented at your company that has a generic financial analyst business package — a preassembled collection of pages and iViews — already set up for you. Great.

You however, are a specialist in a very specific area of finance that is not represented by the generic pages. So you need to pull different data into your portal. Visual Composer makes it simple for you to connect to the particular service on the backend, pull the data object into the workspace, and associate it with a user interface template. You then manipulate the data any way you want to: query, perform calculations, sort — generally live it up, financial analyst style!

Business expert self service

So Visual Composer is the greatest thing since sliced bread, but it only works with SAP applications, right? Wrong. Although it's already tightly integrated with SAP NetWeaver, Visual Composer isn't just for SAP products. Business experts who are specialists in an entire process within your company can access data from any applications that are designated as portal services.

Say that you have an SAP customer relationship solution installed, and you also need to see data from a legacy system, such as a homegrown application built on an Oracle database. You know that data exists on the backend, because you use it every day in a variety of applications. Parts of the data exist in bits and pieces in other iViews, so you know that the portal has access to the data as a service.

Using SAP NetWeaver Visual Composer, you can take inputs from various sources and generate a single composite view. You cannot only view and manipulate information from both solutions, you can even write, edit, and save data back to both solutions simultaneously from within an iView. It's easy to alter existing iViews and only slightly more complicated to create completely new models from scratch.

No developer left behind

Forget developers? Never! SAP NetWeaver Visual Composer provides a number of advantages to the developer, not the least of which is that all those annoying little UI fixes can now be done by the users themselves.

But wait, you say: In some circumstances this could be downright scary — letting Pat in accounting get his hands on the financial database could be a recipe for disaster (nice guy, but not exactly technically minded).

But with SAP NetWeaver Visual Composer, it's okay, because the business logic is kept separate from the creation of the user interface. The *business logic layer* is what enables the portal to connect to the underlying applications, enabling the deployment of data in the portal. And because it's displayed as an object, definitions that limit what data can be used (and in what context) can be built into the object before it's even made available to users.

From the developer's perspective, what users are doing is manipulating the interface and accessing the underlying applications only at the display level. To a developer, most of these changes are superficial — like rearranging the furniture, not building the house.

Another plus for the developer is that a power user, like a business expert, can pull together most of what is needed before calling on the developer for help. Instead of building an entire module from scratch, the business user picks bits and pieces from different iViews and different underlying applications, and then hands them off to the developer with a request that's as simple as, "Now instead of displaying the quarterly *inputs* here, I'd like it to show the quarterly *outputs*." One quick change and the developer has completed what was once a relatively complicated coding task. Best of all, the business logic built into the data object guarantees that information saved back into the underlying application is valid for the application that uses it.

The Parts of SAP NetWeaver Visual Composer Symphony

In practice, SAP NetWeaver Visual Composer works a little like a supercharged three-headed monster (but in a good way). It's really a combination of a diagramming program, such as Visio; What You See Is What You Get (WYSIWYG) HTML editors, such as Dreamweaver or FrontPage; and a coding environment, such as Eclipse. Within SAP NetWeaver Visual Composer, you can perform the tasks that lead you from that sketch on a napkin to a diagram of your process — what you want the final product to do — right through to the final deployment.

Visual Composer uses a framework with four areas that enable you to construct the finished iViews:

- ✔ A Design tab, in which you construct the model of the iView
- ✔ A Layout tab, in which you design the look and feel of the iView
- ✔ A Preview tab, in which you preview the iView and validate its logic
- ✔ A Source tab, which displays the XML structure of the model that is automatically generated as you build the iView

Each tab has a separate toolbox that contains tools specific to that tab.

Fetching data

First, there's the data source layer. SAP NetWeaver Visual Composer is already integrated with SAP NetWeaver and the underlying SAP applications. This means that the framework for connecting data to these applications is built in. For example, you can quickly import, either by searching or by choosing from a list, the relevant Remote Function Calls (RFCs) and Business APIs (BAPI) on which you want to base your iViews.

RFCs and *BAPIs* are the connections to the underlying applications that Visual Composer uses to go get and send back data.

The UI: It's a logical thing

If you just have to have a submit button, an input box, or an output list (and who doesn't now and then?), precoded selections such as these come ready to use within Visual Composer. The UI logic underlying these prebuilt templates defines what the users see, how they interact with the iViews, and how the iViews' data queries interact with the underlying applications. You select, combine, and modify the elements by dragging and dropping representative icons — and as you do, SAP NetWeaver Visual Composer handles the final coding. What could be simpler?

The UI layout shortcut

Don't you just love *templates* (those useful little predesigned files that somebody put together so you can jump start whatever computer task demands your attention)?

If you love templates, you'll be glad to hear that what the end user sees — the sizes, shapes, and colors of the finished product's user interface — is included within SAP NetWeaver Visual Composer as templates. You can easily manipulate these templates using Visual Composer's WYSIWYG customization tools.

Step-by-Step: Designing Workflow

Okay, for you folks who are always creating checklists, here's one. Although you can be very creative and use SAP NetWeaver Visual Composer in almost any way you like to build iViews, we start by showing you an overview of the various steps that you would use to construct a model.

Here are the steps you can follow in their typical order:

1. Open a model (new or existing).

2. Choose the high-level model elements, such as module, page, or iView.

3. Define properties for the high-level model elements.

4. Build the iView.

5. Add data sources.

6. Test the functionality of the data sources.

7. Define the UI logic.

8. Customize the iView layout.

9. Define the iView properties (for example, isolation-level settings).

10. Define additional iViews.

11. Generate model documentation.

12. Compile the model and deploy the portal content.

13. Go home and party — you deserve it!

You can perform these steps in any order. You can start with your UI and then add data sources. You could start with data sources and then design a look and feel. You can add to, subtract from, and change your model at any time. The final iView isn't finished until you choose to compile the code at any point in the workflow.

Basing Your Environment in a Browser

Unlike many development environments, with Visual Composer, you don't have to be connected to the underlying applications while you're in the development stage. Because SAP NetWeaver Visual Composer runs on the server with the underlying applications, it makes the connection independent of your desktop. You can connect and compose iViews from anywhere. (Well, we wouldn't try doing this during a bungee jump, but pretty much anyplace else.)

Inputs and outputs, interactors, and operators

Two of the key abilities of SAP NetWeaver Visual Composer are retrieving and displaying data. For example, you can create an input form for social security numbers and a display for the associated worker's employee record. Within SAP NetWeaver Visual Composer, you can decide what a user should input and design the appearance of the resulting logical form for that input.

However, this is just the beginning of SAP NetWeaver Visual Composer's capabilities. After you have retrieved the data, using all those slick modeling tools, you can modify the data by using what are called interactors and operators. Sound like a bunch of close-knit thespians and phone company employees? Read on for an explanation.

Say you want to pull up your sales team's employee records, sorted by annual sales performance. You can choose a filter to do this from a list, dragging and dropping it onto your output form. (Conveniently, the form retains the ability to sort your list upon deployment.) The information you retrieve is called the *operator*. If you would like the information displayed as a bar graph instead of a list, you can select an interactor. As the name suggests, an *interactor* is the component a user uses to interact with the model, giving or receiving inputs from the chosen application. For example, you might grab a bar graph icon and drag and drop it using the appropriate tool. When you deploy this component, the end user sees your graph.

Runtime

The model itself is a kind of self-contained universe: It contains all the components of the iView, including information about connectors to the backend services, the UI, and associated elements. When you save a model, its structure and all the metadata for it are stored as an XML file within the Visual Composer environment. Further information about your model is stored on the server in a SQL Server database, allowing you to log on from another location and continue working where you left off.

As you build your model, SAP NetWeaver Visual Composer is automatically coding the iView. When it's complete, you use the Preview tab to validate your code. The SAP NetWeaver Visual Composer compiler then converts your code into a format supported by the SAP Enterprise Portal (right now HTMLb (HTML for ABAP) and SAP's own server pages, but also in the future this might include Java, JSP, and HTML). You can deploy the compiled code to the portal from within SAP NetWeaver Visual Composer.

Here's the payoff: At *runtime,* the time when the user actually is utilizing the code you've created, whatever you created functions independently of Visual Composer. These folks can then retrieve and display data in exactly the same fashion as they would any old-fashioned, hand-coded page. The code generated is part of the standard runtime portal logic. This means that when the code is deployed to the portal, the iView can run within the portal framework as an independent application all by itself. Like any other iView, it also inherits its look and feel from the portal, depending on the theme that the user has previously selected.

Figure 15-3 shows how the design time and runtime all work together to create an application.

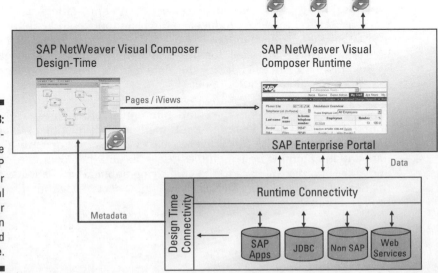

Figure 15-3:
The archi-
tecture
of SAP
NetWeaver
Visual
Composer
at design
time and
runtime.

Using Visual Composer in Concert with Other SAP NetWeaver Pieces

SAP NetWeaver Visual Composer comes as part of the SAP CAF. In the current version, SAP NetWeaver Visual Composer generates code that runs on top of the SAP Enterprise Portal. In the future it's likely that code for Web Dynpro will be created by Visual Composer, and perhaps code for other sorts of user interfaces as well.

To do its job, SAP NetWeaver Visual Composer uses the services described in the business object repository of the mySAP™ Business Suite solutions.

The Future of SAP NetWeaver Visual Composer

Time to look into our crystal ball. For Visual Composer, the future looks rosy. In the future, SAP NetWeaver Visual Composer will be able to model user interfaces for almost every SAP NetWeaver component, including SAP Business Intelligence.

In many different areas of computing, from operating systems to databases, graphical tools dramatically speed learning and development. Visual Composer shows that this can be true even with applications as sophisticated as SAP's enterprise products. SAP has announced that, in the future, all mySAP Business Suite solutions will use SAP Enterprise Portal as a user interface. This means that Visual Composer, in conjunction with applications such as Developer Studio, will become the main tool for creating the user interface for the entire range of SAP products.

Now, as modeling becomes the solution to implementing processes across your enterprise, the drive to bring this method of development to additional areas will continue. SAP NetWeaver Visual Composer is currently able to take data and interactions from multiple processes and then combine, manipulate, and store information back to the underlying applications. It's easy to picture the next stage of growth: creating entirely new services within the same tools, methodology, and framework.

Chapter 16

Composite Solutions

*T*he SAP Composite Application Framework (SAP CAF) is a new way to create applications through modeling rather than writing code. (No swimsuit-clad men or women were involved in the modeling of this framework.)

The fundamental idea of application modeling is that you tell the modeling system what you want an application to do, and then the system creates the application that you want. This is very cool indeed, as you soon see.

The other key idea behind the SAP CAF is that the building blocks it uses are actually pieces of other applications. That's where the word *composite* comes in.

The SAP CAF uses other applications because those applications make themselves useful by presenting their functionality to the SAP CAF as services. The goal of this chapter is to explain the structure of composite applications and the tool that you use to build them.

Don't worry if you don't have this all under your belt the first go round. The SAP CAF is one of the coolest and most powerful parts of SAP NetWeaver™, and getting the hang of it takes a while.

But believe us, it's well worth the effort.

The Anatomy of the SAP CAF

Composite applications are applications built out of parts of existing applications. It's a simple idea and it's increasingly relevant because companies have invested in many different systems to automate the fundamental processes of their businesses in recent years. A composite application takes all that functionality and taps into it.

Although the idea of composite applications isn't hard to understand, building them is far from simple. So SAP went and created a new development tool called the SAP Composite Application Framework (SAP CAF). When you're SAP, you can just do things like that.

The SAP CAF has goals, too

The goal of the SAP CAF is to make composite apps as easy as possible to develop and configure. That means that you can rapidly and inexpensively adapt them to meet your needs. The SAP CAF meets this challenge by working off of innovative ideas such as model-driven development, pattern-based user interfaces, and a choice of role- or process-based definition of an application. (We explain more about each of these later in the chapter.)

When you take a closer look at the challenges, it becomes clear that building composite applications is a tricky proposition. Answer the following questions before you build any composite application:

- How will you create reusable components from your existing enterprise applications?

- How will the data and functionality of one application used for operations such as create customer, close account, or initiate a transaction be made available to other applications?

- How will the components and services that are built from different applications be made to work together in a coordinated manner?

- How will the data across all your enterprise applications be managed?

- How will you construct new user interfaces to take advantage of the various parts that you take from different applications?

- How can all this functionality be made easy enough to be practical for developers?

- How will composite apps be made configurable?

- How can you keep the total cost of ownership (TCO) of composite applications low enough to make them worthwhile?

Tesler's Law of Conservation of Complexity states that you can't reduce the complexity of a given task beyond a certain point. After you reach that point, you can only shift the burden around. The goal of the SAP CAF is to shift as much of the complexity of developing a composite application as possible away from programmers and onto the tool itself.

So what's SAP's strategy for doing this? Well, it involves modeling and packaging parts of programs for reuse via various sorts of objects and services.

What's in it for developers?

The designers of the SAP CAF, in their infinite wisdom, realized that they couldn't provide a solution that would satisfy every situation. Instead, they decided to empower developers in a variety of ways so that they could solve problems as they sprouted up.

The SAP CAF offers developers

- A choice between role-based or process-based modeling, that is, with either the person or the process in the center of the action.

- Elaborate support for user-interface patterns, which are reusable collections of screens and the programs that work together in the same way. Searching for a record and then changing its values is one such pattern.

- Guided Procedures, a sophisticated and configurable container for process instances, which allows the particular process you are running to be altered on the fly, based on what's happening.

- The ability to generate the code for most of an application rather than writing it by hand.

With all this in mind, we take a look at composite applications from the outside in.

Three Unique Perspectives on Composite Applications

Okay, now step into our handy time machine. In Chapter 6, we explain how composite applications consist of two parts: the functionality of an enterprise application that automates processes and the user interface, which includes a hub to connect to and tap into the power of as many applications as you need.

In that chapter, we also point out that the hub portion of a composite application is powered by SAP NetWeaver. In this chapter, you see how the SAP CAF works to create composite applications. We look at SAP CAF from three different perspectives: a user's point of view, the view of the composite apps creator, and from where a developer sits.

Okay, you're the user

The user perspective is perhaps the most important because, after all, they have to use the darn thing. From the user perspective, composite applications are about innovation and automating cool new kinds of processes.

When SAP workers sat down and thought about the user's perspective, they thought of the three families of composite applications (see Chapter 6): those that extend existing mySAP™ Business Suite solutions, one-of-a-kind applications called *custom composite applications,* and those that create new products called xApps™.

As a result, users are frequently impressed by the breadth of what they see in a composite application. Instead of having to jump from application to application to follow a process, composite applications let a user stay in one interface for the whole trip. Here's an example of such a process: A user may start with some Customer Relationship Management (CRM) functionality such as creating a customer record, taking an order, checking the customer's credit limit, and then using the Supply Chain Management (SCM) application to fulfill the order. But to the user, it's like working in a single application with a single interface.

Users benefit big time from this because composite applications excel at combining transactional data, such as the records that describe the sales order for a customer with unstructured data, such as call reports from sales people or market research. Crossing this boundary and bringing along the advanced collaborative capabilities of most composite applications means that the user gets tons of analytic and decision-making power in the bargain.

Perhaps the most important user benefit is the fact that the interface layer of composite applications that the user looks at is constructed from either a role-based or a process-based perspective. You see, many enterprise applications reflect the structure of the database or the transactions that do the work, but the role-based perspective helps the user perform the tasks that he or she needs to get done. The process-based perspective shows the flow of work through the steps of a process as the work proceeds from task to task and user to user.

Because a composite application has a common structure for all the functions that it brings together, it also has common administration and other tools. A control center exists for each role, which is the user interface for each composite application. This provides the equivalent of an inbox for processes that allows easy navigation to any process in the composite application.

For users, then, composite applications provide one interface, one way to get stuff done, and far fewer headaches from playing application roulette.

Now you're the builder

The second perspective to explore is how you create composite applications. These things aren't programmed like traditional applications with hours of sweating over code and coffee. Instead, they're modeled. You see, the SAP CAF is fundamentally an application-modeling tool.

But to use a modeling tool, you first have to understand how the model elements might apply in a particular situation. So we break one down into it's teeny tiny pieces.

For example, Figure 16-1 shows the process for a simple product definition.

The process that we describe here shows the people involved and the way that an idea flows through the product definition process of evaluating, rating, and planning. The different roles are shown, including the tasks that each role is responsible for and the way that each role has a certain responsibility. To use the SAP CAF, a developer might then break the process down further and describe it in these terms:

- User roles
- Different user interfaces
- Processes
- Services
- Objects
- Underlying systems

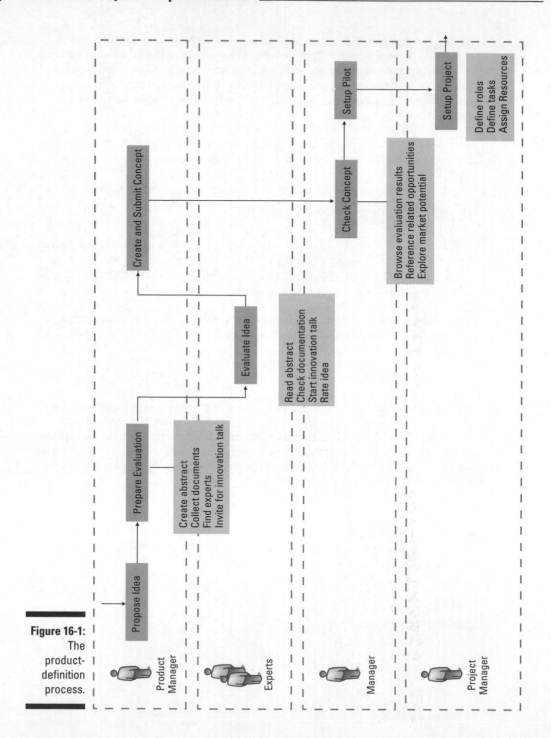

Figure 16-1:
The
product-
definition
process.

These elements are the building blocks of composite applications. We explain them in a bit more detail from the bottom of the diagram to the top:

- ✔ **Systems** are the existing enterprise applications that are used by the composite application.

- ✔ **Objects** are the ways that the raw functionality from the underlying systems are packaged together into useful chunks. Usually, a composite application creates a few new objects that are unique to its particular function.

- ✔ **Services** are operations that transform or create objects. These, too, are either packages created from underlying systems or newly created packages for a particular composite application.

- ✔ **Processes** are the paths that the user guides the application through, the sequences of steps and forks in the road that he takes to get work done.

- ✔ **User interfaces** show all this underlying stuff to the users.

- ✔ **Business roles** define the particular part of the process that a person is responsible for.

From a developer's perspective, all these layers are collapsed into a few elements:

- ✔ **Scenarios:** At the top of the stack are the scenarios, which are the user interface and processes that control the interaction with the user and the business logic.

- ✔ **Services:** The scenarios use services to get the functionality required to do the work of the application.

- ✔ **Objects:** The services are provisioned by objects contained within the application. (The following section describes objects further.)

- ✔ **Agent objects:** The services are also provisioned by agent objects, which are proxies for services that are provided by other applications.

In this way, the work of the application is done through an abstract layer of services that's completely separate from the object layer that implements them.

Finally, you're the developer

Traditional software development tools are focused on writing code. Good developers, of course, are doing much more than just spitting out lines of code when they program. They're expressing in code their vision of how to solve a problem.

Most programmers write complex programs by dividing the data and functions related to that data into collections of data and code called *objects*. A customer object, for example, might include a function or a method to retrieve the first name, last name, or set the value of the social security number.

Programmers can use objects to create an application to transform and process data. Development tools help programmers write code to create objects and to expose the data and functions of those objects in the user interface. Here ends this oversimplification of traditional development.

The starting point for the SAP CAF is the fact that much more is known about how applications are constructed these days than in days of old (say, 10 or 20 years ago). Tool builders such as SAP can now provide the developer with much more help and can automate and simplify many more tasks. This means that developers can build applications much faster and change them much more easily.

A Technical Perspective

Part of the reason that all this is possible is that another decade or two of experience has shown how applications should be constructed. It's now obvious that many user interfaces are similar in key ways.

Patterns, models, and frameworks

Many programs show a list of records and allow the user to click a record to display it. These commonly occurring types of user interfaces are called *patterns*. Patterns are now used all over computer programming so that users can take advantage of them when faced with a new piece of software.

One major way that the SAP CAF simplifies your life is to make heavy use of patterns, especially in the area of user interface. A developer selects a pattern, which does most of the work of creating the application, and then fills in the details of the kind of field that each record should contain and how the information should be displayed.

Patterns are really kind of simple. They're a way to do something that includes steps that are frequently the same and parts that change based on the circumstances. A pattern for cooking might involve the broad steps of shopping for food, measuring the spices, chopping the vegetables and meat, cooking, garnishing, and serving. By changing what happens at each step, all sorts of different meals could be prepared.

Forget code?

Code, you say? What about code? Does this approach make programming languages obsolete? No. Coding in languages such as Java is still part of building an application with the SAP CAF, but they play a much smaller role. The SAP CAF uses the patterns (models prepared in advance that are ready to be configured with metadata) along with other metadata to generate the code that eventually becomes the program. Hand-written code is then used to create application-specific objects and services that are controlled by more metadata that is then plugged into patterns by using the SAP CAF.

Modeling is the second magic bullet that the SAP CAF provides for developers. It turns out that you can think of most applications as involving the basic elements of user interfaces, including roles, processes, objects, services, and in the case of composite applications, underlying systems.

The SAP CAF allows developers to specify the behavior of an application by defining relationships between the elements. This means picking and choosing between high-level elements, such as roles or processes, and linking them to data. Then the developers link data to screens, and so on. (When we say high level, we mean that these elements have a lot of functionality included in them already. This functionality is described and controlled by what is called *metadata,* which is a fancy way of saying data that describes what a program should do.)

It turns out that patterns exist in the way that roles, processes, and user interfaces interact, as well. A developer starts building an application by using a pattern for an application that describes and displays reports, and then tweaks the metadata to make the application perform exactly the way that he or she desires. For example, the process of searching for a particular record, changing it, and saving it, is done through a set of screens that are very similar from application to application.

The reason that this is called model-driven development is that the program is created by changing a description (metadata) of what the program should do. This metadata is used to generate the code that lies under the covers.

Okay, next technical concept: Having an environment into which you can plug components is the notion of a *framework*. A framework is a set of rules for how to build components for a particular purpose. The SAP CAF relies heavily on frameworks, especially in developing the user interface.

Getting back to patterns

To a developer, the SAP CAF is actually a big modeling environment that allows you to define a program in terms of a standard set of model elements that are grouped together into patterns. (Remember patterns, described in the previous section?) Developing the application is generally much faster, and maintaining it is much cheaper because a model is usually easier to update than code.

In this discussion, we emphasize the use of patterns in the user interface. But it's important to recognize that patterns can be used at any level of the application where you discover a common structure. The way that certain parts of the application logic work, the way that data is retrieved from a database, or the way that processes are implemented may be implemented through patterns. Using process patterns, as it turns out, is one of the most productive ways to accelerate application development.

Frameworks are simply standard ways for things to be plugged into an environment. A framework for a meal might be a certain type of vegetable, another type of meat, and a couple of spices. As long as the vegetable, meat, or spice meets the criteria (for example, potato or poultry), it can be plugged into that meal.

Here It Is: The SAP Composite Application Framework

So far, you've seen the big-picture moving parts of composite applications. Now you find out how composite applications get created. You get a closer look at each part of composite applications, how they fit together, how the SAP CAF manipulates them, and how you can use them to design an application.

Here's what you look at next:

- ✔ User-interface patterns and frameworks
- ✔ Role-based modeling
- ✔ Process-based modeling
- ✔ Guided procedures
- ✔ Services and objects

Manipulative modelers

The way that the SAP CAF handles all these different elements is through modeling environments, called *modelers,* that manipulate, configure, and define relationships between basic elements provided by a framework. All the modeling is captured in metadata. For example, the framework for the user interface provides buttons, textboxes, drop-down lists, and so on. The modeler allows those elements to be laid out on a page and to be related to data elements from a database. All the SAP CAF layers share this structure, as shown in Figure 16-2.

The structure of composite applications allows you to construct utilities that you can use with any composite application because they all operate on the metadata and framework elements and don't have to know anything about the application logic.

One of the first of these tools is the *control center*. This little beauty allows a user to list all the roles that she is playing in a set of composite applications, and then the user can look at the user interfaces for each of those applications and see the processes that are underway. This sort of structure allows any composite application to quickly come available to all composite applications.

Good enough. So now take a look at each layer provided by the SAP CAF.

Extending patterns and frameworks

In computer software, patterns and frameworks are all over the place. A very common pattern in software is the menu at the top of the page on most applications. The menu has commands such as File, Edit, Format, and so on. When you click one, it displays a drop-down list of menu items.

The SAP CAF extends that pattern and framework approach from the outside of the interface of a page (what some designers call the *chrome*) into the body of the page. The SAP CAF provides the developer with patterns that are designed to be used with the other elements of the model, such as roles, processes, or guided procedures. A particular pattern might show all the functions available for a particular role, for example.

So now think about this: You can plug various patterns into each part of the framework. In this way, the SAP CAF leverages modeling, patterns, and frameworks to allow maximum usefulness for a developer. Imagine a developer picking a framework for an application, plugging different patterns into each part, performing some configuration, and then having the whole thing generate many thousands of lines of code for him. Geek heaven!

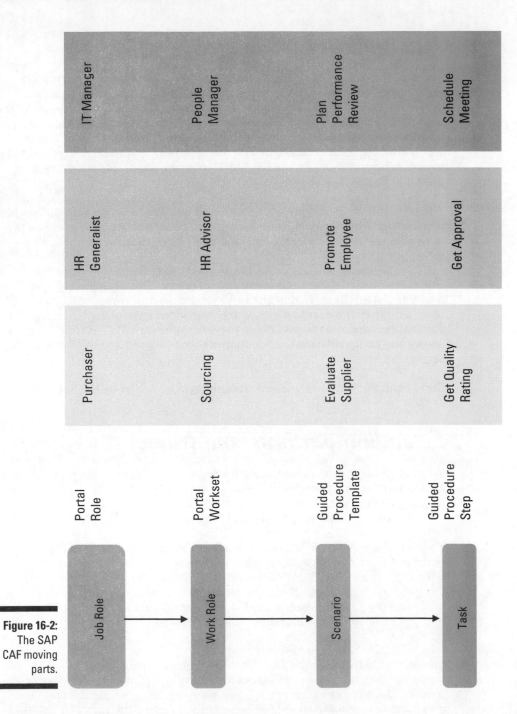

Figure 16-2:
The SAP
CAF moving
parts.

The flexibility of this approach doesn't end with the designer. It's possible (and, in certain cases, desirable) to select different patterns at run time. If some users can only display data but others can edit data, it may make sense to control this access by switching from a display-only pattern to a pattern that allows editing at run time, depending on the identity of the user. The same flexibility can be applied at the framework level, as well.

These concepts and terms aren't easy pickings. Absorbing them can take time. Don't worry: We revisit the SAP CAF and its functionality several times in this book. To get the big picture, just take the SAP CAF one bite at a time.

Roles and processes

We now return to our food analogy. (You can tell it's lunch time for us, can't you?) For dinner at a restaurant, the roles are customer, waiter, busboy, cook, and dishwasher. Each role plays a different part in buying, preparing, serving, and eating the meal. The process of the meal might be defined in terms of setting the table, seating, ordering, cooking, serving, eating, clearing the table, and paying the check.

If you model an application, which pieces should be primary in modeling the application and which in the presentation through the interface? Should you have one interface for each role or divide the interface of the application by the steps in the process?

In general, the answer is . . . it depends. Some applications will be more successful if roles are dominant and others if processes are dominant. The creators of the SAP CAF understood this and supported both approaches.

Go with the role

The idea of the role-based approach is to look at the role as a container. Generally, roles have _deliverables_ assigned to them, some specific thing that will be produced. Inside each role container, the part of the program used to model the role, you place several scenarios. Seat a party of one at a table for two means take one place setting away. Seat a party of five at a table for four means add a chair and a place setting. Different scenarios exist for ordering, serving, and clearing.

SAP embedded the concept of a portal role in SAP® Enterprise Portal 6.0, which is designed to implement a structure similar to an SAP CAF role. This makes the job of the SAP CAF much easier because instead of having to generate all the code to support its version of a role, the SAP CAF can simply use the SAP EP portal role object to do the job.

Figure 16-3 shows how a role-based approach to three different jobs might be modeled. The top row identifies the general role and the second row, the specific facet of the role that is being automated. The third row represents a process, and the fourth row is a step in the process.

It's a process

With process-based modeling, the process — not the role — is at the top of the tree. The main container for the process in the SAP CAF is a business scenario, which has procedures, actions, and services as its components.

In process-based modeling, the idea is that some applications should be described with a set of steps, each with components, with several levels of containment.

Figure 16-4 shows how process-based modeling might describe a task. Instead of the main category being a role, it is a type of process, such as a product launch, project to be managed, or merger. Then, the specific processes are the next level, with the lowest level representing steps in a process.

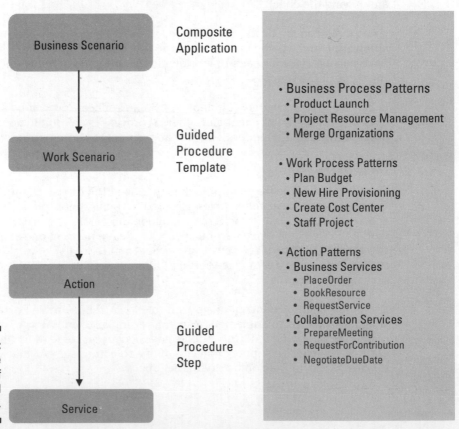

Figure 16-3:
Three examples of role-based modeling.

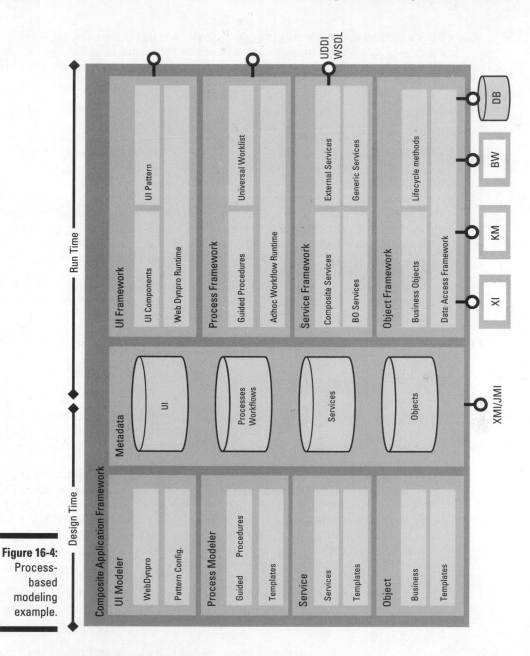

Figure 16-4:
Process-based modeling example.

Choosing among them

When programmers and designers discuss the relative virtues of role-based versus process-based modeling, the debate can become quite heated. (Yes, programmers and designers have no lives and these are the types of things that get them heated, believe us.)

Both approaches have strengths and weaknesses. But the best approach really depends on the application and the way that your company works. Although hard-and-fast guidelines for when to use each approach are difficult to come by, we can give you a few examples and rules of thumb.

Role-based modeling is usually the way to go when a small number of roles or perhaps even just one role is the center of the application. An employee self-service application, for example, where the employee role dominates the application, is a natural for role-based modeling. In this scenario, the phases, actions, and services of the related processes take a secondary role.

Process-based modeling makes the most sense when each role plays a smaller part in the application and different roles become dominant depending on the stage of the process. The most important things for such an application to reflect are how many of the process steps or activities have been completed and which part of the process is currently being performed. Because no one role is dominant, such applications tend to be much more collaborative than those for which role-based modeling makes sense. A good example of this is budgeting, where everyone in the company does the same process at different levels of granularity, and the results are rolled up into one document.

Guiding you through

Another powerful tool that the SAP CAF provides is called a *guided procedure*. Guided procedures are a new kind of tool for developers. They're essentially a simple and easy to use framework for defining a process in a flexible way.

A guided procedure includes a collection of a steps called *phases*. An example of phases would be the steps involved in hiring a new employee. Each phase might have several *actions,* steps such as filling out an evaluation form or performing a specific unit of work. Behind each action is an *enterprise service* that performs some sort of function. As the work proceeds, the guided procedure might collect references to objects, services, documents like resumes, and other guided procedures.

Guided procedures aren't limited to one user. A guided procedure defines steps that are executed in parallel by many different users playing many different roles.

The workflow of a guided procedure is powerful. It allows for looping and branching and dependent execution of a process, or for overriding the standard process for a particular instance of a guided procedure.

Guided procedures also have *templates,* which are like patterns that allow many different sorts of guided procedures to be created from one general definition.

Getting interactive with forms

Guided procedures lead kind of insular lives, never going out on dates or to the mall. So obviously they need a link to the outside world. *Interactive forms* are one way that guided procedures communicate with the world at large.

Interactive forms are standalone documents built to collect information offline from a user. The form is then submitted to a guided procedure, which processes the information. Interactive forms transfer the data back and forth from the guided procedure by using XML.

Interactive forms solve an important piece of the automation puzzle because they provide a mechanism for collecting data that can be used anywhere, on many different devices (such as phones, PDAs, and so on), regardless of connectivity.

Composite scenarios

Another way that guided procedures call the shots is through *composite scenarios,* which perform a neat trick for applications that aren't yet hip to Web services. Composite scenarios orchestrate the behavior of many different applications that haven't yet been made available as services. (*Services* are the collections of functionality used by the various layers of the SAP CAF built out of several different kinds of objects.)

In the composite scenario technique, a guided procedure moves a user from one user-interface screen to another. The user has the impression of a single workflow, even though the screens are provided by different applications. Sometimes a process can be effectively automated as a path through several different applications without modifying them.

This approach, of course, has its limits. The screens don't really know that they're participating in the composite scenario, data may be inconsistent across each screen, and implementing a composite scenario in an environment with many different vendors is difficult. The biggest limitation may be the assumption that the business logic of each application has to be accepted as is, unlike the standard SAP CAF application in which the objects and services are controlled by the developer. With a composite scenario, you have no chance to modify the applications.

Services and objects

Are you still with us? Good. The SAP CAF puzzle has a couple more pieces to fit in place, and then we leave you in peace.

The services and objects from underlying systems come together in a SAP CAF object, which is designed to accelerate the process of creating the objects and services that you need to build a composite application.

Objects, engines, and processes

Business objects are the workhorses of the SAP CAF. They're the gateway to custom functionality built inside an SAP CAF or they provide a path to services that the SAP CAF accesses from outside.

Business engines are another kind of object that provides a utility function, like calculating interest rates. Business engines don't have multiple copies of themselves, unlike a business object, which may have one instance per customer.

Business processes are special extensions to a business object that allow it to keep track of process-related information.

Out of these building blocks, the services used in a SAP CAF come to life.

The object is . . .

The SAP CAF objects are powerful in their own curious way. The power of an SAP CAF object comes from the fact that it starts out with a huge amount of functionality built right in. For example, the SAP CAF objects are able to

- Plug into user-interface patterns.
- Package functions for use as Web services or use Web services from other programs.
- Provide collaborative functionality.
- Provide content-management functionality.
- Store data or instances of themselves through various persistence mechanisms such as databases or XML files.
- Participate in guided procedures.

The goal of the SAP CAF object is to provide functionality and services for composite applications. As such, the SAP CAF objects get created to perform all sorts of different tasks. They aggregate and enhance services from underlying systems. They provide a consistent abstraction layer to encapsulate services. They allow for loose coupling so that objects can hide implementation details and be as reusable as possible.

Accelerating things

One important result of all this power is that when you need a new service to help a process along, it can be whipped up in the blink of an eye. This idea of *accelerated service provisioning* means that not only are applications easier to create, but they're faster to create, as well.

From a design perspective, you can also think of an SAP CAF object as a meta object that has the same relation to an object that metadata (data about data) has to an application. An SAP CAF object acts as a meta object by presenting different views or services depending on who is using the object. This represents a higher and more flexible level of abstraction than is present in a normal SAP CAF object.

With these concepts in mind, the notion of accelerated service provisioning amounts to this: The SAP CAF provides the ability to rapidly assemble new services out of existing objects and services so that new functionality can be created as fast as possible with as little new code as possible.

Reposeful data

The services available in the SAP CAF come from third parties, mySAP Business Suite solutions, and low-level system functions such as one object sending a message to another.

The SAP CAF provides one central service repository that allows quick and easy access to the different types of services, all of which are described in a uniform and consistent manner. They are, in fact, Web services, but with an additional layer of description of the Web service framework, which allows enterprise services to be created by coordinating many lower-level Web services.

For example, deleting an entry in a database is a Web service, but canceling an order is an enterprise service that has a business context and an understanding of the relationships with other business objects that ensures the consistency of the application.

The Future of the SAP CAF

Time to gaze into the future. The future in this case is based on the fact that common metadata structures and frameworks of composite applications provide for new types of utilities and tools. SAP is currently working on two such tools and we thought that you might want to know about them.

One implication of guided procedures and the flexible nature of composite applications in general is that informal collaborative processes (you know, where you and somebody else get together to get something done) are much easier to automate than through traditional methods. These semi-structured processes involve things like discussion forums and management of documents. SAP is working on a general framework for extending all composite applications with collaborative and content-management functionality using model-based development.

Another interesting project involves using *semantic nets* to discover relationships between the elements of composite applications that aren't directly modeled in metadata. What's a semantic net, you say? Well, imagine that you find out that, based on the information in the system, two different customers are actually the same customer, or are in the same family unit. If you discover these relationships, search and content navigation functions can be extended to the semantic level, which means that you can move through data based on meaningful relationships, not just on alphabetical order.

Chapter 17

Tying It All Together: SAP Solution Manager

Software companies sell software, but what software users actually need are solutions for their business problems. For example, when you think, "I need new spreadsheet software," what you really mean is, "I need a better way to create the monthly departmental budget report." The second thought is the business process that you want help with. You buy a spreadsheet package — applications software — because it provides the solution.

The same is true with the SAP large enterprise software. On one side are SAP's software products, on the other your company's business processes. The question is, how can SAP software help you solve your business problems and meet your business goals? A significant part of SAP's answer to this question is a big, powerful product known as SAP Solution Manager.

SAP Solution Manager is what's known as a *central service platform*. This platform is made up of frameworks, tools, and services that can help you implement, manage, monitor, and support your SAP (and, as we explain later in this chapter, non-SAP) business solutions.

The Many Sides of SAP Solution Manager

SAP Solution Manager is a pretty important sounding title. What does this guy actually do, anyway? Well, specifically, SAP Solution Manager helps you:

✔ Centrally manage your SAP enterprise applications.

✔ Minimize the risk and increase the reliability of your enterprise applications.

✔ Reduce your total cost of ownership (TCO) throughout the life cycle of your enterprise applications.

✔ Link your IT infrastructure with your company's core business processes.

✔ Get more business benefit from the IT investments that your company has already made.

Here's the problem

To get a clearer idea of how SAP Solution Manager can help you, imagine that you're the senior VP of IT (a VPIT) at a large corporation. You can name your own salary. The systems you oversee include a long list of enterprise applications, some from SAP, some not, running at locations around the world.

Hold that image. Now imagine that you're sipping your first coffee of the day and worrying about your users. Which users are complaining and about what? Do you have the software patches to address — and, you hope, end — their complaints? With your staff already overloaded, how can you get the patches implemented quickly? And how can you make sure the fixes aren't worse than the problem, snarling other systems as an unintended consequence?

The wizardry of SAP Solution Manager

With the previous example in mind, we take a look at the things that SAP Solution Manager can actually do to help. Think of SAP Solution Manager as kind of like a software wizard for every moment of your enterprise applications' life cycle. When you want to install software, SAP Solution Manager acts like an installation wizard, just like the one on your desktop system. But SAP Solution Manager doesn't stop there. When it's time to implement your systems, SAP Solution Manager acts like an implementation wizard. When it's time to run your systems, SAP Solution Manager acts as your operational wizard. And when it's time to catch and fix problems, SAP Solution Manager is your support wizard.

Take a look at each of Solution Manager's functions.

Implementation: Getting SAP up and running

After the software license is purchased and the box is open, how do you get SAP programs up and running? SAP Solution Manager is an on-site platform that helps you implement SAP applications by

✔ Providing a management overview of projects, including their status and issues.

✔ Defining project scope based on your existing portfolio of applications.

✔ Offering enhanced testing features, including SAP's extended computer-assisted test tool (eCATT) technology, which lets you maintain and execute test scripts on non-SAP software from an SAP terminal.

✔ Helping you manage the handover from an application's implementation team to its operators.

The implementation portion of SAP Solution Manager is supported by a whole family of content. Essentially, SAP Solution Manager acts as a delivery mechanism for *content* — sets of information that provide everything that you need to make SAP programs work. These include best-practice documents, road maps, implementation accelerators, and related services.

Operation: Monitoring all this stuff

Okay, so implemented software is better than software in a box, but you're still not home free. When your system is up and running, you want SAP Solution Manager to help with three kinds of monitoring: service levels, systems, and business processes.

Solution Manager collects data, monitors workflow, and measures workflow against your service-level agreements. It also provides detailed procedures for handling errors and resolving problems. The operation component also includes a family of tools for your operations pleasure.

Support: May I help you?

We all need a little help now and then and, so this component of SAP Solution Manager acts as a gateway or portal to SAP and a ready, willing, and able assistant to your support desk. It helps by

✔ Handling internal customer messages.

✔ Managing SAP Notes customer-support documents.

✔ Integrating SAP support by sending support messages to SAP, receiving status updates, and using Microsoft NetMeeting for application-sharing among end users, power users, and back-office experts.

You could also think of SAP Solution Manager as a container for business content, a methodology for implementing that business content, and a documentation system that helps you track the current state of all your systems.

The Three Faces of SAP Solution Manager

The previous sections give you a general sense of how SAP Solution Manager can help your business. Here we take a peak under the tent flap and see just what's going on.

From a software perspective, SAP Solution Manager is made up of three major components:

- ✔ **Content:** This is not content as you might normally think of it, but software that helps you get the most out of your SAP systems. Among the many goodies here are best-practice documents, services, road maps, and implementation accelerators.

- ✔ **Tools:** Here the word *tools* means software tools, not hammers and wrenches. In this section of Solution Manager are service-level reporting, monitoring, service development, process management, support desk, customizing distribution, and implementation platforms.

- ✔ **Portal to SAP:** You'll be glad to hear that no SAP customer is an island. Solution Manager provides direct links between your shop and SAP Service Marketplace, service delivery, and SAP Notes.

Figure 17-1 shows the detailed services offered at each of these layers.

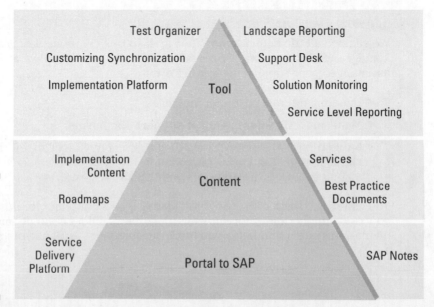

Figure 17-1:
The functionality and content of SAP Solution Manager.

Call the cops!

Another neat gateway feature is SAP EarlyWatch. It works like a virtual police unit, patrolling your systems from various locations and reporting back to SAP headquarters.

SAP EarlyWatch collects data from your systems and then forwards it to your SAP Solution Manager system. If the data gets a red (this is bad) rating, SAP Solution Manager sends a report to SAP, and an SAP service engineer gets in touch with you. If the data's rating is green (this is good) or yellow (caution and look out!),

the data is retained in SAP Solution Manager, and a report is sent to SAP every four weeks for a checkup.

SAP Solution Manager also makes it easy for you to order and receive SAP support services. These include SAP Solution Management Optimization, which can help you get the most from your SAP solutions, and SAP Empowering, which helps you acquire the best core competencies for your solutions.

The following sections examine each of SAP Solution Manager's three main components in a tad more detail.

Content directs the action

SAP Solution Manager provides what SAP calls *business content,* which is what you need to take a bunch of software and turn it into something that helps your company compete in the marketplace. If you want the (ahem) more formal definition, content includes *metadata* (settings that control the way a program works) and software that directs the action of your applications to create a business solution.

Much, though not all, of this content is most useful in the early days of a newborn application's life when the application is being planned, installed, and implemented.

Take a closer look at some of the many types of business content provided by SAP Solution Manager:

> ✔ **Best-practice documents:** SAP Solution Manager defines which processes are performed by various software components (CRM, ERP, and so on), and gives models of how these processes have been successfully set up by other SAP customers and developers. SAP Solution Manager then essentially delivers these business scenarios from CRM and other SAP applications to your doorstep.

- **Road maps:** SAP Solution Manager doesn't want to leave you lost on some back road of IT with a flat tire. So it provides *road maps,* which are methodologies for implementing your software. Just like a paper road map in your car's glove compartment, these show you where you're headed and point out the major landmarks (like the world's largest ball of IT applications). Unlike your paper road maps, SAP's road maps don't rip or get coffee-ring stains!

- **Implementation accelerators:** You're smart, so you've probably figured out by now that knowing and doing aren't the same thing. That's okay, because after SAP Solution Manager loads you up with best-practice documents and road maps, it also helps you put that knowledge into action. It creates checklists for your software implementation of both action items and issues to resolve (or at least consider). It also creates a repository for all your implementation documents. It can create test scripts based on all your documents. Best of all, SAP Solution Manager can do this for solutions that involve new SAP software, older SAP software, and non-SAP software.

I spy: Tools keep an eye out

An important task of SAP Solution Manager is *monitoring.* You see, SAP Solution Manager is a bit of a snoop. The good news is that SAP Solution Manager is on your side and all the spying and snooping it does helps you keep your SAP systems running full tilt.

Here are a few of the many tools included in SAP Solution Manager:

- **Service-Level Reporting:** This function of SAP Solution Manager reports on the performance of your systems on a regular basis. It also improves communication between your IT shop and your business units by setting clearly defined and verifiable business goals. It then monitors and reports on how well you're meeting those goals within a set period of time. For extremely time-sensitive processes, you can even use a secondary feature known as Alert Monitoring to check a system every few hours or even, if you have nothing else to do, every few minutes.

- **Solution Monitoring:** This tool makes a logical connection between your software and your business processes. It collects performance indicators and automatically recognizes situations that require immediate action. SAP Solution Manager provides a graphical user interface (GUI) that displays alert triggers for any of your systems or business processes.

- **Business Process Monitoring:** This tool concentrates on alerts that are related to screw ups with the technical operation of your business processes, such as poor performance of business transactions, processing, hanging, or poorly performing interfaces or background jobs.

SAP Solution Manager to the rescue

This component is like those home security systems that automatically contact the security company or police when a break-in occurs. The gateway features of SAP Solution Manager are your hotline to SAP technical support. SAP Solution Manager collects data from your systems and automatically sends alerts to SAP whenever signs of trouble appear. (Don't worry: The SAP support team doesn't just show up at your door — they call first.)

Another key aspect of the SAP Solution Manager gateway is access to SAP Service Marketplace. This is an Internet portal that helps you collaborate with SAP and its partners. This is a rather exclusive club: In fact, you have to have an SAP username and password to even enter.

SAP Service Marketplace is divided into four main areas:

- ✔ **Support:** Here's where you can find access to SAP Notes, a site where you can order and download SAP software, create customer messages, and find a list of SAP support addresses.

- ✔ **SMB Portal:** Information and tools for small- and medium-sized businesses. This handy portal offers you marketing and sales tools, Solution Development Kits, new-product information, and upgrade reports.

- ✔ **SAP Developer Network:** As its name indicates, this is a portal for developers and their Weblogs (commonly called *blogs*), discussion forums, presentations, and a spot where you can download both software and tools.

- ✔ **More:** Filled with good stuff that SAP didn't know how else to classify, this area contains links to training courses, a directory of SAP partners, and a place for partner leads and referrals.

How SAP Solution Manager Helps Your Business

As you might expect from such a robust little fellow, SAP Solution Manager is no one-trick pony. Instead, it's the package that likes to give, give, and then give some more. The list of SAP Solution Manager key benefits is so long that you could easily think of SAP Solution Manager as several products in one. (That's actually not too far from the truth.) So when you ask, "How can SAP Solution Manager help my business?" get ready for a lengthy answer.

Here are the characteristics that enable SAP Solution Manager to save your corporate neck just about daily. It's:

- **Heterogeneous:** SAP Solution Manager plays well with others. SAP engineers realized that today's IT environment includes both SAP and non-SAP applications. They also saw that business processes often span more than one application, sometimes involving systems in more than one physical location. So they designed SAP Solution Manager to address your *entire* IT environment, regardless of application, vendor, or location.

- **Cost conscious:** SAP Solution Manager helps you reduce total cost of ownership by centralizing support and speeding up life cycle planning, implementation, operation, support, and continuous improvement.

- **Business minded:** This thing wears bifocals: It works on both the technical and business aspects of your IT solutions. It provides a detailed view for your core business processes, not just your components and applications.

- **Risk averse:** No one likes unforeseen expenses, and everyone wants to keep IT operating costs to a minimum. SAP Solution Manager helps on both fronts by ensuring that your entire SAP solution environment is always running smoothly.

- **Smart:** When you work with SAP Solution Manager, you also have access to SAP's best practices and knowledge for on-site service procedures. In effect, you benefit from the trials, errors, and accumulated wisdom of earlier SAP customers.

- **Thrifty:** Like a good Boy Scout, SAP Solution Manager is thrifty, because you pay no extra fee to use it. It's included in your annual maintenance fee for SAP solutions. (Something for nothing — cool!)

Putting SAP Solution Manager to Work

Where many other enterprise solutions are content to do just one task extremely well, SAP Solution Manager is the multi-tasking Leonardo da Vinci of enterprise software. No, it can't paint the *Last Supper,* invent the parachute, or explain just what the heck Mona Lisa was smiling about. But here are some of the many tasks that SAP Solution Manager can help you with:

- **mySAP™ Business Suite implementation:** The mySAP Business Suite solutions built around SAP NetWeaver™ technology go down more easily with content provided by SAP Solution Manager. Use configuration information and a process-driven approach to speed implementation, by providing the blueprint, configuration, and templates for the final-preparation phases of your SAP project. SAP Solution Manager also helps you administer projects by centralizing the control of cross-component implementations. It gives all members of your project team easy access to key documents. It seamlessly integrates information to allow fast, smooth transitions between project phases. It even helps you integrate non-SAP components into SAP by providing process definitions and documentation.

✔ **Global rollouts:** It's a big world out there, and your company may just own several pieces of it in far-flung places. SAP Solution Manager can standardize your processes across multiple locations. SAP Solution Manager centralizes control, which means that you can implement configuration settings just once from a central location and then make those settings take effect at as many local installations as you have. SAP Solution Manager also helps you manage versions at multiple locations and compare and adjust templates. This makes it easier for you to adapt to changing requirements.

✔ **Synchronization of customized settings:** Like the tree falling in the forest without a soul in sight, customized settings made only in the central office might not make a sound. But SAP Solution Manager makes sure that your changes are heard. It reduces manual synchronization efforts by automatically distributing customized settings to various systems at the same time. It also centrally manages all requests to synchronize these settings. The benefits to you are greater consistency, safer administration, fewer errors, and simpler consistency checks. You can also use SAP Solution Manager to set up and configure additional systems for testing, training, and demos.

✔ **Testing:** It's a dirty job, but someone's got to do testing. By creating a single point of access and centrally storing all testing materials and lab results, SAP Solution Manager speeds test preparation and execution. You can also reuse its testing material in subsequent projects. SAP Solution Manager integrates testing with implementation, allowing you to perform tests as process structures get configured. It also integrates testing with issue handling to ensure that problems are handled efficiently.

✔ **IT and application support:** The support desk included in SAP Solution Manager helps you manage your IT incidents more efficiently and with less hassle about support costs. It provides information that improves problem resolution, and its central handling of support messages can boost your support organization's efficiency.

✔ **Solution monitoring:** Does less administrative work sound good to you? We thought so. SAP Solution Manager performs central, real-time monitoring of your systems, business processes, and interfaces. It even monitors intersystem dependencies. All this proactive monitoring helps you avoid critical situations, and automatic notifications help you respond quickly to any issues that come up. Solution Manager even sends an alert to the person or group responsible for dealing with the situation.

✔ **Service-level management and reporting:** Promises, promises, promises. As an IT manager, you make a lot of them, and SAP Solution Manager helps you to keep your word. It helps define service levels and then automatically monitors and reports on them. By monitoring all systems in the solution, SAP Solution Manager provides you with a consolidated report containing exactly the information that you need to make strategic IT decisions. These handy reports contain recommendations for optimizing your systems.

✔ **Service processing:** Wouldn't you like somebody to support you? SAP Solution Manager does just that. It makes appropriate service recommendations and delivers SAP support services. These include SAP Safeguarding services, which can help you manage technical risks and ensure the technical robustness of your solutions; SAP Solution Management Optimization services, which help you get the most from your SAP solutions; and SAP Empowering services, which help you acquire the right core competencies to manage your solutions. SAP Solution Manager makes the ordering and delivery of services easy and enables you to provide self service to your organization independently of SAP.

Take a look at Solution Manager in action in the following examples.

Example 1: Helping with the implementation two-step

Getting started with a new enterprise application can be a slow process — especially if you have to reinvent the proverbial wheel. But SAP Solution Manager helps build strong enterprise-apps implementations in two ways: by providing a best-practices process and by providing business content.

First, SAP Solution Manager helps implement enterprise software by providing models of best practices. Essentially, this is SAP's way of saying, "Other people have gone this way before. Here's what worked for them — and here are the snake pits to avoid."

For example, say that you're the sales manager of a midsized printing company in the MidWest. As part of your latest project, you want to work with your IT group to set up your company to deal with online sales. You know what you want the system to do, but how do you get there? Lucky for you, others have already made this voyage. A best-practices model, supplied by SAP Solution Manager, shows you which components of your existing IT systems need to be activated.

Also, SAP Solution Manager helps your implementation project by delivering business content. This is metadata and other software that controls or directs the actions of an application. SAP Solution Manager is SAP's way of delivering that business content to you. SAP Solution Manager also delivers road maps that provide a methodology for your implementation. Figure 17-2 shows a high-level view of the structure of SAP's recommended implementation process.

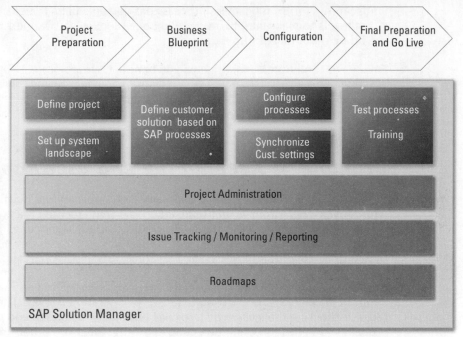

Figure 17-2:
An overview of the SAP implementation process.

Example 2: Upgrade this!

Okay, today you're the IT administrator at a large computer game manufacturer. Your enterprise applications and processes are running, but from time to time you need to make upgrades. SAP Solution Manager can help you. Just as it helps with implementations, SAP Solution Manager provides an integrated road map that guides you through the peaks and valleys of your upgrade projects.

SAP Solution Manager actually checks your systems to determine which pieces need upgrading and when, based on the requirements of your business solution. You can run this test, incidentally, *before* your system actually goes live — a neat way to ensure success from day one. If a piece of the system is not quite up to snuff, SAP Solution Manager also provides proposals for the upgrade process.

So it's Tuesday and you go ahead with the upgrade. SAP Solution Manager manages the end-to-end process of upgrading your software for you so that you can put your feet up (until the phone rings again with some urgent IT-type fire to put out).

SAP Solution Manager checks what's known as *landscape compatibility*. That is, it determines whether you have every software component — the complete landscape — for each business process that you specified. It also compares patch levels to make sure that upgrading one piece of software doesn't throw the other, older pieces into a tizzy.

Finally, SAP Solution Manager helps you handle upgrade projects by giving you tips on how best to get where you want to go. Once again, these tips are based on the real-world experiences of actual SAP customers, so the bodies of IT administrators that went before you went for a good cause.

Example 3: Keeping the end user happy

You're the CIO at a large pet food company with international reach. (All the world loves a pet.) Your team has installed and implemented SAP systems. Now it's time to run those systems. But your company is pushing for end user satisfaction. Because you've gotten this far, you're probably not surprised to discover that, once again, SAP Solution Manager can help.

Here's where you enter what SAP calls the *operational phrase* and where SAP Solution Manager helps with — what else? — operational tasks. These tasks include checking the system on a regular basis, responding to end user requests and questions, and detecting and fixing bugs and other problems.

Your CEO has stated that end user requests are a major issue that you have to address when running your systems. End users not only encounter bugs, but they also have a tendency to forget how to use the systems that their IT department has so painstakingly built. SAP Solution Manager helps keep your CEO happy by either passing along end user complaints and questions to the support team or by pointing end users to solutions that may already exist through a form of knowledge-management system. (*Knowledge-management systems* help companies collect, arrange, and share data, solutions, fixes, and other information that was previously known only to a select few.) Happy end users. Happy CEO. Big year-end bonus!

Example 4: Keeping an eye on your systems

Okay, so today you're a beleaguered IT type just trying to watch the four-ring circus of applications, systems, servers, and users to spot potential disasters. You're smart enough to know that many problems in life are easiest to solve before they've had time to fester. That includes problems with enterprise applications. So SAP Solution Manager monitors your applications and processes for problems and then helps you nip them in the bud. SAP Solution

Manager checks your IT environment, determines the status of your systems, and detects any possible problems.

You can use SAP Solution Manager to monitor most of your systems with the feature known as EarlyWatch. This service offering does a weekly patrol of your systems, compiling the past seven days' worth of operational statistics, consolidating, averaging, and displaying them in a nice, neat little report. For example, your weekly report might show the average data *throughput* (the amount of transactions being executed) for a given system.

SAP Solution Manager also monitors your business processes. This is a more sweeping view of an entire process that isn't limited to just one application or system. For example, SAP Solution Manager looks at your ordering process and sees how orders are created, where invoices are generated, and so on, all the way through the ordering process. This data is then compiled, consolidated, and averaged. So what you see is not a single order for an individual customer, but a high-level view across the entire ordering system, showing you what's working as specified, and what's not. Your hot shot management team just loves this stuff!

Finally, SAP Solution Manager monitors service levels. Service levels are essentially promises made by your IT department to the rest of the company. Say you've promised an average response time of 15 seconds for credit applications. Solution Manager collects the data on the credit program's response time for a week, averages it out, and compares it against your 15-second promise. If Solution Manager shows your average time at just 10 seconds, you have something to crow about; if it's 20, go back to the drawing board — with SAP Solution Manager's help, of course.

How SAP Solution Manager Works with SAP NetWeaver

SAP Solution Manager really does play well with others. One of its favorite playmates is none other than SAP NetWeaver. SAP Solution Manager helps support the applications that are part of NetWeaver. It does this by using a method called life cycle management.

Essentially, SAP Solution Manager cares for an enterprise application from cradle to grave. These *life cycle management* capabilities address the problems that show up at every turn and about which customers are frequently left to fend for themselves.

Life cycle management means that SAP Solution Manager helps you take an application from installation through configuration, then on to operation, and finally to updates and modifications. But even this process can be divided into two parts: the software life cycle and the solution life cycle. The former looks at the application's life cycle from the developer's perspective, and the latter looks at the application from the perspective of the users. What they both share, of course, is SAP Solution Manager.

The Future of the SAP Solution Manager

SAP Solution Manager is a digital dashboard that you can use to observe, monitor, and adjust the end-to-end life cycle of your SAP applications. That won't change anytime soon.

But what is likely to change over time is Solution Manager's huge task list. We can safely predict that it will continue to grow. Solution Manager will evolve to help you further improve your IT operations, reduce costs, and increase reliability. It will take on more information, automate more processes, and provide even more help for running SAP solutions.

Already, SAP Solution Manager and Service Marketplace are on their way to becoming the complete support system from SAP for SAP solutions and for the rest of the IT environment provided by other vendors. Ultimately, SAP Solution Manager may become the best-practice wizard for managing in the IT industry. Now that's one smart program.

Part IV

SAP NetWeaver in Action

The 5th Wave   By Rich Tennant

"The top line represents the cost of ownership of our IT landscape, the middle line represents the cost of integrating, and the bottom line represents the rate of my hair loss over the same period."

In this part . . .

War stories about how you got through a tough project are almost always educational. There you were, in the Congo, with only a simple portal interface in hand to fight off wild animals and your CEO. Yet somehow you survived and saved the IT day.

This part tells typical stories from some of the most common jungles in IT and enterprise computing and shows how, in each case, SAP® NetWeaver™ can help get you out of the Congo with a promotion, raise, and early retirement.

Well, at least you'll build some useful solutions for your business.

Chapter 18

The World of Internal Portals

*I*n an episode of *Star Trek,* a portal might be a cosmic doorway into another dimension. In your office, however, portals are simply one of the most frequently used ways that SAP NetWeaver appears in your company.

In their simplest form, *internal portals* are aggregates of information — high-tech dashboards that provide a visually integrated view of your business and its individual projects.

In the scenario that we describe in this chapter, you see how SAP NetWeaver components all work together to create various kinds of internal portals. You discover the nature of internal portals, the IT problems that you must solve to put them in place, and how SAP NetWeaver can help you out, using one possible staged implementation plan. By the time you finish this chapter, you'll understand why portals can be your entrée to a more efficient business.

Start by Redefining Browser Technology

The ubiquitous Web browser has become one of the most effective tools around for simplifying employee access to information, applications, and a slew of necessary IT functions. Despite its humble origins as a method for accessing dry research documents and obscure Web pages about topics like genealogy for pets, the browser is now the entryway of choice to the IT world.

Many corporations are busy taking the potential of browser technology to the max by developing internal portals. These portals provide the visual interface that makes employee access to the information and applications that they need to do their jobs much simpler. A one-stop resource, portals eliminate the need to pull sources and functions from a hodge podge of systems, all requiring different log-on names, passwords, and user interfaces, and all presenting information in different ways. Portals cut through this mind-boggling complexity by providing a single interface tailored to an employee's needs and position within the enterprise, whether that position is assistant to the assistant whosit, CEO, or outside supplier.

But an interesting phenomenon is going on here: As internal portals are gradually integrated with underlying enterprise software, they evolve, like shape-shifting aliens, from one-way receivers of information into versatile two-way tools. They provide single interfaces with shared authentication and become tools that you can use to

- ✔ Conduct single searches of multiple data sources spread across a dozen servers.
- ✔ Publish documents to targeted groups.
- ✔ Track changes during projects.
- ✔ Interface with legacy applications or new business processes created by the invisible integration of formerly separate software.
- ✔ Foster collaboration and improve teamwork.
- ✔ Conduct employee training.
- ✔ Make hot coffee in the morning — just kidding.

Ultimately, portals provide a flexible gateway — accessible from anywhere in the universe that the Internet reaches (yes, we hear that Internet service providers are available on Mars, now) — to a continually expanding array of applications. Those applications can be running both inside your enterprise and outside of it (for example, on your favorite vendor's network). At each step of the way, portals simplify and personalize information and functions. This makes for happy, efficient workers and an organization that has unburdened itself of many of the chores that it used to do.

Internal Portals: The Magic Bullet for Streamlining Business Processes

Just as Chinese takeout makes your life easier at the end of a busy day, an internal portal is an opportunity to make a user's life easier when dealing with business processes. A portal knits together the myriad bits and pieces of information and applications employees actually need to do what they do. And, by eliminating arbitrary IT boundaries, internal portals cut costs, reduce organizational overhead, save time, and lower employee frustration levels (all without adding MSG).

So, how do you choose the best way to implement an internal portal? Well, that depends on the level of functionality that you need right off the bat and on how easily that level can be upped as employee needs change down the road (and trust us, they always do).

For example . . .

Say that for the last hundred years or so your HR department has distributed a paper form to your employees to update their health plan options at the end of each year. In recent years, HR has started sending these forms out as e-mail attachments, which they consider a triumph of technology. However, some employees still print out the form and return it via inner office mail, while others hastily enter data and e-mail back the form. Now some poor souls in HR have to download and sort through all the attachments and pieces of paper and copy or re-enter the data into the HR system. (We won't even talk about the e-mailed forms that got lost because the mail server was down on Thursday.) Temps have to be hired to process forms, overtime is required, and you inevitably hear a great annual gnashing of teeth.

How could you streamline this painful process? Well, you could put an icon on every desktop that connects directly to HR software, but this would require each employee to navigate through a complex interface targeted to HR professionals. Face it: That kind of interface has way more options than the typical user ever wants to know about.

A portal could bring sanity to the project for the employee as well as the HR department. In this scenario, an employee's personalized portal links to a Web-based form. Now, each employee simply clicks and updates the electronic form, which goes through the portal to the corporate HR system, expediting the process and saving money, time, and aggravation.

Reaping the benefits of portals

It's hard to calculate the savings in employee effort and energy the portal in the example in the previous section provides. This becomes even more obvious when you consider that one fundamental part of a portal's appeal is its ability to select and distribute subsections of existing applications right to the folks who need them.

So suppose that some guy on the 11th floor who is working on a project to renovate the manufacturing plant in Kalamazoo needs only 5 percent of an application's functionality to complete his work. The portal can supply just that functionality. In effect, you grant role-based access to the underlying software through a familiar, streamlined interface that's already integrated with the data and collaborative tools (such as e-mail, instant messaging, or discussion forums) that the employee uses every day.

What does all this mean to your business? It saves the company training costs and improves employee satisfaction. It may also help you avoid a full-scale technology migration (which could cause several nervous breakdowns in your IT department) by preserving delicate legacy systems and updating only their look and feel.

A fully actualized portal, one that goes beyond just providing a pretty face for an application or an intranet, can take the technology a step further: It can create new, more useful interfaces tailored to specific jobs. It can aggregate both information and functionality from applications and allow users to pick and choose what they need to use. It can transform ad hoc business processes (you know, the shortcuts developed over time by frustrated workers used to skipping in and out of multiple applications) into documented best practices. In fact, those best practices are essentially encapsulated by the portal, which looks like one simple solution to the user even though the underlying functionality is provided behind the scenes by a half-dozen applications and databases.

Maximum Overdrive: A Fully Actualized Portal

So, assuming you've seen the light and you're itching to be the first on your block to get your very own internal portal, how do you get the best portal solution for your buck?

If your company wants one of those fully actualized-type portals, you need to select a portal solution that provides the maximum flexibility and integration capabilities. The ideal solution should offer

- ✔ Out-of-the-box integration with both the vendor's and key third-party's systems.

- ✔ Services that support and search structured and unstructured data sources, as well as the alphabet soup of legacy applications and languages used by offices that may be halfway around the globe.

✔ The ability to stitch together applications that use, for example, ABAP in France and Visual Basic in Canada (or such diverse infrastructures within the same department, division, or data center) — and the portal has to do this stitching seamlessly.

As you might suspect, SAP NetWeaver comes to the rescue and provides all of these capabilities, as will be explained in a minute. But first, it is important to examine two challenges that internal portals help overcome: cost and security.

Getting started on a budget

As the kid with the red shoes in *The Wizard of Oz* said, there's no place like home, so why not start with your existing resources? Many companies have in-house IT staff with legacy programming skills that can be leveraged in the open portal environment. By allowing developers to use their existing skills to create new user-interface components, a portal eliminates the need for programmers to migrate into strange and unfamiliar development territory.

But will I have to reinvent my IT setup, which could cost an arm and a leg, you may ask? That's part of the good news. Enterprises under budgetary constraints are often interested in squeezing out a few more years from their legacy systems. A portal allows them to do this, adding fresh user interfaces while running on top of existing back-end systems. This avoids the cost and disruption that you inevitably encounter when you have to rip out working systems and start application development from scratch.

Beware invaders

Like a medieval town that has installed state-of-the-art moats and gates, the comings and goings of people through the portals you install in your company should be of concern to you. As portals gain in complexity and functionality and evolve from simple data aggregators into publishing, collaboration, and search tools, issues such as granting and tracking permissions, user authentication, and overall security come into play in a big way.

One strength of portals for simplifying the life of users is that using a single log-on and password opens an array of Web-based services. To actually make this work to your advantage rather than becoming a security nightmare, the portal must support multiple layers of security and pass authentication along to multiple applications, each of which remembers automatically which slices of functionality are allotted to each user.

Collaborative tools such as instant messaging have to be integrated with the portal as well, and this raises other questions about security. The sad truth is that some popular consumer products have security limitations that make them unsuitable to carry sensitive data.

All these concerns and more must be addressed when choosing an internal portal solution. So, now look at how SAP NetWeaver brings you to the promised land of internal portals.

SAP NetWeaver: An Internal Portal's Best Friend

You probably realize (because you bought this book and know that it's all about SAP NetWeaver) that we're suggesting SAP NetWeaver is your best bet to solve all these internal portal challenges. In SAP NetWeaver, SAP provides a general platform for application development in addition to all the technology needed to build a very cool, flexible, internal portal.

Want proof? Okay, check this out: An effective portal solution must include the following (and you guessed it, SAP NetWeaver does it all):

- **An integrated development environment (IDE)** in which to create components and services that are the building blocks of an internal portal
- **Web services** that make available only the functions of existing applications that users need to do their jobs
- **Master data management** so you can pull information from different data sources, whether structured or unstructured, into a single, searchable interface
- **Collaborative tools** such as virtual workspaces, discussion forums, real-time chat functionality, and secure messaging to connect users anywhere in the enterprise
- **Personalization of the interface** so it's easy to use
- **Publishing and document tracking** to ensure that data is distributed, seen, and processed efficiently

Given its background as a creator of world-class enterprise applications, you probably aren't surprised to find out that brainy types are tucked away in SAP offices all over the world working on many of these areas — interfaces in particular — to make the applications it sells flexible and maintainable. SAP sees portals as the interface framework of the future and is designing its products accordingly.

For these reasons and more, SAP NetWeaver is the platform that we recommend for the evolution to portals. With its suite of tools for building interfaces, extending and integrating applications, and creating Web services, SAP NetWeaver quickly builds portals for aggregating information in a way that lets you add functionality as needed via SAP and third-party applications. All this functionality is packaged in an integrated development platform that offers tons of power.

You also benefit immensely from the fact that SAP is like some whiz-kid overachiever: SAP is the vendor of the platform, the creator of toolkits for content management and business information warehousing, and a leader in deploying secure single sign-on authentication mechanisms. If your company's IT team creates an application in SAP NetWeaver, it utilizes components and services that are designed to work together rather than having to struggle with incompatible, cross-vendor integration problems.

Figure 18-1 shows how the capabilities that are relevant to internal portals are distributed throughout SAP NetWeaver. Elements provide support for user interface, process integration, collaboration, and aggregation of information.

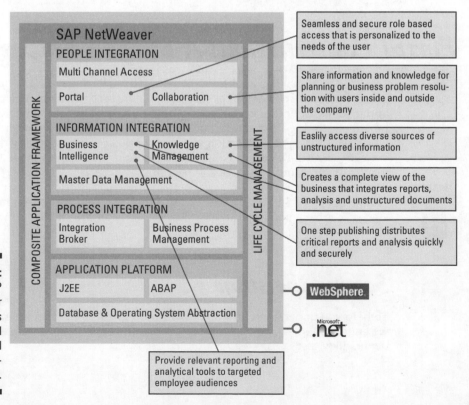

Figure 18-1: SAP NetWeaver features for internal portal development.

We haven't convinced you yet? Okay, another advantage of SAP NetWeaver for portal development is its prepackaged integration of SAP® Enterprise Portal (SAP EP), a robust technology solution for portal creation, with mySAP™ Business Suite applications. Do we hear you asking what on Earth that means? Simply that portals created by using SAP EP are already compatible with a whole bunch of Enterprise Resource Planning (ERP) components and services already used by SAP customers.

This kind of compatibility is a convenience for portal developers and (more importantly) leads to a significant reduction in your total cost of ownership (TCO). How does it do that? The truth is that preparing enterprise applications to be included in a portal is about ten times more expensive than including them from Web services. Having this work done in advance by the application developers saves huge costs and boosts the creativity of programmers who no longer have to work into the wee hours every other Saturday grappling with integration problems.

With this general overview of SAP NetWeaver functionality in mind, take a look at how the different components of the solution play a role in each stage of a fledgling portal's development and evolution.

Portal Construction: A Staged Process

Just as a child reaches adulthood by going through sometimes painful phases, most portals unfold in stages. At each stage, existing enterprise applications and other sources are gradually aggregated and integrated, components are added as needed, and information-gathering and other functions increase. Although the duration and form of this evolution greatly depend on your organization's needs, skills, resources, and desire to innovate, each step results in measurable savings and benefits.

The flexibility of SAP NetWeaver ensures that you can work through these stages relatively painlessly, adding functionality as your needs grow and change.

Setting the stage

To help you understand how an organization gives birth to an internal portal, we give you a sneak preview of the process. In general, portal implementation occurs like this:

✔ The easiest portal to assemble gathers data from various sources to provide employees with a top-level view of the enterprise and individual
projects. Self-service features automate simple tasks to reduce the overhead from tasks such as manual data entry, correcting errors, and need-
less paper forms in departments such as HR.

✔ A second-stage portal adds collaborative tools and publishing abilities
to help people work together and capture and codify the flow of work
processes that are common practice, but not written down anywhere.
These portals first reflect and ultimately strengthen how employees
actually process and transmit data inside the enterprise.

✔ As you integrate more sources of data and underlying SAP applications,
you gradually extend the abilities of internal portals outside the enterprise. First, you use data warehouses to finish the integration of information inside the portal, and then you enable enterprise applications to
securely communicate and exchange data with vendors and customers
outside the enterprise. Eventually, you can make life even easier by
automating these functions.

All of this adds up to an elegant progression, starting with easier steps and
moving to harder ones, as shown in Figure 18-2. From a humble portal for
employee self service of tasks such as address changes, a mighty portal for
automated B2B collaboration can emerge.

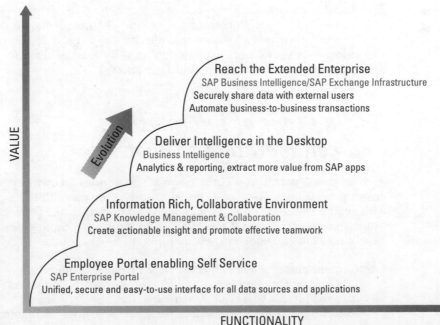

Figure 18-2:
Possible
stages of
internal
portal
develop-
ment.

Building the framework: Portal construction 101

Now we go a little deeper into the care and feeding of an infant portal. Step one of portal construction involves building the actual portal and laying the groundwork for you to extend its capabilities in the future.

Using SAP EP, your development team implements a simple digital dashboard to improve decision support and performance management by pulling together information. Essentially commonly used reports and screens from enterprise applications are brought together in a single screen. This is done via several processes:

- ✔ The SAP EP iViews framework provides a complete library of *portlets* (portions of Web pages) that collect and display data arriving from SAP applications. A built-in *eventing* system allows iViews to interact and update one another based on user input.

- ✔ SAP EP becomes the standard user interface for the new generation of all mySAP Business Suite solutions.

  The Web Dynpro framework for developing these interfaces will be included in the next version of the SAP® Web Application Server (SAP Web AS), further reducing the cost of the rapid development of portals.

- ✔ An ad hoc workflow function that allows definition of the steps in a task on the fly enables users to define workflows through simple step-by-step interfaces without all your employees having to get a degree in programming. A universal work-list function acts as a kind of inbox for tasks and individual steps outlined in these workflows.

Adding tons of information, and collaboration to boot

As your young portal grows in size and scope, it does its own version of outgrowing its diapers. To meet its growing needs, you can add to its capability with search features that make it easy to find data and take actions, collaboration tools such as instant messaging, and publishing capabilities. These capabilities are embedded in several different SAP products.

- ✔ Content management and knowledge-management features of the SAP EP pull raw data into repositories and then create categories (called *taxonomies*) for that data. At the same time, SAP® Business Intelligence (SAP BI) performs a similar task for structured sources of information such as data about customers, sales, or other transactions. After you integrate SAP EP and SAP BI, they enable portals to index, search, and navigate through dispersed pools of data, adding the crucial ability to share documents.

✔ SAP EP also includes built-in secure collaboration tools, including instant messaging and virtual workspaces, and provides document publishing and tracking capabilities.

✔ The Business Workflow process control framework of SAP Web AS can describe and automate all of the steps in a complex process with lots of moving parts using a model-driven approach. This means that complex processes are defined by dragging and dropping instead of laborious programming.

Delivering intelligence to the desktop

Your portal baby is now crawling all over the place and it's about time for it to start walking . . . in this case, right to the users' desktops.

When portal users are actively sharing data and accessing applications through a single interface — which guarantees the integrity of the data they're using — the next step is to make that data accessible to any and all enterprise applications inside the organization.

SAP BI is the answer. Not only is SAP BI a standard data warehouse, it is also pre-integrated with SAP EP. This allows many of its standard reports and displays to be saved as iViews for rapid integration with portals. When you have these reports and displays in place, you've gone a long way to making data accessible throughout your enterprise.

Reaching out to the extended enterprise

Now that you have nurtured your internal portal and helped it become big and strong, it's probably asking to borrow the car and head out on its own. It's time to take the final step in portal development. This involves extending the reach of this new information-rich and collaborative environment by bringing in yet more information from as many sources as you like and extending the portal functionality to new groups of users.

SAP® Exchange Infrastructure (SAP XI) can describe data arriving from other SAP applications as XML messages. This is cool because that XML data can then be turned into iViews that you can include in an internal portal or use in conjunction with an array of adapters to extend application functionality into the portal.

You can get even more integration functionality based on Web services by using SAP Web AS.

Looking Forward

Unlike the guy in Franz Kafka's *The Metamorphosis* who wakes up one morning to discover he's a bug (honest, you should read this book, it's weird), when you wake up with internal portals in place, you have a much more pleasant surprise. You discover that your business world has changed for the better. That's because building even the simplest of portals leads to an immediate shift in perception about how employees actually use information and applications.

Being a proud parent of a portal, you also come to realize that you've laid the groundwork for future components and services that can be combined and recombined inside a single interface in ways that reflect how IT is actually used inside organizations. (What a concept!) If you create these services with an eye toward manageability and reuse, they provide a dramatic increase in the flexibility of your company's IT infrastructure.

With portals built on SAP NetWeaver, you can rework interfaces to extend the life span of your legacy applications and invent new services by invisibly combining existing applications. Forward-looking companies (like yours) create a set of components and services that can easily be recombined in weird and wonderful ways to meet your future needs.

This kind of flexibility is the goal of Enterprise Services Architecture, a set of principles, values, and guidelines identified by SAP. Enterprise Services Architecture provides a practical road map for step-by-step progress toward a service-oriented architecture. Based on a comprehensive view of your enterprise, this road map allows you to do two really important things: You can use this flexibility to build a rapid cycle of innovation and business process evolution and you can react quickly to change without spending a fortune.

In fact, the people at SAP must be really smart because all portions of SAP NetWeaver are designed to resolve compatibility and integration issues. This means that your business can move gradually toward the level of Enterprise Services Architecture that you need to transport your business efficiency to a whole new dimension.

Chapter 19

Deploying Web Services

*W*eb services are a universal three-pronged plug for connecting applications. They provide a way to piece together a variety of features from different applications on various platforms and make them useable by anybody in weird and wonderful ways.

As we make clear in Chapter 5, Web services have a profound effect on the world of IT. They seem to show up everywhere, at every level of every application. They can connect one application to another, hook up an application to a portal, or let a cell phone or other mobile device access an application online. Web services have the potential to make any application into a server with its own functionality.

Thankfully, years of hype have given way to actual progress in this field. This chapter reviews the forces driving companies to deploy Web services and shows how SAP NetWeaver, guided by the principles of SAP Enterprise Services Architecture, can bring Web services to life.

Wanted: Flexible Business Systems

Every enterprise today needs business processes that are nice and malleable. If you can rework a process rapidly and extend it — internally and externally — in response to market changes, you've got what it takes to send your competition into a tizzy.

The bad news is that the IT systems underlying most business processes are notoriously brittle and difficult to modify. This is even more pronounced when you've got a group of systems that have been cobbled together using inflexible technology.

The good news . . .

The good news is that there is now a powerful new technology available to make malleable IT systems (and we just told you malleable is good, right?). It's Web services technology and it's revolutionary.

Web services technology encapsulates existing applications and makes selected portions of their functionality and information available to other applications. This all happens in a highly standardized and reusable way.

What does that mean to you? Stitching together software pieces in brand new ways makes use of all your existing investments in skills, software, and hardware. Web services software paves over differences between underlying architectural elements, such as operating systems, programming languages, and even hardware design. That just happens to make it the most powerful and flexible integration technology available today.

You can get more detailed information about Web service technology and how SAP is using it to advance enterprise technology back in Chapter 5.

Okay, but what can I do with it?

With Web services software, you can — with relative ease — integrate virtually every kind of legacy system, mainframe application, client/server application, and Web-based system. From them you can create new applications that sit on top of existing systems. These new species of composite applications can support vital business processes currently in place and enable those processes to evolve.

Essentially, Web services software *decouples* the IT function from the business process, allowing you to continuously innovate in both of those arenas without major disruption.

Although business processes may be your most pressing need, you probably need even more functionality from your IT systems. After all, you have to meet mounting competitive pressures and more sophisticated customer expectations. Web services software, implemented in stages and based on a broad view of your company and its needs, helps you achieve your business goals more effectively and efficiently.

Business User Wish List

You can look at Web services as an ideal way to find solutions to several vexing problems. The solution most in demand? A common user interface.

You ought to be in pictures . . .

Business users want existing applications presented to them on the desktop on a platter: a platter that has one look and feel. They're tired of contending with systems in which each application provides its own peculiar user interface, perhaps Web enabled, perhaps not. A common user interface, available across a bunch of applications, reduces the need for training, saves time and aggravation, and increases productivity. Equally important, a common user interface lowers maintenance costs because IT only has to support one user interface instead of many. Lucky you: Web services technology provides a gateway to new user-interface paradigms.

More than a pretty inter-face

Users also want to be able to change the business processes under the snazzy interface as easily and rapidly as possible. This requires that IT systems supporting those processes be extensible and flexible. It also requires closing the gap between how users describe business problems and how IT managers understand them. They don't always speak the same language.

Users like business process change to be reflected immediately through a reprogramming or reorganizing of the appropriate IT stuff in the back room. In this kind of system, the user designs and describes a complete business process in familiar, business-oriented terms, then hands that description off to the computer, which translates it into executable code that uses all the existing applications to bring the business process to life. Is it IT magic? No. Web services technology enables any application to participate in business processes.

Start with what you have

When it comes to IT, leveraging what you've got is the name of the game. Rather than writing new systems from scratch or installing new packaged products, IT organizations are always looking for new ways to reuse the software and systems they've already developed and licensed. They're also looking for ways to integrate existing applications with new ones — easily and cheaply, of course.

Here's the problem, though: Although most enterprises are swimming in information, that information is usually scattered in any number of incompatible application and database pools. It's tough to view or analyze as a unified whole. Hard-coded integration techniques can help, but these techniques not only lack technical standards, but they're also *brittle* — meaning that they can be broken by just making a small change — and costly to implement. Web services open up your company's trove of existing functionality for reuse.

Reaching out to customers

The last piece of the Web services puzzle is the ability to reach new customers with as much speed, as little friction, and as much transparency as possible. Amazon.com is a good example of this kind of reach. It can sign up thousands of Web sites, many of them quite unsophisticated technically, to sell its books. In fact, Amazon.com even lets customers use its Web site to resell books to other customers, provided these books are purchased at Amazon.com. These business-model extensions work largely because Amazon.com requires virtually no work on the part of its many partners. Web services can codify, model, and automate the terms of a business relationship.

So, lots of companies today are opting to outsource things as a way to cut costs and improve efficiencies. But it's becoming clearer every day that outsourcing is not a panacea if it results in you losing control over a critical portion of a business process. Whether you want to outsource services to maximize a business process or sell your company's wares to a business partner, success depends on your ability to integrate a bunch of IT systems — those within your enterprise and those operated by outside partners. Web services provide a way for you to quickly create flexible integrations that you can maintain cheaply.

What'll We Do about IT?

Poor IT. Not only does it have lots of challenges, but it's chasing a moving target every day trying to keep pace with the frantic evolution of technology. Web services can address the IT types' very pressing needs and technical goals, which include

- ✔ Supporting service-oriented architecture and applications.
- ✔ Presenting non-Web–enabled applications on the Web.
- ✔ Maintaining applications. (This is a perennial concern for IT and threatens to become a bigger challenge as IT systems become more complex and begin harnessing the functions of more applications).
- ✔ Extending existing applications and building new ones on top of them.
- ✔ Dealing with the costs involved in developing skills and professional expertise.

Here's what Web services bring to the table to help with these problems:

- ✔ Integrated development tools used to compose Web services store their definitions in repositories so you can share across project teams and maintain them over time.

- ✔ SAP® Enterprise Portal (SAP EP) technology constructs a common user interface for use across multiple, otherwise incompatible, applications and presents non-Web–enabled applications online.

- ✔ Web services, by holding applications and presenting them in the form of well-defined, well-behaving services, promises to keep maintenance costs in check.

- ✔ Many applications haven't been designed with extendibility in mind; they don't provide the right elements needed to create a strong platform for building new applications. Web services expose software functionality in a way that makes the functionality reusable.

- ✔ The introduction of new system architectures has, in many cases, substantially driven up the costs of IT skill development and training. For example, when companies moved from mainframes to client/server computing, an IT employee's assembly programming skills didn't transfer well to the new object-oriented paradigm. Web services, however, makes good use of well-honed Java programming skills and related skills for system analysis and program design.

Indeed, Web services are based on and work hand in hand with a variety of open technologies and standards, including Java and XML. IT organizations find these standards really useful for lowering development costs and improving system interoperability.

As you try to get more flexibility in your business processes, your IT organization has to come up with ways to integrate applications in a more loosely coupled way. This means making available not only information, but also related functionality from applications. And this is precisely what Web services are designed to do — integrate applications at a more abstract level that keeps data and function in the context of each other.

SAP Gets Its Arms around Web Services

SAP was one of the first technology providers to embrace Web services technology, and it seems the company is determined to help customers use that technology in the most effective way possible. That's where SAP NetWeaver comes in. It helps you employ Web services in support of SAP Enterprise Services Architecture.

Enterprise Services Architecture

Used on their own, Web services are handy but fairly low-level software development tools. Used as part of the Enterprise Services Architecture, Web services let you build adaptive business solutions and provide lower total cost of ownership.

Enterprise Services Architecture supports something called *process-centric* computing. Consider an example: An order-management system must provide a mechanism or service for you to delete an order. When called into action, this "delete order" service simply purges an order object from the system by erasing the appropriate records in a database. This sort of service, which acts in the context of one application, is called an *application service.*

An *enterprise service* is a broader concept. Canceling an order typically involves much more than that one action. Instead, a "cancel order" enterprise service triggers a whole sequence of actions that may involve any number of IT systems, as well as input from several pre-designated individuals. You may need to take the order out of production, run back the supply-chain plan, send notifications to the customer, suppliers, and logistics providers, and so on. At some point the "delete order" application service will be invoked in the order-management system as well.

A fair amount of high-level orchestration is required to make sure each of these tasks gets done with proper attention to security and in a way that avoids failures in individual processors, applications, or data networks.

Hey. Wouldn't it be great if this entire set of actions was described just once and then made available for reuse in any number of business processes in the form of an enterprise service? Ah ha! That's exactly what SAP Enterprise Services Architecture makes possible.

In this example, at a business level the architecture defines just what actions an enterprise service named "cancel order" has to accomplish. SAP NetWeaver then maps those actions to the appropriate set of Web services available from specific applications. Those applications could include the company's own systems, as well as those operated by its suppliers, out-source services providers, customers, and other business partners.

This higher-level service, which is aware of the broader processes and inter-application context, is called an *enterprise service.* SAP Enterprise Services Architecture enables IT and business managers to work together designing and constructing business processes by essentially selecting and organizing pre-defined enterprise services.

One more thing: SAP Enterprise Services Architecture serves as a blueprint that allows you to decouple business processes from low-level business objects and applications, each of which is encapsulated as a standards-based Web service. By using this architectural blueprint, managers can determine the speed at which the enterprise creates and adopts innovations in process and technology. SAP Enterprise Services Architecture can also simplify out-sourcing and help extend your company's value chain to include new business partners and to reach new customers.

Three key ingredients

SAP Enterprise Services Architecture isn't rocket science, but it is a sophisticated idea that a lot of smart people took a long time to develop. If you want to keep things simple, just keep in mind that SAP Enterprise Services Architecture is made up of three main ingredients:

- ✔ **IT systems.** Each makes its functionality available as a set of Web services for use by other applications.

- ✔ **An integration platform.** With this you can create a homogeneous and harmonious view of what is usually a mish-mash of heterogeneous, incompatible applications, databases, and previously built integration linkages.

- ✔ **New composite applications.** Through the precise orchestration of new and existing Web services, these applications emerge from underlying systems and deliver just the right functionality to support current and future business processes.

SAP NetWeaver is the integration platform that puts Web services to work in support of Enterprise Services Architecture, and it does it in such a way that all important elements of IT and business are unified — people, information, and business processes.

SAP NetWeaver: Time for a change

By now you've figured out that SAP NetWeaver provides an open and extensible platform for the development, deployment, and management of Web services. (That's why this chapter is in THIS book.) It's based on open technologies and standards, is fully interoperable with Microsoft .NET and IBM WebSphere, and is tightly integrated with mySAP™ Business Suite solutions, which makes it an ideal tool for Web services.

Figure 19-1 gives you an overview of the SAP NetWeaver capabilities related to Web services.

Here's a rundown of these capabilities:

- ✔ A portal can consume Web services by creating role-based interfaces that bring together the functionality of many applications.

- ✔ Composite applications are Web services that can be constructed on top of the application platform creating an intermediate layer that allows Java code to communicate with existing applications and then present the functionality as a Web service.

✔ Messaging, integration broker, and business process management (BPM) features enable the portal to use Web services as part of a role-based user interface.

✔ BPM capabilities that orchestrate the Web services from third parties that are available in many different parts of SAP NetWeaver, such as the Remote Function Calls (RFCs) and Business Application Programming Interfaces (BAPI®s) in mySAP Business Suite solutions.

✔ Powerful development tools that fully support the J2EE standard while allowing ABAP developers to continue using the familiar ABAP Workbench to create Web services.

✔ An SAP Composite Application Framework (SAP CAF) that uses a model-driven approach to create larger applications built on Web services components. This approach simplifies the work of developers who use multiple applications or legacy systems with SAP NetWeaver.

✔ SAP NetWeaver Developer Studio, which provides a development environment for Web services using proven ABAP technology and J2EE's innovative open standards.

✔ Life cycle management capabilities for overall control.

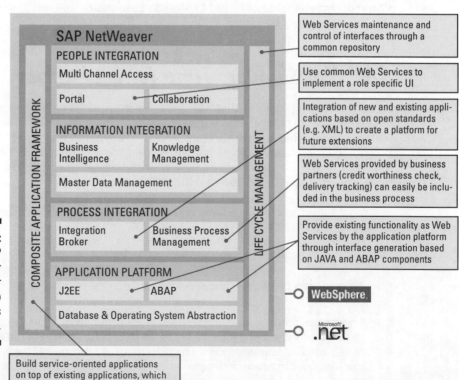

Figure 19-1:
SAP NetWeaver support for Web services deployment.

A staged approach via Web services

Every journey may begin with a single step, but with so much capability on hand and so many issues that need addressing, it's hard to know where to start with Web services. Instead of forcing you to deal with an all-or-nothing proposition, SAP encourages and enables a four-stage approach that minimizes disruption while maximizing your cost savings.

✔ Implement a role-specific user interface.

✔ Provide R/3 functionality.

✔ Create a platform for the future.

✔ Roll out your Web services to partners.

Figure 19-2 outlines how to get your feet wet in Web services.

Next, take a good look at each of these steps.

Step 1: Getting the user interface right

Start slowly. The first low-risk step forward is to use Web services as part of an internal portal implementation that connects the employees of a department in a context everybody already understands. This involves using the SAP® Enterprise Portal component of SAP NetWeaver. The portal provides the framework for building new user interfaces. Its iViews and ad hoc workflow functionality incorporate and orchestrate many different Web services and processes.

Step 2: Using R/3 functionality for a Web service

Now for a gutsier move. Add to the functionality of portals and other applications by unlocking useful functionality from R/3 through Web services. To do this, use the SAP® Web Application Server (SAP Web AS) component of SAP NetWeaver. This allows both Java and ABAP programmers to create Web services. This, in turn, allows your IT organization to take full advantage of existing skills and capabilities.

SAP NetWeaver allows all R/3 and mySAP Business Suite solutions' RFCs and BAPIs to be automatically accessed as Web services. This gives developers a vast amount of functionality to help them enhance portal offerings or build enterprise services.

Step 3: Creating a platform for future extensions

The next step extends your reach as you build and control applications using the integration broker and BPM capabilities of SAP NetWeaver. During this process, you knit together mySAP Business Suite solutions and third-party applications to either form new applications or a collection of reusable Web services.

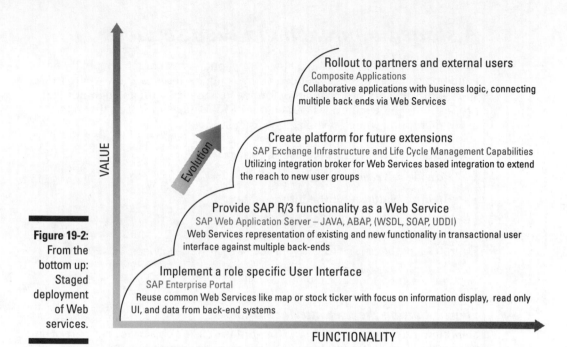

Figure 19-2:
From the bottom up: Staged deployment of Web services.

(Chart — vertical axis: VALUE; horizontal axis: FUNCTIONALITY; arrow labeled "Evolution")

Rollout to partners and external users
Composite Applications
Collaborative applications with business logic, connecting multiple back ends via Web Services

Create platform for future extensions
SAP Exchange Infrastructure and Life Cycle Management Capabilities
Utilizing integration broker for Web Services based integration to extend the reach to new user groups

Provide SAP R/3 functionality as a Web Service
SAP Web Application Server – JAVA, ABAP, (WSDL, SOAP, UDDI)
Web Services representation of existing and new functionality in transactional user interface against multiple back-ends

Implement a role specific User Interface
SAP Enterprise Portal
Reuse common Web Services like map or stock ticker with focus on information display, read only UI, and data from back-end systems

Here's how this process works: Applications move data and functionality through a central hub provided by SAP® Exchange Infrastructure (SAP XI). The hub uses and creates Web services. Next, the integration repository defines and generates Web services interfaces.

SAP NetWeaver life cycle management functions control the rollout and updates to a suite of Web services.

Step 4: Rolling out services to partners and external users

Step four may be the trickiest, but it has the biggest payoff. Here's where you create full-blown applications and use Web services to automate both internal and external processes.

Use the SAP CAF, a model-driven development environment, to create composite applications. These applications are based on different kinds of services — not just from SAP NetWeaver and mySAP Business Suite, but from the tools and applications of any number of vendors. The flexibility of this model-driven approach lets you optimize newly customized composite applications, without expensive redevelopment and testing.

Chapter 20

SAP R/3 and Then Some

● ●

In This Chapter

▶ Meeting the growing demand for flexible solutions by extending SAP® R/3®

▶ Solving the integration challenge through SAP NetWeaver™

▶ Mapping a solution through incremental implementation

▶ Preparing an architecture for the future

● ●

If SAP NetWeaver were a school teacher trying to make a point, it would write on the blackboard in huge letters: *Make the most of existing investments in enterprise applications.*

Given that enterprise resource planning (ERP) is the mother of all enterprise applications, the drive to innovate frequently means reusing some part of SAP R/3, and this definitely makes the most of your precious investments. This chapter shows you why companies find it beneficial to extend R/3 and shows you how SAP NetWeaver can make it happen for you.

The Flexible, Extensible Rag

You've heard it before: Today's rapidly changing marketplace demands technology that adapts and expands as new market forces shape new business needs. Business Economics 101, right? But how do you get that kind of competitive edge?

Well, some companies run around trying to find flexible, extensible solutions that go out and get information and applications from all around the organization and even beyond the corporate walls. Meanwhile, their users are demanding increasingly complex and sophisticated systems that take a broad array of people, information, and processes and make them work together like a well-tuned engine every step of the way. IT departments are asked to somehow get older systems to give 110 percent on their last wing and a prayer, while they simultaneously burn the midnight oil creating the next generation of technology — a technology designed to confront tomorrow's unforeseeable challenges and address business needs that aren't even yet a glimmer in any CEO's eye.

Now, you'd be surprised how many of these challenges can be resolved by delivering old-fashioned SAP R/3 to new audiences. When you extend the R/3 capabilities, you can add new functionality or create custom applications that integrate R/3 modules with multiple vendor systems. Of course, this often requires custom-designed functionality, enhancements, modifications, or applications that leverage all your organization's current IT resources into the future.

So given all this, how does your business position itself for the future? By using SAP NetWeaver to extend R/3 to the Web and then gradually implementing completely custom-designed composite applications. (See Chapter 23 for more about composite applications.) That's what this chapter is all about.

The Integration Two-Step

IT departments are hotbeds of pressure: pressure to reduce costs, increase the value of current investments, and develop new applications that address moving target business needs and a here-today, gone-tomorrow parade of technology standards. Particularly on enterprise-level systems, this means taking advantage of your initial investment by extending the functionality of your platform to as many points as possible.

Business users from Timbuktu to Toledo demand multichannel access to key systems, as well as the ability to use these systems via browser-based interfaces on desktops at work, handhelds on a plane, and cell phones. You have to manipulate, exchange, and store data in lots of locations using lots of mixed systems — both inside your company's borders and in the great world beyond.

Making the choice

Why do IT departments opt to extend their company's SAP R/3 functionality and develop custom applications? In many cases, they are responding to their company's decisions to

✔ Increase returns on its IT investments by moving its R/3 modules to the Web.

✔ Use Web technology to extend SAP R/3 by combining R/3 functionality with technology from another vendor's application or other installations of SAP R/3.

✔ Migrate to SAP R/3, which requires leveraging existing user training and comfort levels by duplicating the look and feel of a legacy application while relying on R/3 as back-end support.

✔ Require new functionality that relies on existing SAP R/3 data or modules but meets some specific need that is unique to the company or industry.

✔ Deliver rapidly on an innovation unique to their company or industry, or deliver an innovation not yet available from vendors.

✔ Develop a custom product to enhance a relationship with a business partner.

✔ Rapidly assemble information from SAP R/3 and different custom data sources for decision support.

Wait a minute, it's not that easy . . .

To meet these needs, your IT team has to overcome a whole variety of challenges — particularly if your company has a large investment in multiple technologies.

For example, different departments and company locations often have a variety of data, management, and application environments (including different databases, support systems, and middleware). Your IT team must be prepared to support diverse technologies throughout their life cycle. Over time, the team has to move business units along from one technology to another, transferring them seamlessly to modular-, client/server-, or Web-based systems. Hopefully, this change happens without expensive additional training. Duplicate systems have to be ditched and redundant legacy applications shown the door. And IT has to do all this while integrating the data that lives in functional silos into central, standardized systems.

Within your IT department itself, all the resources of SAP R/3 have to be deployed without extensive training in new programming languages. That sounds fine, until you consider that only a single, standards-based development environment can support a variety of programming languages (ABAP and Java, for example) and allow developers to use their existing skills to manage the overall application development process.

Across your enterprise, there's potential for a project management nightmare. Communication, team, source, and life-cycle support are vital in projects involving a large number of developers or a programming staff spread out over several continents. On the most minimal level, simply to prevent developers from overwriting each other's code willy-nilly, there's a need for check in/check out, version control, and transport for sources and configurations. And controlling the process from development through testing to deployment is not enough. Companies also have to anticipate and control the entire life cycle of an application *beyond* deployment. Updates or enhancements you deploy down the road also must take into account the variations among individuals or departments.

Want a handy checklist of things to worry about? Here are just some of the issues facing those charged with developing R/3 extensions or custom applications:

- ✔ Assemble, manipulate, exchange, and cache data from multiple sources in a custom application while retaining data integrity.

- ✔ Return data altered by a custom application to its original primary application or data source.

- ✔ Translate incompatible data formats into one format.

- ✔ Create reusable services from existing enterprise applications.

- ✔ Use prebuilt components or services for content management, search capabilities, and so on.

- ✔ Rapidly create and improve user interfaces.

- ✔ Support role-based access to information.

- ✔ Create configurable processes that run the hodge-podge of all modules and services.

- ✔ Integrate with systems for application security, single sign-on, and operational monitoring.

- ✔ Implement best practices for software life cycle management and maintenance.

The Envelope, Please: It's SAP NetWeaver (You Peeked!)

SAP NetWeaver pulls together all the elements you need for continuous development into one neat package any IT team would love. Because SAP NetWeaver supports programming languages such as Java and ABAP in a single, standards-based development environment, your IT teams can work with their existing skill sets, tools, and codes using this single integrated platform for managing your company's software life cycle. This miracle product even enables you to deploy browser-based user interfaces that extend your current technology to the Web. And, if developing composite systems using pre-existing code, services, and new applications is your fondest wish, you can do that, too.

In short, this is one solution that allows you to deploy all the resources of SAP R/3 alone or in combination with your older systems — without sending the IT kids back to programming school.

One other perk: Because SAP NetWeaver is based on open technologies and standards, it's fully interoperable with Microsoft .NET and IBM WebSphere.

Each piece plays a role

As you know by now, SAP NetWeaver is a collection of cool components, all used in this complex enterprise solution. Here's how each plays a part in extending R/3.

SAP® Web Application Server (SAP Web AS) ensures that new applications will work hand in hand as extensions to your existing SAP solutions. All the components of SAP NetWeaver are tightly integrated and are built to work with R/3 and with each other.

Java developers will be happy to learn that they can use powerful tools that fully support the J2EE standard, while ABAP developers will turn handsprings because they can continue to use the familiar ABAP Workbench. You can control overall development through SAP NetWeaver's life cycle management tools. And don't forget developers using multiple applications or legacy systems in conjunction with the SAP NetWeaver solution: They will have all the resources of the SAP Composite Application Framework (SAP CAF) at their disposal.

The SAP NetWeaver Developer Studio, which is based on the Eclipse open-source development environment framework, offers all the standard equipment expected of an integrated development environment (IDE) including editors, debuggers, and life cycle management tools. Integrated with Developer Studio is Web Dynpro, the SAP framework for building adaptable user interfaces. This provides both a graphical modeling environment and a runtime environment.

As the foundation of the entire SAP Enterprise Services Architecture, SAP NetWeaver Developer Studio provides a development environment for Web services that uses proven ABAP technology and the innovative open standards of J2EE.

The most important capabilities for SAP R/3 integration are shown in Figure 20-1.

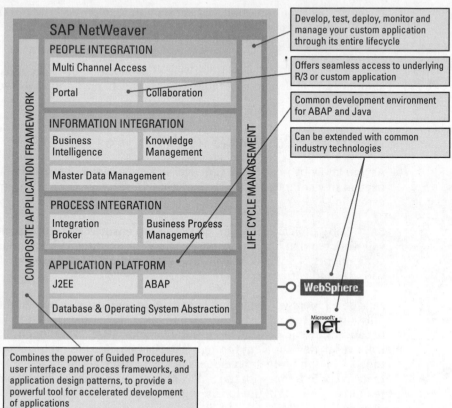

Figure 20-1:
SAP
NetWeaver
support for
extending
R/3.

Hitting the highlights

Highlights of the SAP NetWeaver solution include the following:

- ✔ **A portal** that enables creation of Web-based interfaces, bringing to new audiences R/3 functionality adapted to the needs of particular processes and roles

- ✔ **An application platform** that enables developers to access RFCs and BAPIs and create and orchestrate new Web services to meet the needs of new functionality or integration with other applications

- ✔ **Support for both J2EE and ABAP development**, which allows existing skills to be applied to extended R/3, reducing the need for retraining and expanding the pool of developers

✔ The **SAP CAF,** which allows services from R/3 and other applications to be created quickly and assembled through model-driven development into applications that are quickly developed and easy to change

✔ **Life cycle management features** that handle the details of managing complex development projects across large teams in distributed locations — features that include source-code management, staging, customizations, and upgrades

The key advantage of SAP NetWeaver is that it is already integrated with SAP R/3. This integration ensures that each enterprise application comes with a significant number of components and services ready to participate in integrations and in the creation of new applications to extend R/3.

Software Integration: It's a Staged Process

Didn't your mother tell you never to rush things? (Okay, she was probably talking about chewing your food more slowly when you were rushing to get outside and play.) But implementing SAP R/3 extensions and custom applications works best if you take it in three easy-to-digest bites. This means your folks can build skills at low cost before moving on to more complex customization challenges.

The implementation path follows these general guidelines. (See Figure 20-2.)

1. You create portal-based user interfaces to demonstrate the power of extending underlying R/3 applications to a broader audience via cool Web technology.

2. You create an application that combines data from multiple sources and allows the user to interact with it in a coherent and friendly way. (Always be friendly to your data.) To meet new needs as they come up, the SAP Web AS allows existing R/3 functionality to be recombined into new forms that you access through J2EE or ABAP components and Web services.

3. You deploy full-fledged composite applications using role-based user interfaces, SAP NetWeaver integration tools, multiple components from mySAP™ Business Suite, legacy applications, and applications from other vendors. This step extends R/3 to support and optimize new business processes.

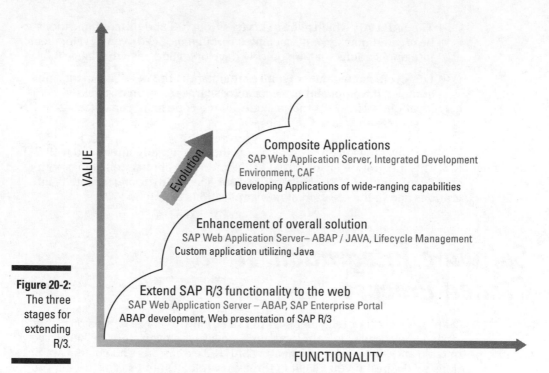

Figure 20-2:
The three
stages for
extending
R/3.

Step 1: Turning on R/3 functionality

Ladies and gentlemen, start your engines: The first step for extending R/3 is
to use the always-handy SAP® Enterprise Portal (SAP EP) to provide new,
easy-to-customize interfaces for specific purposes. The portal provides the
framework on which you can build these interfaces with iViews, and an ad
hoc workflow engine that allows users to quickly and easily define a set of
steps on the fly to organize the work of a team and orchestrate different services and processes.

SAP Web AS, a powerful runtime system, hosts components based on ABAP
or J2EE technology. This allows the portal to easily access and knit together
RFCs and BAPIs using the most convenient technology at hand.

Step 2: Moving toward the overall solution

Ready, set . . . the next step is to create applications that add extended and
customized functionality to SAP R/3. You do that by using

✔ **SAP EP** to provide the framework for creating a new user interface that includes the extended functionality.

✔ **SAP Web AS** to construct new Web services based on ABAP or J2EE — services that supplement R/3 functionality with new custom components and allow the portal access to the widest possible variety of functionality and information. This also brings the largest amount of developers into the loop.

✔ **Life cycle management features** to keep the maintenance of these new components and solutions under control so that you can coordinate the work of large development teams and manage versions and upgrades.

Step 3: Building on a framework

Go! The most advanced step is to use the composite application framework and services from SAP R/3 to create entire new applications that build on everything that's gone before.

The SAP CAF brings in a whole bunch of different kinds of services from SAP NetWeaver and mySAP Business Suite, along with tools and applications from other vendors, into a model-driven development environment. What does that do for you? It allows the core R/3 functionality to inform and help automate many different applications, which lets you make good use of all the information and knowledge about R/3 that you've acquired. The model-driven nature of the framework allows you to optimize the composite application without expensive redevelopment and testing.

SAP® Exchange Infrastructure (SAP XI) uses its integration broker functionality to reach out through XML messages to other applications, regardless of which vendor you got them from, and bring their data and functionality into an application right alongside those from R/3.

Extending SAP R/3 creates services that allow you to reuse data and functionality between applications. If you do it right, you'll cross the finish line and see a dramatic increase in the flexibility of your company's IT infrastructure.

Where Is SAP NetWeaver Taking R/3?

As your company determines which parts of its architecture need to respond rapidly to business conditions (well, that would be just about everything these days), you can use SAP NetWeaver to construct more components and services for those areas. *Rapid response* is a business strategy you implement using custom applications and component-based integration. These are developed by assembling existing components and services and using the frameworks for development, user interface, process control, security, and administration provided by SAP NetWeaver.

Forward-looking companies are already busy creating an IT strategy that can easily be recombined to meet future needs. This is the goal of Enterprise Services Architecture.

In Enterprise Services Architecture, applications such as SAP R/3 provide what are known as *application services.* These application services can be combined to form enterprise services, which are built to understand and handle the complexity required for automating the core processes of a business. Although an application service performs an important function in transforming the state of an application — for example, deleting the records that hold a sales order — the enterprise service understands the entire process and deletes the sales order from all systems, both upstream and downstream.

Chapter 21

Making Sense of Data: Analytics and Reporting

This is the Information Age. Information is the Holy Grail for today's businesses, and with good reason. Knowing exactly how well your organization is running and making the right moves to succeed based on that information requires plenty of business intelligence.

Not only do you need a steady flow of information from every layer of your enterprise, but you also have to sort and analyze fresh data before it rots somewhere in the bowels of your operation.

Now, this would be a tall order even if data arrived speaking a single language, using a shared format, and coming from one place. But real life is seldom that neat: Your company probably runs on top of a thicket of separate applications that work with data arriving from inside and outside the company, that resides in databases, and in transactions occurring every second, accessed through assorted (and often inconsistent) interfaces.

As you rethink your business processes and begin integrating those applications, implementing an analytics and reporting solution guarantees that you can make smart decisions based on a truly complete set of business data, data tailored to the needs and position of everyone in the enterprise. Then this data has to be delivered at the right time, in the right format, arriving at a desktop or PDA, and the data has to be viewed by the right person, whether that's the CEO or a valued customer.

In this chapter we explore how SAP NetWeaver, in conjunction with other SAP components or alone, begins to lay the groundwork that enables your organization to make sense of the data it generates, lowers your total cost of ownership, and saves time.

Business Drivers

Imagine that a NASCAR team has been granted an unlimited budget by its owner. After the top-flight pit crew has been assembled and after a car equipped with top-shelf components has been built, winning races still depend on the car and driver's symbiotic, well-tuned performance. That performance will be reviewed, adjusted, and refined based on expected and completely unanticipated mid-race changes.

Today's enterprise has no clearly defined pit stops at which to take stock of the business, but the principle is the same — after spending billions of dollars to generate, aggregate, and distribute information, corporations don't spend nearly enough time or money analyzing that information and reporting the results to those within the organization who need it — from the CEO's digital dashboard (the user interface on his laptop), to the desktops of the analysts in the CFO's department, to customer service reps using analytic applications to guide day-to-day interactions with customers.

What would an analytics and reporting solution look like?

An analytics and reporting solution has to retrieve data from any and every aspect of the enterprise to answer questions such as

- How is the company performing today?
- How well did it perform yesterday?
- What should the employees, partners, suppliers, and managers do differently?

Performance, of course, is based on the objectives of your organization — but most organizations need to answer questions about profitability, gross sales, customer retention, and other key performance indicators (KPIs).

To get at your information, you have to store it properly. So any analytics and reporting solution has to start with a flexible data warehousing foundation. Having already invested millions of dollars over many decades in legacy applications or contemporary Enterprise Resource Planning (ERP) software that was often never intended to communicate one with the other, corporations need a layer of data warehouses that can pull data from everywhere, whether that's a legacy HR implementation running in Des Moines or relevant data outside a corporation's immediate control — a supplier's inventory system, for example.

A data warehouse has to be flexible enough to read and sort data arriving from a near-infinite range of heterogeneous sources and formats. Then it has to be scalable enough to gather that data and prepare it for business analysis and reporting by tracking and monitoring based on parameters of the reports. Beyond asking how many widgets the company sold today, can the software extend itself to handle more in-depth or entirely different sorts of queries?

Any data warehouse worth its salt has to do so without unduly burdening your company's transactional system. Thousands of users performing queries tend to slow down systems to a snail's pace and lead to delays.

To provide access to important data and take a huge burden off transactional systems, that important data has to be extracted. The data warehouse should be able to aggregate information that shows the state of your business over time and then shuttle that data into a separate environment for reporting and analysis. This reduces the strain on the software and provides an environment that promotes a much better understanding of what the heck is going on.

Using what you get

But implementation is just the first step. When an analytics and reporting solution is up and running, the next goal looms ahead — ensuring that an organization's workflow and IT infrastructure are geared to make maximum use of all this great information. Another key is finding ways to distribute information to the right spot and in a secure form, where it can have an impact, whether it is a report, e-mail, or wireless alert.

While traditionally buried deep in the heart of the CFO's office, today analytic applications, or at least slices of their functionality, are making their way to the desktop of almost everyone inside the enterprise. Customer service reps have access to analytic features that help them actually service customers, for example.

The data that lies underneath those neat reports and analyses that are now zipping around your company have to be flexible enough for global delivery through a desktop application, as an element in a Web-based internal portal, or on a Wi-Fi-equipped PDA. Connecting reports to collaborative tools allows users to not only study results in their ivory towers, but actually act on them, whether that's planning for the future or solving problems through e-mail or instant messages.

At each step, as information and insights travel further and further away from their snug little data warehouses, and as more sources are connected to those warehouses, guaranteeing data integrity becomes incredibly critical. With certain kinds of data, this integrity isn't optional: The United States and

European Union regulatory acts, Sarbanes-Oxley and Basel II, respectively, put an onus on corporations to maintain the strictest standards in the generation and processing of financial data, for example.

Analytics and reporting solutions have to be just as adept in their handling of metadata — tracking how a number was derived, where it was derived from, and determining (before the CFO signs off) whether data integrity was maintained — because documenting that integrity may have greater long-term ramifications than the data itself.

SAP NetWeaver-based Solution

Being in the solution business, in SAP NetWeaver, SAP has provided a comprehensive solution. This consists of a general platform for application development that packs in all the elements that meet challenges for extending the analytics and reporting capabilities of an underlying SAP® Business Intelligence data warehouse. This solution is illustrated in Figure 21-1.

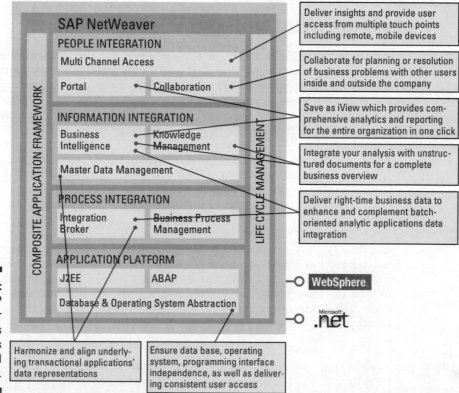

Figure 21-1: How SAP NetWeaver supports analytics and reporting.

Running down the features

At the risk of having you grow tired of hearing how many features SAP NetWeaver has (yes, there's a lot packed into this little beauty) here's a rundown of its features for analytics and reporting:

- ✔ An integrated development environment (IDE) to create components and services that are the building blocks of an internal portal.

- ✔ Master data management that provides a system for harmonizing and unifying master data stored in many different enterprise applications. (*Master data* is data about your business, such as customer and product data that spans many transactional events.)

- ✔ An automatic process that keeps replicated data in synch.

- ✔ Adapters and integration brokers that translate one format to another.

- ✔ Messaging technology to move data between applications, both inside and outside of the enterprise.

- ✔ A portal framework for integrating analytic applications into employees' customized and familiar interfaces right on their desktops.

- ✔ Collaborative tools, such as virtual workspaces, discussion forums, real-time chat, and secure messaging to connect users anywhere in the enterprise.

- ✔ A mobile device distribution framework to make information in reports available to wireless devices for people who live on the road.

Wow! How does it do all this stuff?

Given its background as a creator of world-class enterprise applications, SAP has been working on many of these problems — and data warehouses in particular — since you were just an enterprise youngster. SAP NetWeaver is the result of this evolution.

The SAP® Web Application Server (SAP Web AS) for example, delivers an underlying infrastructure that provides an RDBMS- and OS-independent platform for the SAP Business Intelligence (SAP BI) applications running atop it. These acronyms may be Greek to you, but they just mean that you can run SAP BI on almost any database or operating system in the market. SAP Web AS also ensures that you can tailor a user's access and interface as you like, while remaining consistent across all transactional, analytic, and reporting solutions.

SAP NetWeaver also extends SAP BI's capabilities with prepackaged components for data management, portal development, collaboration, and application integration. This last is key for delivering the freshest possible data for *right-time* analytic processing and reports that actually mean something in context and deliver information when it can make a difference.

The SAP® Enterprise Portal (SAP EP) unifies all the different information, applications, and services from multiple systems into a single, personalized, Web-based interface. This happens alongside any other ERP solution, third-party data and applications, and commonly used tools such as instant messaging and e-mail. You can easily add an analytics and reporting solution to the mix without disrupting either underlying applications or the Holy Grail of the great user experience.

SAP® Exchange Infrastructure (SAP XI) stores definitions of XML data formats and Web services in its integration repository so they can be easily used over and over again. That means that the SAP XI built into SAP NetWeaver provides an open and reusable approach based on Web services and open standards that connect to legacy systems as easily as to mySAP™ ERP modules. SAP XI can even link an organization's systems to applications running on a strategic partner's system. SAP XI automates data retrieval for sorting and analysis, speeding up reporting cycles, and pushing your enterprise toward the elusive goal of real-time reporting or at least right-time reporting — providing fresher data than you actually need to make your decisions.

Solution evolution

The previous sections in this chapter discuss some of the ways that SAP NetWeaver does its magic with analytics and reports. This section examines the steps in each stage of the evolution of an analytics and reporting solution.

Most solutions unfold in stages. At each stage in an analytics and reporting solution, the scope and functionality steadily increase as existing data sources, transactional applications, and interfaces are integrated, calling on more components as you need them. This evolution is based on your organization's needs, processes, resources, and desire to innovate, but you'll probably find that measurable savings and benefits happen at every step. And the flexibility of SAP NetWeaver means that you can add more functionality as your company's needs grow and change.

Figure 21-2 is an illustration of the stages of implementing an analytics and reporting solution, which include the following:

1. Build a data warehouse and a business intelligence foundation capable of aggregating and analyzing data, converting it into relevant business information, and guaranteeing its integrity to ensure a "single version of the truth" for knowledge workers. Then add a layer of Web services to provide a foundation for improved access.

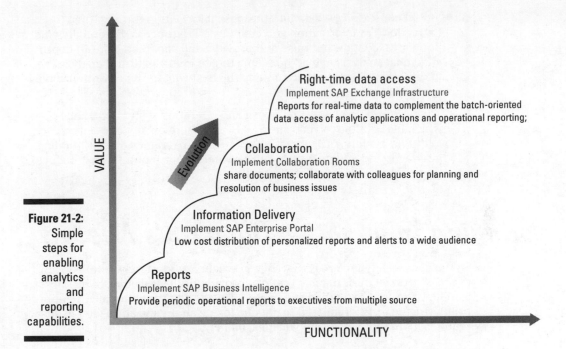

VALUE

Right-time data access
Implement SAP Exchange Infrastructure
Reports for real-time data to complement the batch-oriented
data access of analytic applications and operational reporting;

Evolution

Collaboration
Implement Collaboration Rooms
share documents; collaborate with colleagues for planning and
resolution of business issues

Information Delivery
Implement SAP Enterprise Portal
Low cost distribution of personalized reports and alerts to a wide audience

Reports
Implement SAP Business Intelligence
Provide periodic operational reports to executives from multiple source

FUNCTIONALITY

Figure 21-2:
Simple
steps for
enabling
analytics
and
reporting
capabilities.

2. Integrate customized analytic applications and reports into employees' portals and other interfaces to give them instant functionality at a level and through an interface they can easily understand.

3. Add collaborative tools to make the lessons learned by reviewing the reports immediately actionable. Document sharing enables employees to plan around results, while tools such as secure instant messaging promote problem solving through action.

4. The most comprehensive solutions automate data delivery into the analytics and reporting solution, leading to fresher data arriving on the desktop in a timely way, and therefore to more relevant reports. Ultimately, you can get a right-time view of your enterprise — one that's more detailed than your decision makers are used to seeing.

Reports

Before you can implement an analytics and reporting solution that provides not just reports full of words and numbers, but meaningful insights, an extensible data warehouse capable of collecting and sorting data from a wide range of sources has to be built. Here's how SAP NetWeaver does this:

- SAP BI converts raw data into business information through the Extraction Transformation and Loading (ETL) process. Essentially, this populates a data warehouse and provides full capabilities for in-depth statistical analysis and ad hoc reporting to investigate and analyze the information. Then it can determine the best way to run or optimize business processes.

- The SAP Web AS ensures database and operating system portability, which means that you can run SAP BI anywhere on any computers. In addition, it offers authentication abilities and a framework for building interfaces and adding future Web services. (It's a mouthful, but believe us, you'll appreciate all of this stuff.)

Bringing Information Where It's Needed

So things certainly look rosy: SAP BI can create appropriately detailed views of organizational performance that can provide brilliant flashes of business insight. Great. But extending and customizing SAP BI's functionality to appropriately deliver this great stuff to anyone inside an organization who needs it requires a few more bells and whistles, namely:

- SAP EP's ability to integrate analytics and reporting into a Web-based portal. This is an effective way to deliver business intelligence to users through a familiar interface that requires little or no additional training.

- SAP® Mobile Infrastructure (SAP MI) or the multichannel access of SAP NetWeaver. This one expands the scope of an analytics and reporting solution beyond the desktop to a wireless PDA- or WAP-enabled cell phone.

Getting Along with Others: Collaboration

After the guy in the third cubicle from the elevator runs an analytics application or receives a report, enabling him to collaborate in a secure, context-appropriate environment is the next step. Here's how SAP NetWeaver achieves this collaboration:

- SAP EP and SAP Web AS include built-in secure tools for collaboration around KPIs and metrics, including IM and virtual workspaces. They also provide document publishing and tracking capabilities.

- SAP Knowledge Management enriches the structured information of the data warehouse by establishing connections to unstructured data that SAP Knowledge Management has indexed, linked, and made searchable. This means you can generate market research data and then connect it with analysts' commentary and insights stored in documents.

Getting Your Data When You Actually Need It

The niftiest analytics and reporting solutions automate data collection for the warehouse, and then they generate analytical models and reports with the freshest possible data. This means you can spot problems shortly after they occur instead of a week later; the way you make decisions gets better and better, because it's based on good, timely data.

Here's how SAP NetWeaver speeds data collection and delivery:

✔ SAP XI provides a framework so you can pass standards-based data and metadata between heterogeneous systems. That data is eventually routed into a data warehouse. The standards can be set by a company, by an industry, or by a government, usually in XML to allow for easy translation from one format to another.

✔ SAP® Master Data Management creates a unified, central repository of data that uses SAP XI to synchronize replicated data. This is a necessary step for automated data warehouses to continually extract data from transactional applications.

✔ SAP Web AS builds Web services that allow one application to retrieve data from another.

So, What's the Future?

In the race to integrate and aggregate as many sources of data as possible and distribute that data as broadly as possible, analytics and reporting solutions lay the foundation for making sense of that data. Simply adding a data warehouse capable of knitting together so many disparate and rapidly proliferating databases is key. It paves the way for future components and services that you can combine and recombine with the data warehouse to perform more in-depth analysis.

What SAP BI can do is create a repository that is broad enough, deep enough, well-organized enough, and flexible enough to become the base on which you build a new generation of centralized services. It is services like these, which have a comprehensive view of all the data needed for a particular purpose, that can truly fulfill the promise of Enterprise Services Architecture. Such enterprise services provide companies with the flexibility to rapidly innovate and stay ahead of competitors and changing market conditions.

Chapter 22

Doing the Application-to-Application Thing

We have no doubt that someone (probably your mother) taught you that it's good to share things. Why? Because it's the right thing to do, it's the nice thing to do, and otherwise it's right off to bed with no supper.

Application-to-application integration is all about sharing data and functionality for the greater good. The reasons and the techniques are as many as politicians have promises, but A2A integration is rarely easy and most of the time if you're ready to consider such a solution, the business motivation is urgent.

This chapter takes a look at what drives companies to want to make applications talk to each other in the first place and how SAP NetWeaver helps you carry on the conversation.

Why Applications Should Get Along

Whether you're managing the supply chain, improving customer relationships, processing orders, or tracking finances, you have to rely on a variety of quite separate software applications. Typically, each application is set up to handle its own range of tasks; each has its own internal organization and definition of data; each gets tended to by its own support staff; and frequently you've purchased each from a separate supplier.

As you rethink your business processes and shoot for new levels of efficiency, you'll probably find that it's a good idea to make these applications work together as intimately as possible. That means you have to overcome technical differences and get different software brands and categories to exchange information and execute transactions as if they were two peas in one software pod. To reduce redundancy, applications also have to be able to talk to one another. To reduce costs, the system has to be able to migrate data and functionality to one application. This is no easy feat, believe us.

The practice of creating connections between parts of your IT infrastructure is called *application-to-application (A2A) integration*. A2A integration has one fundamental goal: creating a new software landscape whose total function, performance, and productivity are considerably greater than the sum of its parts. Achieving this goal can squeeze the slack from a collection of applications and, ultimately, from the business processes those applications embody. So, it's no wonder that A2A integration is now a top priority and an enduring challenge for virtually every IT department in the world.

The techniques you use to implement A2A integrations vary considerably based on the nature of the applications themselves. The integration process can be lengthy and complex. That's why IT organizations frequently choose to build their skill levels gradually, beginning with simple, read-only, A2A integrations that are easier to work with because these applications don't change each other's data. Then you can move on to more complex integrations.

Making Integrated Software a Must

Generally speaking, application integration involves providing the data or services of one application in the context of another. While processing an incoming order, for instance, application A may need to reach out to application B and request current product prices. When it receives that data, application A can use it as if it had been generated locally. Likewise, two pieces of related data, each generated by a different application, may show up next to each other on the same Web page. The information is given a common context, and the user finds it more meaningful.

Finding an integration needle in a stack

Two separate systems' *interface,* or ability to interact, could take place at any layer of the application *stack* (the different layers that make up a program). Consider the possibilities:

- ✔ **User interface integration.** This might occur in a portal, for instance, when a chunk of the user interface of one application is included in another application. Application X could leave an opening in the Web page it generates, with the expectation that application Y will supply the required data, perhaps in the form of a graphic.

- ✔ **Process integration.** Selected functions could be extracted from two or more programs and stitched together behind the scenes to create what appears to end users as a new, perhaps highly specialized application that implements a process using functions from many applications. This is very much like a composite application.

- ✔ **Application programming interface (API) integration.** To perform some discrete function or to execute a complex transaction, several applications might be set up to pass carefully defined pieces of data from one to the other in a specified sequence. The APIs of many programs may be involved, say to change the name of a customer in many different applications from one program.

- ✔ **Data integration.** Information from disparate applications can be brought together, organized, and stored for shared use in a central data warehouse.

In practice, you could use any combination of these methods to accomplish a specific task. The choices you make about where to connect different pieces of software should account for runtime performance, programming and maintenance ease, and flexibility in adapting to new business conditions.

Introducing . . . which applications?

It's a great big world of applications out there. Just search online for software and you'll be blown away by what's available. Integration projects could involve any combination of these.

Obviously, the more commonality there is between applications, the easier it is to have them exchange information while preserving context and semantic consistency. Sticking to well-defined, standards-based interfaces can make all the difference. It's also important to use robust integration tools designed specifically to serve multivendor IT environments. This reduces the cost of maintenance and implementation and gains the maximum reliability.

When deciding which applications to integrate, don't be intimidated by potential barriers: Integration can take place across virtually any boundary, be they technical, organizational, or geographical. The different systems could operate within the same corporate department, the same division, or the same data center — or not. Today's standards-based intranets, providing high-speed connections between servers located almost anywhere on the planet, provide a robust communications medium for most integrations.

TECH TERM

Looking good

Encapsulating applications is another important, if less obvious, reason to integrate. Here, the goal is to hide a legacy program's workings and user interfaces while using its functionality. For example, an older, homegrown customer information system may work just fine, but its *green screen* 3270-type interface is obsolete. Once this system is encapsulated and integrated with a newer system that sports a rich GUI, end users can work directly with the newer application and benefit from the older system's logic and database. Encapsulation doesn't happen automatically, but only when the IT architect bases the integration on a layer above the application, frequently doing so by using a Web service that does the encapsulation.

Consider situations where you want to provide knowledge workers with a more integrated experience. You can easily grasp the potential efficiencies gained from A2A integration. These individuals spend their workdays with all kinds of applications via keyboard, mouse, and screen. The rich graphical user interface (GUI) on today's desktop computers makes it easy to have almost any number of applications running at once. But prepare for a painful experience if one application's output has to be reentered into another and workers have to switch between windows. What's more, retyping information from one application into another inevitably introduces errors.

SAP NetWeaver Meets A2A Integration

This may come as no surprise, but because SAP NetWeaver is an open integration and application platform, it packs a powerful set of A2A integration capabilities. It supports the integration of applications within your enterprise, independent of vendor, design, function, location, or owner.

The platform is also ideal for integrating systems across company boundaries, called *business-to-business* or *B2B* integration.

Figure 22-1 shows how capabilities from the all different layers of SAP NetWeaver help achieve A2A integration.

To support A2A integration effectively, a solution has to include the following things. Coincidentally, SAP NetWeaver has them all.

 ✔ An integrated development environment (IDE) to create components and services that are an A2A integration's building blocks.

✔ Master data management capability that enables you to pull a variety of data sources into a single, well-organized database.

✔ An automatic replication and distribution process that synchronizes duplicated data.

✔ An integration broker with messaging technology and adapters to translate one format to another, to move data between applications, and to centralize the shared knowledge.

✔ Web services to expose *slices,* or selected functions, of existing applications that other programs can use.

✔ Advanced business process management (BPM) you can use to design, execute, automate, and monitor application-spanning processes by describing the way applications interact in a flexible format. This allows you to adjust the processes as you need to.

A key advantage of SAP NetWeaver for A2A integration is its preintegration with mySAP™ Business Suite solutions. *Preintegration* means that each enterprise solution of mySAP Business Suite comes with components and services already integrated with SAP NetWeaver, making integration a product, not a project. This is really important if your existing SAP applications account for more than 70 percent of all integration point flow.

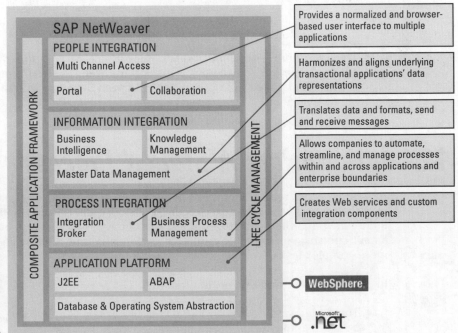

Figure 22-1: SAP NetWeaver features that support A2A integration.

Lining Up the Components

SAP NetWeaver support for A2A integration depends on how your enterprise approaches your integration project. Here's a rundown of how you might end up using various components in your A2A adventure:

- Focused on data? You're likely to use the SAP® Exchange Infrastructure (SAP XI) integration broker and its functionality for creating adapters, exchanging messages, and translating formats between one application and another.

- Focused on APIs? You'll get heavy use from the SAP® Web Application Server (SAP Web AS) and its ability to create Web services that can use APIs from any number of applications and support standards-based connections between two applications.

- Your developers will rely heavily on the SAP NetWeaver Developer Studio, a fully functional IDE that provides services that support a model-driven development. This marks a crucial step forward in productivity because it allows all of the various components and services from mySAP Business Suite and SAP NetWeaver to be described using metadata, then glued together through modeling, rather than programming. This means that applications are composed from parts rather than coded by hand.

- Web Dynpro, the SAP user framework, allows for rapid assembly of user interfaces based on modeling and common patterns.

- The SAP Composite Application Framework allows components to be stitched together sans coding. This and the Web Dynpro framework are the most advanced examples of model-driven development environments available.

A2A Integration: A Staged Process

A2A integrations typically proceed in stages, each one involving planning, experiments, and then gradual execution. Risk is reduced and the impact of a failure lowered when you stage things. Most companies wisely decide to start small. They take on lower-risk projects, build skills, and then move on to more complex tasks.

In general, A2A integration occurs this way:

- The easiest and least risky initial step involves a simple data exchange between applications.

- The next step might involve handing off a transaction that began in one application and is continued in the next.

✔ More advanced integrations might include moving back and forth between applications, with each changing the state of the other in significant ways.

✔ Here you're running with the big boys. The most powerful A2A integrations orchestrate the behavior of several applications through a many-to-many message flow that streamlines execution of business processes with increased monitoring.

Figure 22-2 shows the progression in complexity of A2A integrations, in which each layer builds on the previous layers, increases in difficulty, but also provides more business value.

Step 1: Data integration

The essence of data integration is making the data from one application available in another. SAP NetWeaver offers several different methods for doing this:

✔ SAP XI passes messages containing the requested data between applications. The openness of the SAP XI adapter framework allows the deployment of various adapters to translate virtually any format.

✔ SAP Web AS constructs Web services that allow one application to retrieve data from another.

✔ SAP® Master Data Management (SAP MDM) creates a unified central data repository that several different applications can use. Using this method, SAP MDM employs SAP XI to synchronize replicated data.

Step 2: One-way process integration

Now you're ready to move all data required in a cross-functional process from one application to another. This means you're ready to perform a *one-way process integration*.

Traditional stovepipe integrations used only APIs from each application. This resulted in brittle integrations that were expensive to maintain. SAP NetWeaver, on the other hand, offers a configurable approach, building on the capabilities for data integration of the following components:

✔ SAP® Enterprise Portal (SAP EP), the user-interface framework for all mySAP Business Suite solutions, can also be used to create either role-based or process-based views of cross-application processes.

✔ SAP XI can move data from one application to another.

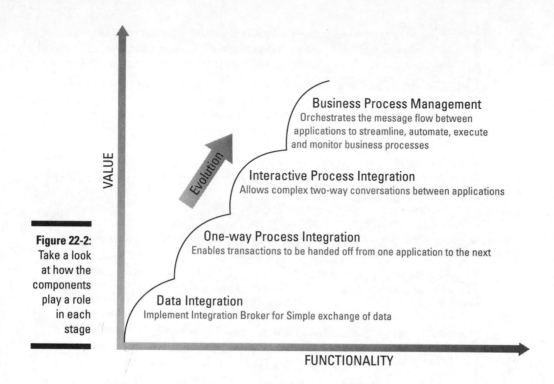

Figure 22-2:
Take a look
at how the
components
play a role
in each
stage

Step 3: Interactive process integration

So you've mastered one-way process integration. Now it's time to look at a more interactive experience. A two-way conversation between applications requires not only the user interface and data integration, but much more sophisticated process control and synchronization. You also need to be able to encapsulate various functions through Web services, standard adapters that allow one program to use the data and functions of another.

SAP NetWeaver provides advanced process automation at two levels, to coordinate users and to coordinate other applications. On one level, the business workflow management system of the SAP Web AS models, controls, and automates the business processes taking place within a software component. Once defined, the automated workflow serves to coordinate the activity of users working with the business processes.

On another level, cross-component business process management (BPM), a function of SAP XI, drives and controls complex business processes across business applications and between different companies. For both types of process automation, the process is controlled by a modeling language that you manipulate through a graphical user interface.

You can use Web services constructed on SAP Web AS to encapsulate communication between applications. These services also provide primitive operations — the ability to perform individual steps in a process — that can be orchestrated by process control frameworks.

Step 4: Business process management

You've mastered integration, now's it time for the advanced course. Advanced A2A integrations involve automating complex interactions, such as automatically determining if a purchase order can be fulfilled and routing the order to the lowest cost supplier. These occur between two or more applications. Building on all the functionality you've already heard about, SAP offers two ways to help manage complex integrations: the BPM capability and the SAP Composite Application Framework (SAP CAF).

✔ BPM has a very cool process-modeling environment that handles asynchronous coordination of processes between all your different applications. This means a process can be started, and then hours and days can go by and the BPM engine waits for steps to be completed. As a result, you can use modeling, rather than coding, to orchestrate all the messages and services for data exchange and process management that span days, weeks, and even months.

✔ The SAP CAF lets you create advanced applications in a model-driven development environment. What's that mean? Just this: Not only the processes, but all aspects of an A2A integration can be modeled and configured using parameters. With this method, you can construct new views of a process's progress across applications and actually compose new applications out of the parts created for A2A integration.While A2A integration ranges from the simple and direct to the fiendishly complex, it is usually a challenging implementation project. Taking the project in stages as we suggest increases the chances of a successful implementation that creates enormous business value.

Chapter 23

Custom Made: Composite Applications

*P*art of the joy of custom application development has been reinventing the wheel at every turn. You had to start from scratch and repeat other people's mistakes until you got it right. This gets really tiresome — really fast.

That's where SAP NetWeaver can be a big help. It allows you to start with a huge amount of functionality already at your disposal. This changes the landscape for custom application development by making it faster, more efficient, and less costly.

This chapter takes a look at the continued need for custom applications and the way that SAP NetWeaver helps by providing great tools for building custom composite applications.

Custom Processes, Custom Applications

Just a few years ago in the Dark Ages of enterprise computing, when business users requested IT support for new business processes, the IT department had one of three choices: purchase new software and customize it, build a new application from scratch, or extend an existing application to meet the need. In most cases custom coding for new functionality or integration was a big part of the picture. When any one application in the value chain was updated or upgraded, the custom programming would have to all be redone. It was a time-consuming, complex, and costly process, and not a soul in IT looked forward to it.

Now it's a new millennium. (Remember Y2K?) You're entering an era in which your IT department is armed with more proven tools and reusable functionality than ever before. Instead of cumbersome coding by a team of programmers, a new paradigm has been developed called *composite applications,* which are applications created from parts of other applications using Web services. Under this paradigm much of the development process consists of picking and choosing among existing components that match your business's process. With this approach, coding is minimal; instead, modeling is used. This approach works even if your company requires the development of your own unique applications to work across a whole ton of organizational units and processes.

Because they reuse existing functionality from many different applications, composite applications make the most of any IT investment. They are able to streamline the end-to-end process or extend the system while leaving current applications untouched.

The opportunities for custom development have changed because of the aggressive development of enterprise applications along with the growth of tools such as Web services, enterprise application integration, business intelligence, and portal technology. What makes the leap to composite applications possible is a new framework that allows developers and even business analysts to compose new custom composite applications that define an end-to-end process from the data and functionality existing in enterprise applications. They don't need to know all the details of the underlying technologies, application program interfaces (APIs), and tools — and they can do all this at a cost that won't put your budget in traction.

In this chapter we take a look at the kind of custom composite applications that are likely to make sense in your current IT environment, and how you can build them in a way that maximizes their value to you today and many years into the future.

The Eternal Need to Customize

An enterprise is a complex animal and you don't want to go poking a stick in its face before you understand just how complex it can be. At the enterprise level, it's possible to have hundreds of systems from different vendors, purchased at different points in time, operating in different locations throughout the organization. The brutal experience of building, launching, and maintaining a custom application that draws on a whole bunch of data sources in this environment can make grown programmers weep. It's an extremely painful and expensive process to make most systems work together, and your IT department will complain that they just can't spend months of coding and development every time an application needs upgrading. And they're right.

With about as much impact on your life as the decision to have kids, the decision to pursue a major custom application should not be taken lightly. You should consider it only if the following conditions are met: The reward is potentially quite large, you can find a cost structure that makes sense, and you can demonstrate incremental progress as the application is being built.

Some common motivations for building custom applications include

- Automating an innovation in a business process that has proven successful — a best practice or next practice (see Chapter 2 and 7 for more details on these) that is unique to a company or industry and not provided by vendors.

- Automating an important relationship with a customer, partner, or supplier.

- Reducing the risk of costly errors.

- Rapidly assembling information for decision support.

- Capturing collaborative processes that require human beings to play together to get stuff done.

- Creating highly customized, end-to-end processes to support innovation and beat the competition.

Where did we come from?

Historically, custom development meant starting from scratch, beginning with database design, and then proceeding through the parallel design of the user interface and application logic. Take a trip down memory lane with us for a moment and contemplate the custom development landscape way back when many tools that are now mature parts of the computing landscape were in their early, standalone infancy:

- Systems for content management, business intelligence, and search were just poking their heads out as stable commercial products.

- Toolkits for XML messaging and transformation, enterprise application integration, Web user-interface design, and business-process management were just baby technologies or did not even exist.

- Custom applications frequently implemented their own mechanisms for access control, security, and operational monitoring, instead of reusing a pool of systems for all the functionality you needed to incorporate.

Where are we now?

Today, you live in a brave new world. A custom application may have elements that are new, but almost always it employs and orchestrates the data and functionality from a variety of existing applications.

However, very few applications still allow you to design, execute, and monitor a process that spans multiple systems. Rather, typically a tight link exists between the applications and where the process is tracked, extracted, and controlled. That's because the people who built the current generation of application tools weren't psychic. They didn't understand that their applications would be presented to the user in a layer that was fed into by multiple resources and that the process that was being implemented would be managed from outside the application itself.

Where are we going?

In the modern day, any custom application has many applications, platforms, and toolkits at its disposal. Perhaps the hardest task for the custom application architect in today's environment is not designing the system, but assembling a sufficiently deep understanding of all that is practically possible with all the functionality available.

Here are the challenges that custom application architects face regarding the functionality of custom applications:

- Assembling data from a wide variety of sources in a coherent form for processing by a custom application.
- Broadcasting changes made in a custom application back to the underlying applications and data stores.
- Translating incompatible data formats into a unified format through an integration broker.
- Creating services from existing enterprise applications.
- Creating services from platform component systems, such as content management, Enterprise Application Integration (EAI), and search.
- Rapidly creating and improving user interfaces.
- Supporting many role-based interfaces.
- Creating configurable processes that direct the orchestration of all this functionality.

✔ Integrating with systems for single sign-on, application security, and monitoring operation.

✔ Implementing best practices for life cycle management, maintenance, and upgrade of the software.

With the arrival of SAP NetWeaver, you have just taken a step into the future of composite application development. That's because SAP NetWeaver is a general platform for application development that includes elements that solve all of the challenges mentioned here in a nice, neat, pre-integrated environment.

Bringing Composite Applications to Life

So, life is rosy, and building composite applications is similar to taking a walk in the park in spring, right? Well, life is still challenging, but trust us, it's way closer to that stroll on the grass than it used to be.

As the provider of the platform for enterprise applications, the toolkits for all major functionality, and the development environment, SAP offers a whole new way of building apps. Now when you create an application in SAP NetWeaver, it's simply a matter of combining components and services that are designed to work together instead of struggling to overcome cross-vendor integration problems. The power of modeling is having the ability to create and customize applications and bring them to new audiences such as business analysts through tools such as SAP Visual Composer.

A whole new thing

The SAP NetWeaver development environment is unique in that it reflects the new world in which developers aren't starting from a blank slate, but are using multiple modules or applications to build on existing functionality.

The reality is that developers today often have trouble seeing the forest for the trees. At the enterprise level, any single developer has a difficult time understanding the multiple systems, technologies, and tools that are necessary to create a composite application. SAP NetWeaver provides a set of tools, code repositories, and visualizations that give developers some perspective. They can now reuse the strengths of the tools that they prefer and make use of the investment in code that the organization has already made.

Building software isn't the end of the process. You also have to manage software throughout its life cycle. Any new application has to be created in an installable unit and then you have to install it, test it, configure it, operate it, monitor it, upgrade it, and, eventually, retire it.

With SAP NetWeaver, the enterprise gains perspective on all these events and alerts at all levels: portal, business intelligence, and application server.

In addition to all this great functionality, SAP NetWeaver also provides greater agility because you can leverage the underlying legacy applications without messing up the status quo. And because it augments existing IT assets while allowing you to compose new business processes, SAP NetWeaver gives you another effective way to lower your total cost of ownership (TCO).

Capable composites

The previous sections give you a rough idea of what SAP NetWeaver brings to the table when it comes to building composite apps. But exactly which pieces of SAP NetWeaver do this stuff?

The most important tools that you need for the development of composite applications are shown in Figure 23-1. In SAP NetWeaver, these appear in the following components:

- **Portal:** Providing the framework for building new user interfaces and workflow, the SAP® Enterprise Portal incorporates and orchestrates different services and processes.

- **Integration broker:** Allowing the portal to easily access and knit together Remote Function Calls (RFCs) and BAPI (which are defined in Chapter 4) by using the most convenient choice from a host of technologies, the integration broker helps you instantly create Web services from SAP R/3® functionality.

- **Support for both J2EE and ABAP development:** SAP® Web Application Server is a powerful runtime system that hosts components based on ABAP or J2EE technology. For companies with substantial investments in ABAP or Java code, SAP NetWeaver takes advantage of them both by placing them in the same engine and in the same environment. Other technologies, such as .NET and WebSphere, can also be used and extended.

- **Application platform:** Providing the ability to access RFCs and BAPIs, the application platform allows you to create and orchestrate new Web services that you assemble by using model-driven development to support new functionality or integrate with other applications.

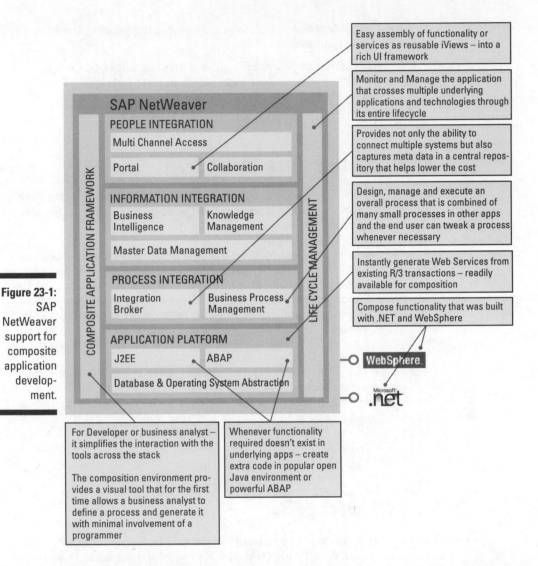

Easy assembly of functionality or services as reusable iViews – into a rich UI framework

Monitor and Manage the application that crosses multiple underlying applications and technologies through its entire lifecycle

Provides not only the ability to connect multiple systems but also captures meta data in a central repository that helps lower the cost

Design, manage and execute an overall process that is combined of many small processes in other apps and the end user can tweak a process whenever necessary

Instantly generate Web Services from existing R/3 transactions – readily available for composition

Compose functionality that was built with .NET and WebSphere

SAP NetWeaver

COMPOSITE APPLICATION FRAMEWORK

LIFE CYCLE MANAGEMENT

PEOPLE INTEGRATION

Multi Channel Access

Portal | Collaboration

INFORMATION INTEGRATION

Business Intelligence | Knowledge Management

Master Data Management

PROCESS INTEGRATION

Integration Broker | Business Process Management

APPLICATION PLATFORM

J2EE | ABAP

Database & Operating System Abstraction

WebSphere

Microsoft .net

Figure 23-1: SAP NetWeaver support for composite application development.

For Developer or business analyst – it simplifies the interaction with the tools across the stack

The composition environment provides a visual tool that for the first time allows a business analyst to define a process and generate it with minimal involvement of a programmer

Whenever functionality required doesn't exist in underlying apps – create extra code in popular open Java environment or powerful ABAP

✔ **Business Process Management:** Providing the ability to model business processes using special languages designed for that purpose, often with graphical tools, so that the way applications work can be easily modified and optimized.

✔ **SAP Composite Application Framework:** Using a visual tool to extend the modeling approach, the SAP CAF allows a business analyst to define a process and generate it without requiring much time from a programmer.

This is possible simply because you assemble the process from handy configurable components.

✔ **Life cycle management:** Handling the details of managing complex development projects across large teams in distributed locations, life cycle management includes source-code management, staging, customizations, and upgrades.

Who can use this thing?

So developers can now easily design, manage, and execute processes that span multiple applications, but what about the poor guy on the other end who has to use those processes?

SAP NetWeaver just happens to allow a ton of freedom for the business user. The environment you compose applications in provides a tool called SAP Visual Composer, which is the part of the SAP CAF that is used for modeling by unsophisticated business analyst types. But SAP Visual Composer does more: Users also can instantly generate Web services from existing SAP R/3 transactions, connect to multiple systems, initiate a process in one system, get a response event back, and continue the process in another system.

In this kind of environment, the type of people using the system shifts from programmers to business analysts. Now these number crunchers can define what they need as a process and automatically generate the code. Business users don't need to understand how these super-sophisticated tools work because technology is doing just what it should — managing complexity but remaining invisible to the user.

Taking It in Stages

This is all swell, you say. You're really happy that building composite apps is now as easy as falling off a log (and a lot less painful). But where exactly do you begin?

We've said it before but it's worth repeating: It's important with a technology as powerful and comprehensive as SAP NetWeaver to think big but start small. You've got to make progress through incremental steps that provide immediate value and bring you closer to a services-oriented IT infrastructure that allows change but keeps a lid on cost.

Figure 23-2 shows a four-stage incremental implementation road map. This gives you an example of how to gradually build skills at low cost before moving on to more complex and costly customization. The stages are

- Data integration
- One-way process integration
- Interactive process integration
- Business process management

Each stage uses an SAP NetWeaver component to solve a specific problem and provide the foundation for further growth.

Information aggregation

Most implementations start with a data scavenger hunt where simple portal interfaces bring the power of the underlying enterprise applications to new audiences. Begin by creating portal-based user interfaces (UIs) that extend underlying SAP R/3 applications to a broader audience by using Web technology. Implementing a portal gives your company a quick win because it

- Allows users to aggregate information from multiple systems in a personalized and easy-to-reuse fashion.
- Gives developers a simple implementation with high value.
- Allows users to become familiar with the overall system — how it presents data and how it allows multiple system access in a coherent interface.
- Allows developers to add functionality without complicating user adoption.
- Is the ideal environment to bring together all the levels of a composite application framework.
- Permits personalization in environment, simple navigation, consistent look and feel, and the ability for the end user to reuse parts.

Turning transactions into Web services

Are you still with us? Good. The next step is to create an application that combines data from a lot of different sources and allows the user to interact with it in a useful and user-friendly way.

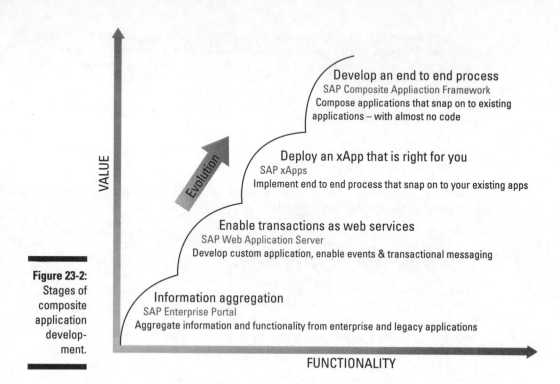

Figure 23-2:
Stages of
composite
application
develop-
ment.

SAP® Web Application Server (SAP Web AS) to the rescue! SAP Web AS allows you to recombine existing SAP R/3 functionality into new forms that you access through J2EE or ABAP components and Web services.

When you've got multiple components at work, you can orchestrate them directly by using other components, or through various process control mechanisms, which include the following:

✔ **SAP® Enterprise Portal,** which provides the framework for creating a new user interface that includes extended functionality.

✔ **SAP Web AS,** used to construct new Web services based on ABAP or J2EE that supplement SAP R/3 functionality with new, custom components. This allows the SAP Enterprise Portal access to the widest possible variety of functionality and information. It also brings the largest number of developers into the loop. (Developers love being in the loop.)

✔ **The life cycle management features,** which keep the maintenance of these new components and solutions under control, so you can coordinate the work of large development teams and manage versions and upgrades.

Deploying SAP xApps that fit the bill

Composite apps in a box? Amazing, but true. SAP NetWeaver provides the platform to build true SAP xApps (packaged composite applications). SAP builds them by using the SAP CAF and then sells them as products to make your life much easier.

In addition to flexibly integrating existing systems and new functional components into a business process, SAP xApps

✔ Drive business processes across different applications, technologies, and organizations.

✔ Enable on the fly or spontaneous team collaboration as part of your most essential business processes.

✔ Provide you with greater agility, because you can leverage your underlying SAP and existing legacy applications.

✔ Put knowledge and structured information within the context of a business process.

✔ Are triggered by events, can aggregate and contextualize information, and finally drive collaboration and transactions.

The good news continues: These applications work seamlessly with other components of SAP NetWeaver, such as the SAP® Enterprise Portal. Because the functioning of these applications is not limited by environment or platform, SAP xApps are the ideal solution for automating processes that cross through many systems in any IT landscape. This enables you to apply best practices without killing yourself in the process.

Developing an end-to-end process

You made it. The last step has a few pieces to it. Here's where you deploy full-fledged composite applications by using the following tools:

✔ Role-based UIs

✔ SAP NetWeaver integration tools

✔ Multiple components from mySAP™ Business Suite

✔ Legacy applications

✔ Applications from other vendors to extend SAP R/3 to support and optimize new business processes

Okay, it's a mouthful and not the easiest nor cheapest of the four steps by a long shot. But if you've gotten this far, you've already obtained great value and seen where SAP NetWeaver can take you, so knuckle under and get going.

In this step, you use the composite application framework and services from SAP R/3 to build entirely new applications. Here's how:

✔ Building on everything that has been created so far, the SAP CAF brings in the widest possible number of different kinds of services from SAP NetWeaver, mySAP Business Suite, and tools and applications from other vendors into a model-driven development environment. This allows the core SAP R/3 functionality to inform and help automate many different applications, thereby leveraging the information and knowledge about SAP R/3 to the max. The model-driven nature of composite application framework applications allows you to optimize them rapidly without expensive redevelopment and testing.

✔ SAP® Exchange Infrastructure (SAP XI) uses its integration broker functionality to reach out through XML messages to other applications (regardless of which vendor made them) and bring their data and functionality into an application right alongside applications built from SAP R/3.

Looking Forward

When you create custom composite applications using SAP NetWeaver, you create components and services that make the data and application functionality from enterprise applications available through Web services. If you design 'em right, these Web services become reusable units of functionality that can serve the needs of more than one composite application.

As your company determines which parts of its architecture need to be dynamic to allow you to quickly respond to business conditions, you can construct more components and services by using SAP NetWeaver. This rapid response is really a business strategy that you implement in the form of composite applications and component-based integration. You do this by assembling existing components and services that are provided by SAP NetWeaver: frameworks for development, UI, process control, security, and administration.

Part V
Rolling Out SAP NetWeaver

The 5th Wave   By Rich Tennant

"Before we explain the integration plan, let me ask you a question. Theoretically, can your IT department actually all work 24 hours a day?"

In this part . . .

A talented rookie golfer may go for the green with every shot, try to drive over that creek, and hope to make the perfect hole-in-one on every par 3. The pro plays it safe and beats the rookie by 20 strokes. What does that mean?

When it comes to rolling out an SAP® NetWeaver™ solution, there is plenty of help available from SAP and many other sources. Why not take advantage of it? With the right coaching and advice, and by benefiting from the experience of others, your early adventures in SAP NetWeaver will be a success.

This part explains how to get the help you might need from people, from quite a few sources of information, and from processes that embody best practices for getting the job done right.

Chapter 24

Plans and People

● ●

In This Chapter

▶ Planning for SAP® NetWeaver™

▶ Discovering people who can help

● ●

*N*ow that you understand how SAP NetWeaver works and what benefits it can bring to your organization, you're probably eager to get started using it without further delay.

Well, what you mainly need to get started is a plan and people to execute it.

So, dig in!

Planning for Success

SAP NetWeaver, being a complex and multi-faced animal, is something of a chameleon. You can use it more than one way. In fact, you can use SAP NetWeaver nearly as many different ways as there are companies.

SAP has had some 30 years of experience working with customers, and during those years, it has observed the *best practices* (which are tried and true, standardized business processes that have been established as the "best" way to do something) of the most successful among them. By following these best practices, you can greatly improve your chances for SAP NetWeaver success.

Here are some of the best practices of successful SAP customers. You can apply the following to your own SAP NetWeaver project:

   ✔ **Figure out where you can apply SAP NetWeaver:** You want to get the most bang for your buck, so figure out where to start by asking yourself, "Where in my organization could SAP NetWeaver provide the most benefits?" Your answer to that question is a great starting point.

✔ **Know thy process:** As Socrates (an early SAP consultant) said, know thyself. Early on, develop a clear understanding of the business processes to which you intend to apply SAP NetWeaver. Don't make the mistake of assuming that, because SAP NetWeaver is an IT solution, you need understand only the technology. Instead, assume that the more you know about your own business processes, the better your ultimate results will be.

✔ **Set your goals:** Develop a clear understanding of what's in it for you — that is, the business benefits that you hope to obtain from SAP NetWeaver. Make a list and make it as specific as possible. Here's an example of a good start: "We will create a portal where internal users have access to vital business information." Next, you could go on to list the measurements you will use to ensure that the portal has achieved its goals.

✔ **Count those pennies:** Determine whether return on investment (ROI) is a factor in your SAP NetWeaver implementation. Sometimes it's not. But if ROI is important to your organization, you need to do the arithmetic, either on your own or with help from an SAP or third-party consultant. Start by estimating how much the SAP NetWeaver implementation will probably cost and how long it will take to complete. Then calculate the benefits SAP NetWeaver is likely to deliver over that time period. How long until you earn back your initial investment? How long before the benefits outpace the expenses?

✔ **Know who's who:** Identify the players and roles for all your SAP NetWeaver project stakeholders. Who's on the team? What are their roles? How are they evaluated and measured? Who are the internal customers? Are there other partners, perhaps outside the organization, also involved? Try not to leave anyone out. The more complete and detailed your list, the better.

✔ **Get the powers that be behind you:** Line up internal support for your SAP NetWeaver project *before* you get started. A project of this size and complexity requires substantial resources and time. Make sure that your company's top IT and corporate executives understand this and, more importantly, buy into it. Spend time with the doubting Thomases and Thomasinas and you'll enjoy their unqualified support later.

✔ **Go with the (work)flow:** Understand your organization's unique culture, especially its pace and style of decision-making. Then work within the system to set expectations and garner valuable support.

People Make It Happen

Now that you know the best practices for SAP NetWeaver success, look at another important factor: people. Ah, people. Can't live with 'em, and for the purposes of an SAP project, you definitely can't live without 'em.

Launching an SAP NetWeaver project is like embarking on a lengthy sea voyage: You don't want to travel alone. In fact, to reach your destination, whether on a ship or with SAP NetWeaver, your success depends on a large and highly skilled crew. Some crew members you will find within your company (perhaps even lurking in your own department), but others will take a little tracking down.

Take a look at the many people that you want to enlist as the crew aboard S.S. SAP NetWeaver.

The quarterbacks: SAP account executives

One person who simply must be on your SAP NetWeaver team is your SAP account executive. Yes, your account executive is essentially an SAP salesperson. But these people are typically very good and can bring a lot to the table. They can be trusted advisors, but more than that, your SAP account executive is your single point of contact for the entire, 30,000-employee SAP organization.

This person's job is to ensure that you, as an SAP customer, are receiving lots of good service. Your account executive is also on hand to help you understand which SAP products and services might be useful to your company. He or she also ensures that you receive whatever support you need from a wide variety of SAP experts.

In short, SAP account executives are the quarterbacks for the whole SAP team and they work with your company.

If your company already uses SAP products or services, finding an account exec should be easy. Just ask around your company, starting in your purchasing or IT departments. When you identify this person, make an appointment to talk things over.

If your company does *not* already use SAP products or services, finding an SAP account exec is still relatively easy. Simply go to the SAP main Web site (www.sap.com) and click Contact SAP. The link takes you to a Web-based e-mail form. Fill in your request and contact information and submit it.

You can count on hearing from someone at SAP very quickly.

Technical players: Solution engineers

If a picture is worth a thousand words, how much is a good product demo worth? SAP solution engineers can tell you. They're another group of people that you should definitely have on your SAP NetWeaver team. A solution engineer is probably not the first person at SAP you should talk with. But after you decide that SAP NetWeaver might be for you, solution engineers provide you with another level of information. These technically savvy people understand the nitty-gritty details of all SAP products and they're ready and willing to demonstrate the current and future functionality of the company's products.

The high-level demos provided by solution engineers are not your usual, one-size-fits-all affair. On the contrary, solution engineers begin by discovering as much as they can about your industry, company, business challenges, and technical requirements. Then and only then do they produce an SAP NetWeaver demo that's tailored to your specific needs. Here, one size definitely doesn't fit all!

Getting engaged: Customer engagement managers

After you decide to purchase SAP NetWeaver and become an SAP customer, a funny thing happens: Your crew quickly gets much, much bigger. Don't worry, your account executive still remains involved. But a new, important person enters your life: the customer engagement manager (CEM).

SAP customer engagement managers are responsible for planning your SAP NetWeaver implementation. Suppose you need consulting services from SAP during your SAP NetWeaver implementation (and you probably will). Well, it's your CEM who makes all the arrangements. These folks are on hand to make sure that your SAP NetWeaver voyage goes smoothly, in the right direction, and on schedule. They direct you to whatever resources and SAP specialists you might need.

Building solutions: Technical solution architects

One of the SAP specialists likely to be pulled onto your project by a customer engagement manager is the technical solutions architect. These single-minded professionals have just one goal in life: to help you (and other SAP customers) architect a successful SAP NetWeaver solution. They help provide a strategy for your SAP NetWeaver rollout and also recommend the best approach for your implementation.

More specifically, a technical solution architect is an expert on SAP products. Although this person is not quite as technical and hands-on as the consultants (see the following section for more about consultants), they do know just about everything there is to know about the high-level features and functionality of SAP products. This high-level view can come in very handy when you're in the middle of an SAP NetWeaver implementation.

Also, your technical solution architect is likely to have a good deal of experience with previous SAP NetWeaver implementations. That means this person has already discovered the shortcuts, figured out to avoid the pitfalls, and can guide you on the most direct route.

SAP consultants and third-party system integrators

As your SAP NetWeaver implementation gains momentum, you'll need to take on new crew as you go. Most SAP NetWeaver installations, at some point, need the help of consultants from either SAP or third-party system integrators. These third-party firms include Accenture, Cap Gemini/Ernst & Young, Bearing Point, and IBM Global Services at the high end, as well as a long list of smaller specialty firms.

What's the difference between working with SAP and working with a third party? SAP has its own internal group of consultants who can give you detailed support for your SAP NetWeaver (or any other SAP product) implementation, regardless of your industry. By contrast, system integrators are companies that have formed partnerships with SAP. They act as extensions of SAP's own consulting team, filling in gaps or bringing in specialized industry or technology expertise.

The choice of who to work with is yours, of course, though most customers opt to work with a mix of both SAP and non-SAP consultants. A typical arrangement may have SAP consultants working on some of the high-level planning issues, while the third-party system integrator works on the implementation areas of the project.

No matter what you decide, SAP consultants are available to provide whatever help you need. For example, SAP consultants can attend important meetings with third-party system integrators, provide product and technology information, and otherwise help the proceedings go as smoothly as possible. Also, because these consultants are SAP insiders, they're usually the first to know about new and forthcoming products and features — information that could be a big help to your own SAP NetWeaver project.

Teacher's pet: SAP education

You need to know how to drive before you take that 25-state road trip. You need to know how to speak French before you try to immerse yourself in Parisian culture. And you need to know how to use SAP NetWeaver before you can take advantage of its many business benefits. The key to all this is education and training.

Lucky for you, SAP offers a rich education and training curriculum. The company employs professional trainers and provides public training on SAP NetWeaver and its many products. If you prefer to stay within the comfort of your office, SAP also offers virtual training and eLearning over the Internet. (eLearning takes place in a virtual classroom that you attend online. It's just like watching TV.) These are all valuable resources that you should consider making available to all your SAP NetWeaver project team members.

Most SAP customers use training in two ways. First, the techies find out how to implement and then customize SAP NetWeaver. Second, the end users of the tools find out how to use SAP NetWeaver solutions like pros.

Tutti-frutti: SAP Custom Development

Some installations of SAP NetWeaver go far beyond the plain-vanilla types and, in fact, involve quite a bit of custom programming. If your implementation falls into this category, the next group of people you're likely to meet is the SAP Custom Development team. This team gets called in, like a hi-tech S.W.A.T. team, whenever special coding is needed.

How do you know whether you need Custom Development? Consider using them only if your other SAP consultants and account representatives tell you that SAP lacks off-the-shelf software that can handle a part of your project. If that's the case, SAP Custom Development can be used to build custom software for you.

Unexpected help: Colleagues and SAP customers

Using an enterprise version of the water cooler, one great way to find out about SAP NetWeaver is to talk with people who are already using it to meet business challenges similar to your own. These real-world users can help you identify key benefits, avoid the worst pitfalls, and generally make your SAP NetWeaver voyage much more pleasant.

More specifically, SAP NetWeaver customers — especially those in your industry or function (such as marketing or sales) — can help you by answering these questions:

- How long did it take them to install SAP NetWeaver?
- How much did their installation cost?
- How did installation cost compare with original estimates?

✔ What sort of return on investment are they achieving, and how does that compare with their original estimates?

✔ What challenges did they encounter along the way and how would they recommend that you deal with those same challenges?

Their answers to these questions and more provide you with invaluable inside information.

But how do you find these SAP NetWeaver users? No huge water coolers exist in an industrial office complex somewhere on the outskirts of towns, where SAP NetWeaver users meet on alternate Thursdays, right? Well, in a way, such water coolers do exist, and you can find them here:

✔ **ASUG:** Start with ASUG (www.asug.com), the Americas' SAP Users' Group. ASUG bills itself as the world's largest independent, not-for-profit organization of SAP customer companies and partners. In fact, it claims more than three out of every four SAP customers in the U.S. and Canada as members.

✔ **SAP conferences and trade shows:** Another good source for real-life SAP NetWeaver users are SAP conferences and trade shows. Check out Chapter 25 for details about ASUG conferences and vendor fairs and SAP's own conference, SAPPHIRE.

✔ **IT and business press:** Yet another source for locating SAP NetWeaver users is the IT and business press. Most IT and business magazines and newspapers publish case studies. To find case studies that deal specifically with SAP NetWeaver users, try using the search engines on these publications' Web sites. *InformationWeek* (www.informationweek.com) and *Computerworld* (www.computerworld.com) are two good ones to start with in the IT world, and the following big three of business are worth a look, too:

  • *BusinessWeek* (www.businessweek.com)

  • *Fortune* (www.fortune.com)

  • *Forbes* (www.forbes.com)

Analyze this!

IT industry analyst firms are a reliable, generally unbiased source for information about IT products, vendors, and markets. They can help you compare SAP products with those of other vendors from price, functionality, and technology standpoints. Leading analyst firms include Gartner, Forrester, META Group, and IDC, but you may also want to consider smaller specialty firms.

Many of these firms offer both research and consulting services. That is, they can sell you reports that give you a sense of SAP's marketplace, technologies,

competitors, and future direction. But they can also advise you on your own
SAP NetWeaver installation and implementation.

Just be aware that the services of analyst firms do not come cheaply. A single
report is likely to set you back several hundred dollars. And their in-depth
services can cost tens of thousands of dollars a year, or even more if you
spring for all the bells and whistles. But they are quite popular in the IT community and thousands of companies rely on analyst information to help make
decisions.

Eye-ess-vee (ISV, to you)

Another useful member of the SAP NetWeaver ecosystem is the independent
software vendor (ISV). These companies partner with SAP to offer industry-
specific and function-specific software. Essentially, they fill in the SAP gaps
for specific industries or business processes.

For example, say your company is in the oil-exploration business. That's a
case where not every Tom, Dick, or Mary can understand the complexity of
what you do. You probably need to work with an ISV that specializes in oil
exploration.

You may find that SAP acts as a reseller of the ISV's software. If that's the
case, the ISV software is already included in your SAP NetWeaver package.
Otherwise, you need to work directly with the ISV's sales team. Again, SAP
coordinates most of this for you, arranging the meetings and helping you
figure out what you need.

Regardless of whether you buy ISV software bundled with the SAP software
or as a separate package, you'll have help from the partner ISV. You can turn
to them for expertise on whatever their software does, whether it addresses
a particular industry, business process, or technology.

So glad you came: SAP hosting

Another option that SAP offers is what's known in the industry as *hosting*.
Sorry, hosting in this case doesn't involve cocktails and hors d'oeuvres!
Instead, this kind of hosting occurs when SAP runs your SAP NetWeaver
system from its data center. In other words, SAP hosts your SAP NetWeaver
software on its computers, which you in turn pay the company to run and
maintain.

Why would you want to do this? It's like buying a data center and data-center
staff in a box, saving you the overhead and headache of running your own. If
you work for a large corporation with one or more data centers already in

place, hosting probably isn't for you. But if your company is small or medium-sized, it's an option to consider.

Calling Dr. SAP Support

Does SAP leave you in the lurch as soon as you're up and running? Not at all. When your SAP NetWeaver project is a go, you make the acquaintance of a new team: SAP Support. These folks like nothing better than keeping your SAP NetWeaver system purring like a contented kitten.

The SAP Support team works in two ways: *They're proactive* and *reactive*.

Reactive is like the times you go to the doctor because you've got a nasty rash or the flu. It means that in the unlikely event that you find a software bug or some other problem in your SAP NetWeaver system, you can call SAP Support and they quickly make a fix or repair. SAP has teams of experts who can resolve any problem quickly and effectively. They've seen it all before.

Proactive is more like your annual physical. It means that SAP Support ensures that your SAP NetWeaver system runs at its optimal levels. A subset of SAP Support, called SAP Safeguarding, checks your system, looking for opportunities to optimize and improve it and eliminate risk from your project. Can your system support the volume of data that you're pushing through it? Could you benefit from selected upgrades or new features? The SAP Support team finds out and lets you know.

Chapter 25

Information Station

. . . .

In This Chapter

▶ Locating information about SAP® NetWeaver™

▶ Using SAP NetWeaver resources

. . . .

*E*ven with the best IT staff on earth, your SAP NetWeaver project team is still not complete. That's because you can't master a platform as complex and feature rich as SAP NetWeaver all at once. Instead, you need to take advantage of the many information sources available to you, both from within SAP and without.

A wise driver, before setting out on a long driving trip, fills the gas tank. In the same way, start with a full tank of information before you embark on an SAP NetWeaver project. This chapter shows you the most important pit stops for information about SAP NetWeaver and other SAP products and services.

It's Portable, It's Yellow . . .

That's right: It's *SAP NetWeaver For Dummies!* The fact that you're reading this book right now is a very good step toward getting the right information about SAP NetWeaver. We designed this book to serve as a ready reference about SAP NetWeaver, so keep it handy as your project starts to take shape.

The SAP Web Site

www.sap.com is SAP's main business-oriented Web site. It's your one-stop shop on the Web for just about any SAP product information you may need.

www.sap.com is a big site — really big. In fact, a complete list of everything you can find there would probably fill another book. So instead, here's a general list of the main information categories and what you can find:

✔ **Solutions:** Here's where you can find everything that you need to know about SAP NetWeaver the product, including business benefits, key capabilities, and customer success stories. You can find links to the mySAP™ Business Suite, industry solution portfolios, the packaged composite applications known as xApps™, and much more.

✔ **Services:** The other half of SAP's product-services dynamic duo, this section includes articles on return on investment (ROI), consulting, listings, and links to SAP hosting.

✔ **Education:** This is the place to go to find links to local training and education programs in over 50 countries, including eLearning, and user education.

✔ **Partners:** SAP, being such a friendly company, has literally hundreds of partners. This portion of the site offers a partner directory (actually, several of them), information on how to partner with SAP, partner news, and more.

✔ **Company:** Here's everything you might want to know about SAP, the company. Links to investor relations, corporate governance, annual reports, press releases, events, and jobs listings — they're all here.

✔ **Contact SAP:** Just as the name would lead you to expect, it's a Web-based e-mail form that you can use to get in touch with SAP to ask questions or get more information about anything you need to know about SAP and its products. This page also has a link to a listing of local SAP sales offices.

✔ **SAP Community:** The company's version of a public soapbox, this is a public online community for the SAP world. Here SAP experts, would-be experts, customers, and business leaders gather to exchange insights, solve problems, and share ideas. You can also watch event replays, attend product Webinars (online seminars in which you watch the presentation and ask questions of the presenter via online chat), and sign up for the SAP Business Flash, an e-mail newsletter that keeps you up to date on all the news coming out of SAP.

SAP Developer Network

SAP's other main SAP NetWeaver Web site is the SAP Developer Network (www.sdn.sap.com), also known as SDN. It's for software developers and other techies. If your idea of nirvana is getting *very* technical, this is your site.

SDN is where you can find all the detailed technical information about SAP NetWeaver. How to install it. How to use it. How to build with it. How to . . . well, just about anything.

SDN is organized a bit differently than the SAP Web site. When you're logged in, you get access to Weblogs *(blogs)* run by SAP experts, original articles and white papers, moderated discussion forums, downloads, and quite a lot more. Plus, SAP makes all the latest and greatest SAP NetWeaver evaluation tools available on SDN, so you can "try it before you buy it."

SAP Service Marketplace

You are among the elite when you become an SAP customer, and so you can use another SAP Web site, known as the SAP Service Marketplace (`www. service.sap.com`). It's a collection of portals that helps SAP customers and partners to collaborate.

Some areas of the site are public, but to get the full benefits of the SAP Service Marketplace, you need to register and log in.

The Service Marketplace was designed primarily for customers who are in the middle of installing or implementing SAP products and services. For this reason, the Support Area is a key part of the SAP Service Marketplace. The Support Area offers links to SAP Notes, customer messages, and local and regional SAP support centers.

If you'd like to discover more about SAP NetWeaver service and support, go to `www.service.sap.com/netweaver`.

Online Support System and SAP Notes

The Online Support System is for SAP customers and partners only and is used to report problems and get a quick resolution. When you find a critical problem, contact SAP here. Your interaction is tracked in the Online Support System, accessed exclusively through the SAP Service Marketplace. Information about the problem, all the customer interaction, and the problem's resolution are all recorded in the Online Support System. This great little troubleshooting feature is available to all SAP customers.

SAP Notes, also on SAP Service Marketplace for the exclusive use of SAP customers and partners, are the public version of information that's discovered during the process of resolving problems. If someone finds a bug in a product, an SAP Note describes the bug and explains a way to work around it or how to get a patch. SAP Notes also are written to explain what's new in a release or to cover other important questions that come into the support department. SAP Notes are one of the most popular methods of getting help on SAP products.

Using User Groups

Other great sources of information are SAP customers who have already made the SAP NetWeaver journey. They know through experience what works best. The good news is that you don't have to search them out one by one. Users cluster in user groups.

Even better, SAP user groups form wherever SAP users live. You can find the Americas' SAP Users' Group (ASUG) for the U.S. and Canada. In Europe, you can find user groups in Belgium, France, Sweden, and other countries. SAP user groups exist in Turkey, South Africa, Israel, and many other countries. Each group has its own Web site; you can also find a list of SAP user groups on SAPGenie (www.sapgenie.com/usergroups), a consultant site that isn't affiliated with SAP.

Most user groups let you get even more detailed information from their special interest groups (or SIGs, pronounced *sigz*), which are arranged by industry, technology, and business process. Say you're involved in supply-chain planning and you want to find a SIG. You can find eight or more supply-chain management SIGs within ASUG. (For a complete list, go to www.asug.com/groups/index.cfm.)

Getting involved with a user group is a great way to help influence the future direction of SAP products and services. SAP representatives attend the user group conferences and they listen — very, very carefully.

Books and Trade Publications

The printed word is another good source of information about SAP NetWeaver.

You are holding one of the (ahem) best books in your hands right now. But you may not know that SAP has its own press that offers useful guides. SAP Press (what else did you think they would call it?) runs a Web site (www.sap-press.com) that provides detailed information on specific titles. You can even order books online.

The following trade publications and their Web sites are good sources for information about SAP NetWeaver and other SAP products and services:

- *SAP Info* (www.sapinfo.net) is a monthly magazine that focuses on strategy, technology, best practices, and interviews. It's sent to all SAP customers and partners.

- *SAP Insider* (www.sapinsideronline.com) is read by some 100,000 professionals who use, manage, and develop applications for SAP systems.

- *The SAP Professional Journal* (www.sappro.com) is written for SAP administrators, developers, consultants, and technical and project managers.

In addition to SAP-specific trade publications, some independent publishers produce trade magazines that you may find useful. CMP Media, IDG, and Ziff Davis Media are the big three IT publishers in the U.S., but many smaller and more specialized publishers and publications are also worth exploring. The magazine section of a large bookstore, your public library, and the Web are all good sources for locating information.

Events

Whether you need to expand your professional network or you're simply looking for an excuse to get out of the office, you can choose from a long list of SAP and SAP NetWeaver-related live events.

The biggest of them all is SAP's own SAPPHIRE. This annual business and technology forum for SAP customers (www.sap.com/company/events) is sometimes described as an SAP love fest. But it's really a chance for SAP customers, partners, and employees from around the world to get together and find out about the latest SAP products and services. SAPPHIRE includes presentations, hands-on sessions, lectures, workshops, and much more. It's held in venues all around the world, reflecting SAP's international reach. For example, recent SAPPHIRE forums have been held in Sydney, Tokyo, and Las Vegas.

A related group of SAP-run events are called SAP TechEd (www.sap.com/company/events/teched). These technical conferences cover the technologies behind SAP's mySAP™ Business Suite, SAP xApps™, small- and midsize company solutions, and various services.

Finally, SAP also sponsors business forums, seminars, and smaller conferences for the people who dislike big crowds. Business forums (www.sap.com/company/events/forum.asp) assemble SAP experts and customers to explain how SAP products and services can help meet real-world business challenges. By contrast, seminars and conferences tend to focus on specific business processes, including logistics and supply chain, financials, and HR.

Chapter 26

Nifty Implementation Processes and Swell Software

● ●

In This Chapter

▶ Discovering processes for implementing SAP® NetWeaver™

▶ Understanding the kind of software that can help you implement SAP NetWeaver

● ●

*E*very SAP NetWeaver project is like a three-legged stool. The first two legs are the people you meet and the information you gather along the way. This chapter reveals the third leg of implementation: processes and software.

The following methodologies and products can help you take your SAP NetWeaver project from a dream to reality.

SAP Solution Manager

The SAP Solution Manager, which was explained in detail in Chapter 17, has to lead into any discussion about making SAP NetWeaver work for you. Lusting after your very own administrative and monitoring interface may not keep you awake at night, but if you're embarking on an SAP NetWeaver project, it can be a very handy thing to have around. SAP's Solution Manager is just that and a lot more as well. It helps customers implement and manage their SAP solutions relative to their core business processes. Solution Manager helps you change settings, processes, and upgrades to make the most of your SAP NetWeaver solution.

Solution Manager takes advantage of the fact that every SAP solution includes a large number of administrative interfaces. Even at wildly different types of companies (think banks and movie studios, for example), these interfaces end up being very similar. So SAP cleverly created just one approach to these interfaces: the Solution Manager. It essentially embeds SAP's best practices for installation upgrades and software maintenance in a single, handy tool.

ASAP Methodology

The longest journey starts with the first step, right? Well, in the case of implementing, I won't kid you: You have to take quite a few steps. *ASAP methodology* is the step-by-step process that takes you through implementing SAP NetWeaver or any other SAP product. It includes a variety of software tools, templates, how-to kits, and white papers that show you the best ways to implement SAP NetWeaver.

If you remember your history (and who doesn't?), Gaul was divided into three parts. The ASAP methodology does Gaul two better, being made up of five distinct phases: project preparation, blueprint, customization/realization, final preparation, and go-live cutover when the application is launched. We look at each phase separately:

1. **Prepare your project.**

   In this phase, you lay the groundwork: You organize your SAP NetWeaver project team; define project standards; document your project plan in detail; solidify the project scope; resolve issues; and define processes. Now's the time for you to identify and prepare everything that may be needed along the way for your SAP NetWeaver project.

2. **Create a blueprint.**

   You wouldn't try to build a skyscraper without a blueprint, right? Well, think of your SAP NetWeaver project as a software skyscraper (and if you like, yourself as Superman or Superwoman). In this phase, you define your SAP NetWeaver solution in minute detail. Your team scurries about, gathering information on the business processes that SAP NetWeaver must integrate, and then your eager team members determine what the final product will look like. Along the way, you can use questionnaires to determine how many roles the team needs, what reports have to be configured, what customization you need to do, and much more.

3. **Make the blueprint a reality.**

   Time for the SAP NetWeaver blueprint created in phase two to start becoming a reality. In this phase, your team custom-codes the basic SAP NetWeaver software to meet your company's specific needs. Also, you execute conversions and create ports. This phase is a lot of work: Realization is typically the longest phase of the ASAP methodology, so be sure to have lots of coffee and popcorn in the break room when you start out.

4. **Make the final preparations.**

   You've been very patient, so you'll be glad to hear that you're nearly ready to cutover to a production environment — but not quite. In this phase, you ensure that your SAP NetWeaver system executes properly and that your team has fully tuned its performance. You also stress-test your system to make sure that all applications are fully integrated. If stress-testing reveals any problems, now's the time to fix them. This is also when you make sure you train your end users. Finally, handle all change-management activities now, including establishing a support desk.

5. **Make the final cutover and go into production.**

   You've made it! Your SAP NetWeaver system is live, all systems are go, and you should have one very happy project team on your hands. Go ahead, celebrate! Gatorade for everyone!

Solutions in a Box

Packaged solutions are software starter kits and they are to your SAP NetWeaver project what a brownie mix is to a bake sale. They can get your SAP NetWeaver project off to a quick start — and help keep it going full tilt. Check out `www.sap.com` for what's available.

Before you get SAP NetWeaver up and running, you have to deal with a long list of preliminary settings and definitions. An SAP starter package is one type of packaged solution that basically collects all the business content you need in a single box. It also provides a step-by-step guide to SAP NetWeaver's installation and configuration.

When your SAP NetWeaver project is underway, SAP also offers an upgrade assessment package. This helps by giving you an organized way to think about assessing, planning, and installing possible future upgrades.

Jumpstarting with Partner Implementation Packages

Sometimes an SAP partner comes up with a solution so perfect that they just have to share it with the rest of the SAP community. That's where Partner Implementation Packages — because you're now SAP savvy, you can call them PIPs — come in.

PIPs offer repeatable solutions. For a software package to qualify as a PIP, it must be specific enough that SAP doesn't already offer it, but generic enough that it can be useful for companies other than the one for which it was originally developed.

One good example of a PIP is SAP's BW (Business Information Warehouse) Rapid Implementation Package. It helps SAP customers implement a data warehouse in a pre-defined number of weeks with a pre-defined scope. Though originally developed by an SAP partner for a specific client, a more general version of the BW solution is now available to anyone who wants to build a data warehouse without reinventing the wheel.

Hurry Up! Accelerated Implementation Packages

Take the PIP concept, put a time limit on it, and you have what SAP calls an Accelerated Implementation Package or AIP (pronounced *ay-eye-pea,* not *ape*). Every AIP has a pre-defined duration, scope, and estimated cost. It's basically a PIP in a hurry.

AIPs may be what you need if you're looking for an easy, step-by-step way to implement a standardized aspect of your SAP NetWeaver project. *Standardized* is the key here. AIPs aren't designed for custom coding. But if you need another quick tool, sitting an AIP on top of your accelerated ASAP methodology could be just the ticket.

Most of what you find in an AIP includes common implementation practices and requirements that SAP has seen over and over again with its customers. The AIP packages them into a solution that's easy to understand. That, in turn, means an AIP can help reduce duplicate work on your project. For example, if the same process needs to be implemented in multiple components of your SAP NetWeaver project, using an AIP can make that repetition easier, faster, and more efficient.

Get a Product Road Map

Lewis Carrol's Cheshire cat said (more or less) that if you don't know where you're going, any road will take you there. With apologies to Lewis, if you don't know where you're headed with an SAP NetWeaver implementation, it's a no-brainer that you're going to get lost.

The road map for an SAP product, which can be found on www.sap.com, is SAP's vision for how the product will evolve. Keeping a close eye on the product road map provides a great foundation for planning the future of your SAP systems.

In addition, SAP is constantly asking its customers what sort of features they need in its products and which features are the most important to add next. The name for this process is the *requirements roll-in.* Participating in the requirements roll-in process by joining in with groups such as influence councils helps keep the voice of you, the customer, loud and clear in this process.

Ramp Up

Like a freshly mown lawn in the spring, SAP products never stop growing. In fact, SAP spends so much time rolling out new product releases to its customers, it even has a phrase for the process: ramp up. It could be very much to your benefit to find a way into the ramp-up process, and here's why.

A *ramp up* is the organized process of rolling out new SAP product releases, which starts by identifying ramp-up customers. These are folks who are ready for an upgrade and work as a test site when a new product release may not yet be ready or available for the general customer public. SAP issues a call for papers, and if you want to be included, you can submit your reasons to the company. Assuming you pass muster, SAP then scopes and estimates your project. Finally, SAP identifies consultants to participate in your ramp up. SAP also ensures that those consultants are fully trained on the latest SAP NetWeaver releases.

The biggest advantage of being a ramp-up participant is early access to both SAP NetWeaver upgrades and highly skilled, well-trained consulting help. One possible downside is that you become a guinea pig for new software that may still have some bugs. But even that grey cloud has a silver lining: If you do discover bugs, your consultants report them back to SAP for a programming fix, which benefits the next wave of customers using the upgrade. Later, you may benefit from some other ramp-up group's efforts, so what goes around, comes around.

Solution Review: Giving Your Project the Once-Over

When your SAP NetWeaver project is running, SAP wants to make sure it's running *well.* That's where the Solution Review Program comes in. Administered by SAP's consulting services, this is a way for you to ensure the quality of your SAP NetWeaver installation.

How it works

When you participate in an SAP Solution Review Program, your SAP NetWeaver project's structure and organization are evaluated by a consultant who did *not* work on the original installation. Often, this evaluation is done before the system goes live so that any last-minute tunings and adjustments get made before the big date.

Questions that the SAP consultants may ask (and you may want to use as a checklist to ask yourself) include:

✔ Do you have the right people in place?

✔ Are they doing the right things?

✔ Do you have a project plan?

✔ Do you have the right project documents in place?

What if your answers don't entirely impress them? They can also show you via formal presentation how making a few changes could improve your SAP NetWeaver operation and increase your benefits from it. When a report contains a high number of risk areas, some customers have even delayed their go-live date: Better safe than sorry!

SAP xApps™

As you read about in Chapter 7 and Chapter 23, one relatively new concept in IT circles is known as a *composite application.* The idea is that a group of applications can be bundled to create software that acts like a unified business process rather than an unconnected collection of applications. SAP sells composite applications as products called xApps™ (www.sap.com/solutions/xapps).

Chances are that you already have a composite application on your very own desktop system as we speak. Every word-processing package is a kind of composite application that includes all the tools you might need to work with text, drawings, tables, charts, and so on. Rather than presenting you with separate applications for typing, spell-checking, formatting, and printing, the word-processing application combines these into one easy-to-use application.

Now, take that idea and make it bigger — much bigger. Imagine a composite application that could, for example, do all the tasks related to an HR department's payroll process: calculating bonuses, tracking vacation time, deducting taxes, printing checks, and much, much more. The essential quality of a composite application is that it does its work by using services provided by existing programs, instead of starting from scratch. That's the promise of composite applications on an enterprise scale.

SAP calls its version of the composite applications concept SAP xApps. These combine existing, heterogeneous SAP systems into cross-functional, end-to-end processes that, when used properly, can increase your company's competitive agility.

SAP xApps are *cross-functional,* meaning that they can combine different applications, technologies, and departments, such as accounting, human resources, or sales. They mix together existing applications into a business process, and because they're collaborative, they can help hastily assembled teams to work together. Also, SAP xApps are *content-driven,* meaning they relate knowledge in the context of a specific business process. Finally, they're *event-driven,* meaning an event sets off a set of automatic reactions by the systems.

SAP xApps tend to address a specific process. One SAP xApp, for example, was designed to help manufacturers manage their plants' greenhouse gas and carbon dioxide emissions. Another is a toolkit for mergers and acquisitions. A third streamlines product design.

Several SAP partners offer xApps designed for specific industries. Using a specialized xApp™ can give you a head start and save a pretty penny.

Part VI
The Part of Tens

The 5th Wave   By Rich Tennant

"We're looking for applications that work well on a particularly open and distributed network."

In this part . . .

SAP® NetWeaver™ is like an encyclopedia of technology. The information in the encyclopedia could be
used to write thousands of different books. So it is with
SAP NetWeaver. So many solutions can be built that it is
hard to know where to begin.

The chapter in this part shows (almost) ten ways SAP
NetWeaver can help. It focuses on ways to be successful
with SAP NetWeaver and could be your best friend as you
start your SAP NetWeaver adventure.

Chapter 27

Ten (or so) Ways to Get Started with SAP NetWeaver

In This Chapter

▶ Getting started with SAP® NetWeaver™

▶ Serving up suggestions for projects

So you're really excited about SAP NetWeaver and you can't wait to get started. But where, oh where, do you begin?

Like the old Hindu proverb goes, "How do you eat an elephant? One bite at a time." Try to approach SAP NetWeaver the same way.

Here's a quick list of good first steps for a variety of situations. Remember the best mantra with SAP NetWeaver is, think big, start small.

Upgrade Your SAP R/3® System to mySAP ERP

Basically, mySAP™ ERP is just SAP R/3® plus SAP NetWeaver. SAP went and took the newest version of SAP R/3 and optimized it to run on top of SAP Net-Weaver. So, you can take advantage of all the new capabilities of SAP NetWeaver during your next upgrade cycle.

You don't have to swallow SAP NetWeaver all at once. Analyze all the different capabilities and build a road map for adopting them one by one.

Buy Just One mySAP Business Suite Application

All the mySAP Business Suite solutions (see Chapter 6) come pre-bundled and integrated with SAP NetWeaver out of the box. So, why not try out just some of the pieces of SAP NetWeaver for that solution?

After you've installed SAP NetWeaver on a smaller scale for, say, mySAP Customer Relationship Management, you can expand on that to enable other applications. Gradual adoption is the key. Small projects, short implementations, and fast return on investment (ROI).

Build Your Next Custom Application in the SAP Web Application Server

Because SAP® Web Application Server (SAP Web AS) is a J2EE-compliant application server, you can easily build an extension to your SAP system or a new application that ties into SAP without a lot of expense or effort. (Chapter 13 covers SAP Web AS in more detail.)

Give it a try and see how much effort you save by not having to set up a separate application server, separate hardware, separate database, and so on. Plus, because it's built inside the SAP architecture, you don't have to worry about creating all the little connections between the two systems.

Let Your Employees Do It Themselves

This is a really easy step that can have a huge impact on your bottom line. Roll out SAP® Enterprise Portal with the Employee Self-Service (ESS) business package. Most implementations take a matter of weeks and you'll experience very few hiccups. (Chapter 8 covers SAP Enterprise Portals.)

Plus, the HR department will love you forever because they no longer have to answer all those pesky phone calls from employees who still can't figure out how to record their vacation days.

Keep AP from Going Ape

The Accounts Payable (AP) folks would give their left arms to avoid all those phone calls from suppliers asking them when they're going to get paid. Now, we don't know if you're in need of a bunch of left arms, but to make the AP folks happy, why not roll out SAP Enterprise Portal with business packages for sharing orders, confirmations, invoice verification, and payment information? Then add some analysis from SAP® Business Intelligence to figure out which suppliers are giving you the best service.

Your suppliers will love the self-service tools and the AP folks will be able to actually get back to making payments.

Start Using Some Simple Web Services

Web services aren't scary. Identify a couple of areas where third parties offer some simple Web services that your company could get some value out of. Use the SAP Web AS to build the interface and see what happens.

Try integrating a stock ticker or weather map into your portal (see Chapter 18 for more on portals) or maybe integrate an external credit-reporting system into your account qualification process. Start by crawling and then work your way up to walking. In no time you'll be entering the Web Services Marathon.

Give Your CEO a Birthday Present

It's a well-known fact that fish can't live without water and CEOs can't live without pie charts. Set up SAP Business Intelligence for a very focused weekly report on her pet project. After she's got the hang of how to analyze the value of golden parachutes, she can find all sorts of other areas to slice and dice. (Chapter 10 covers SAP Business Intelligence.)

Supplier performance, employee performance, production efficiency, toilet paper usage — they'll all end up getting analyzed before the CEO is through with you.

Set Up Manager Self-Service

Some managers don't even have the time to learn the names of all their employees, much less what their skills and backgrounds are. This can be important when picking the best resource for the right job, right? Why should Monster or HotJobs, two job resource Web sites, know more about your employees than your managers do? They shouldn't.

Set up the SAP Enterprise Portal with the Manager Self-Service (MSS) business package to put all your employee data close at hand. Your managers and employees will jump for joy. (See Chapter 8 for info on SAP Enterprise Portal.)

Clean Up Your Master Data Act

A clean desk might be the sign of a sick mind, but tidiness is a prerequisite for understanding the whole picture painted by your master data. Clean up the mess caused by multiple systems with multiple variations of master records and start figuring out what's really going on with your customers, suppliers, inventory, and employees.

To do this, set up SAP® Master Data Management to consolidate, harmonize and centrally manage data from all of your systems. (For the scoop on SAP Master Data Management, flip to Chapter 11.)

Mobile-Enable Your Applications

Whether your sales workers need up-to-the-minute customer data on their handhelds or your shop floor supervisor needs to order inventory or repair services on the fly, SAP® Mobile Infrastructure can make their lives much easier and liberate them from that hefty PC dependency right away. (For more about SAP Mobile Infrastructure, see Chapter 9.)

Integrate Multiple Applications

It's all about *communication,* so why settle for applications that refuse to talk with each other? If your applications need a marriage counselor, set up SAP® Exchange Infrastructure and get them chatting like newlyweds again. (Can't get enough SAP Exchange Infrastructure? See Chapter 12.)

Appendix

About the CD

About This Appendix
▶ Looking over the system requirements
▶ Using the CD
▶ Checking out what's on the CD

Can't get enough stuff about SAP® NetWeaver™? No problem. We've included a CD with this book that will give you hours of SAP NetWeaver fun, including the following:

- ✔ Lots of detailed white papers and product overviews to help fill in the gaps on SAP NetWeaver capabilities
- ✔ Real-life stories about customers who are using SAP NetWeaver today
- ✔ Demos that show SAP NetWeaver in action
- ✔ A directory to tell you where to go for more information

This appendix shows you what you need to use the CD, how to install the programs on it, and a bit more about what you'll find on the CD.

System Requirements

Before you use the CD, make sure your computer meets the minimum system requirements given in the following list. If your computer doesn't match up to most of these requirements, you may encounter problems in using the contents of the CD:

- ✔ A PC with a Pentium or faster processor
- ✔ Microsoft Windows 98, Microsoft Windows NT4, or later versions of Windows
- ✔ At least 64MB of total RAM

✔ Adobe Acrobat Reader (To download a free copy of the Acrobat Reader, go to www.adobe.com.)

✔ A CD-ROM drive (Okay, you probably knew about this one.)

Using the CD with Microsoft® Windows

This CD is configured to automatically run when inserted (providing that you have that capability enabled on your PC), so you don't have to do much of anything.

To manually run the CD from your CD drive, follow these steps:

1. **Insert the CD into your computer's CD-ROM drive.**

2. **Click the Start button and choose Run.**

3. **Type D:\ (where *D* is the letter of your CD-ROM drive), and then click OK or press Enter.**

   A window lists the contents of the CD in the drive.

4. **Double-click the** START.EXE **file.**

What You'll Find

Like to know what you're getting into before you take the time to install this thing? Okay. The following sections provide a summary of the contents of the CD (kind of "SAP NetWeaver's Greatest Hits").

SAP NetWeaver product details

This is official-type information from SAP itself about SAP NetWeaver capabilities and components. Ever-popular white papers and product overviews for each capability, as well as general information about SAP NetWeaver, are included.

SAP NetWeaver customer success stories

Get the scoop from real customers who are using SAP NetWeaver today to reduce their total cost of ownership (TCO), enable flexibility in evolving their business processes, and accelerate innovation. You'll find success stories on each of the SAP NetWeaver components in a variety of industries and locales.

SAP NetWeaver demos

A picture is worth a thousand . . . you know. See SAP NetWeaver in action by viewing the demos. We include three business scenarios and illustrations of SAP NetWeaver capabilities.

More SAP NetWeaver information

Follow the links in this directory to find more resources on SAP NetWeaver and to get information on how to contact SAP.

Index

• C •